T5-CRE-170

Cambridge Middle East Library

Jordan in the 1967 war

Cambridge Middle East Library

Editorial Board

ROGER OWEN, EDMUND BURKE, SERIF MARDIN, WALID KAZZIHA, AVI SHLAIM, BASIM MUSALLAM

Also in the series

Medicine and power in Tunisia, 1780–1900
NANCY ELIZABETH GALLAGHER

Urban notables and Arab nationalism: the politics of Damascus, 1860–1920
PHILIP S. KHOURY

The Palestinian Liberation Organisation: people, power and politics
HELENA COBBAN

Egypt in the reign of Muhammed Ali
AFAF LUTFI AL-SAYYID MARSOT

Women in nineteenth-century Egypt
JUDITH E. TUCKER

Egyptian politics under Sadat
RAYMOND A. HINNEBUSCH

Nomads and settlers in Syria and Jordan, 1800–1980
NORMAN N. LEWIS

Islam and resistance in Afghanistan
OLIVIER ROY

The Imamate tradition of Oman
JOHN C. WILKINSON

King Abdullah, Britain and the making of Jordan
MARY C. WILSON

The Ottoman Empire and European capitalism, 1820–1913
SEVKET PAMUK

Merchants of Essaouira: urban society and imperialism in southwestern Morocco, 1844–1886
DANIAL J. SCHROETER

The birth of the Palestinian refugee problem, 1947–1949
BENNY MORRIS

Jordan in the 1967 war

SAMIR A. MUTAWI

CAMBRIDGE UNIVERSITY PRESS

CAMBRIDGE
LONDON NEW YORK NEW ROCHELLE
MELBOURNE SYDNEY

THE UNIVERSITY OF TOLEDO LIBRARIES

Published by the Press Syndicate of the University of Cambridge
The Pitt Building, Trumpington Street, Cambridge CB2 1RP
32 East 57th Street, New York, NY 10022, USA
10 Stamford Road, Oakleigh, Melbourne 3166, Australia

©Cambridge University Press 1987

First published 1987

Printed in Great Britain at the University Press, Cambridge

British Library cataloguing in publication data

Mutawi, Samir A.
Jordan in the 1967 war. – (Cambridge
Middle East library)
1. Israel–Arab War, 1967 – Jordan
I. Title
956'.046 DS127.9.J6

Library of Congress cataloguing in publication data

Mutawi, Samir A.
Jordan in the 1967 war.
(Cambridge Middle East library)
Bibliography.
Includes index.
1. Israel–Arab war, 1967 – Jordan.
2. Jordan – Foreign relations.
I. Title. II. Series.
DS127.9.J6M88 1987 956'.046 87-33451

ISBN 0 521 34352 6

CE

DS
127.9
.J6M88
1987

To all those I love
my parents, my wife
and my children
without whose support and love
this book would not have been

Contents

Preface

The seeds of the idea for this book, and indeed the seeds of the war itself, were sown at the first Arab summit conference in Cairo in 1964. Like many fellow Arab journalists, I was excited to be covering an event that marked, for all intents and purposes, the beginning of a new era of Arab politics, and more importantly, of joint Arab action. I had grown up in the 1950s and early 1960s with feelings of great frustration over the fragmentation of Arab opinion on the Palestinian question and the total lack of understanding of Jordan's legitimate defence problems against Israel.

To most Arabs, the summit represented a real opportunity of overcoming these problems, particularly as Nasser himself had called for the conference. Nasser was seen at that time, by the Arab masses and intellectuals alike, as the only leader capable of uniting the Arabs in their common goal of facing up to the Israeli danger.

While talking to some officials who had attended the closed sessions, I had discovered that the Syrian head of state had accused the Arab leaders of cowardice because they refused to confront Israel. He claimed that Palestine could be liberated in six hours if they did decide to fight. Even with my little knowledge of military logistics, this exaggeration was difficult to swallow. To drive a car from Safad in the north to Gaza in the south, would probably require twice as long. How then, I thought, could an Arab leader think he could overrun Israel in six hours? I left Cairo with grave doubts, despite the general euphoria surrounding the summit.

This unease remained with me, and on the morning of 5 June 1967 it proved fully justified. I was in London working for the BBC Arabic Service as a producer of current affairs programmes. Although the news of the outbreak of the war was not totally unexpected, it still filled me with apprehension. My first duty was to try and treat the events as dispassionately as possible, in conformity with the BBC's code of objectivity and professional conduct. I had to put aside my own feelings as a Jordanian whose hometown, Jerusalem, had been captured by the Israelis. I did survive the next six days, but have failed to overcome the war's traumatic effects to this day.

The June 1967 war was, arguably, the most shattering event in recent Arab history. While the 1948 war lost the Palestinian Arabs the larger part of their homeland, they did at least retain an area that included such vital cities as Jerusalem, Nablus and Hebron. The three days of fighting on the Jordanian front between 5 and 8 June 1967 left all this area under Israeli occupation, and forced another huge wave of frightened refugees to run for their lives. For Jordan, the results of the war were equally catastrophic – the army and air force had been decimated, leaving the East Bank defenceless; half the country had been lost to Israel; the economy had been shattered beyond any short-term repair; and a new wave of refugees had arrived on the East Bank. I returned to Amman shortly afterwards to see all this for myself, but nothing had prepared me for the chaos that confronted me.

My immediate reaction was that if this was the price that Jordan had to pay for its commitment to Arab solidarity and brotherhood, then it was a terribly expensive price. My second reaction involved questions that have haunted me ever since. Why did it happen? How did it all start? Could it have been averted? Were only Arab leaders to blame or were Arab masses just as guilty?

In this book I have attempted to answer some of these questions, exploring the motives behind Jordan's decision to enter the war, and its position immediately before the outbreak of hostilities. While Jordan's unreserved participation in the war came as a surprise to most observers, it did not surprise Jordan's decision-makers. No effort, therefore, is complete without the main decision-making institutions being examined and the prominent role of King Hussein being stressed. This is thoroughly examined in chapter 1, and the values and images of the King's formulation of foreign policy are fully analysed in chapter 2. In chapters 3 and 4 the outbreak of war is placed against the background of inter-Arab rivalries, which dominated the Arab world in the years prior to 1967, and Jordanian perceptions of Syria's role in encouraging Arab–Israeli conflict in the immediate period before. In subsequent chapters I have examined in some detail the events of the war itself, including an accurate restructuring of all that went on in the operations room and in the field minute by minute. I have also looked at Jordan's position in the post-war period, including the rebuilding of the Jordanian armed forces and the Jordanian–Israeli confrontation in the Jordan valley town of Karameh in March 1968.

I have interviewed all the surviving Jordanian participants, politicians, military commanders, intelligence personnel, and most importantly, His Majesty King Hussein. I was also given permission by the Army Commander-in-Chief, General Sharif Zaid Ben Shaker (himself commander of the 60th armoured brigade in the June war), to research all the relevant army documents.

I have restricted my study to Jordan's role in the 1967 war because I felt that a tragic misunderstanding of Jordan's intentions by both Arabs and Israelis was a major cause of the war, and indeed a continuing source of friction. First, as to the reasons behind Jordan's policy of non-confrontation with Israel, and secondly, as to the depth of Jordan's commitment to the Arab cause and to the cause of Palestine.

I also wanted to correct, in some way, the imbalance in the literature currently available on the 1967 war. There are many detailed accounts of Israel's role in the war, but none of Jordan's. I do not know whether this is because of a lack of information from the Arab side, the natural disinclination of the defeated to talk about the war, or as some would claim, a general prejudice against the Arabs. I hope this book does convey the balanced picture that I have tried to achieve.

Acknowledgements

I am truly grateful to H.M. King Hussein, whose kind and detailed answers to my questions enriched my experience and knowledge of the crucial period of Jordan's history this book covers. My sincere appreciation also goes to General Sharif Zeid Ben Shaker, Commander in Chief of the Jordanian Armed Forces, for permitting me to research army records and documents related to the 1967 war. Brigadier Fawzi Ebeidat, Commander of the Royal War College, deserves a special thank you for his directions to me on military and strategic issues.

Prime Minister Zeid Rifai, Adnan Abu Odeh, Minister of the Royal Court, Marwan Al-Kassem, Chief of the Royal Diwan, and other politicians and military commanders were very helpful, not only in responding patiently and objectively to my questions but also in contributing invaluable comments and views. I wish to record my sincere appreciation to all of them. The same goes to Professor Peter Campbell, Dr Avi Shlaim and Dr Peter Woodward who guided my efforts while I was preparing my thesis at Reading University.

To all these and others who contributed their expertise and knowledge to the making of this book, I say a special healt-felt thank you.

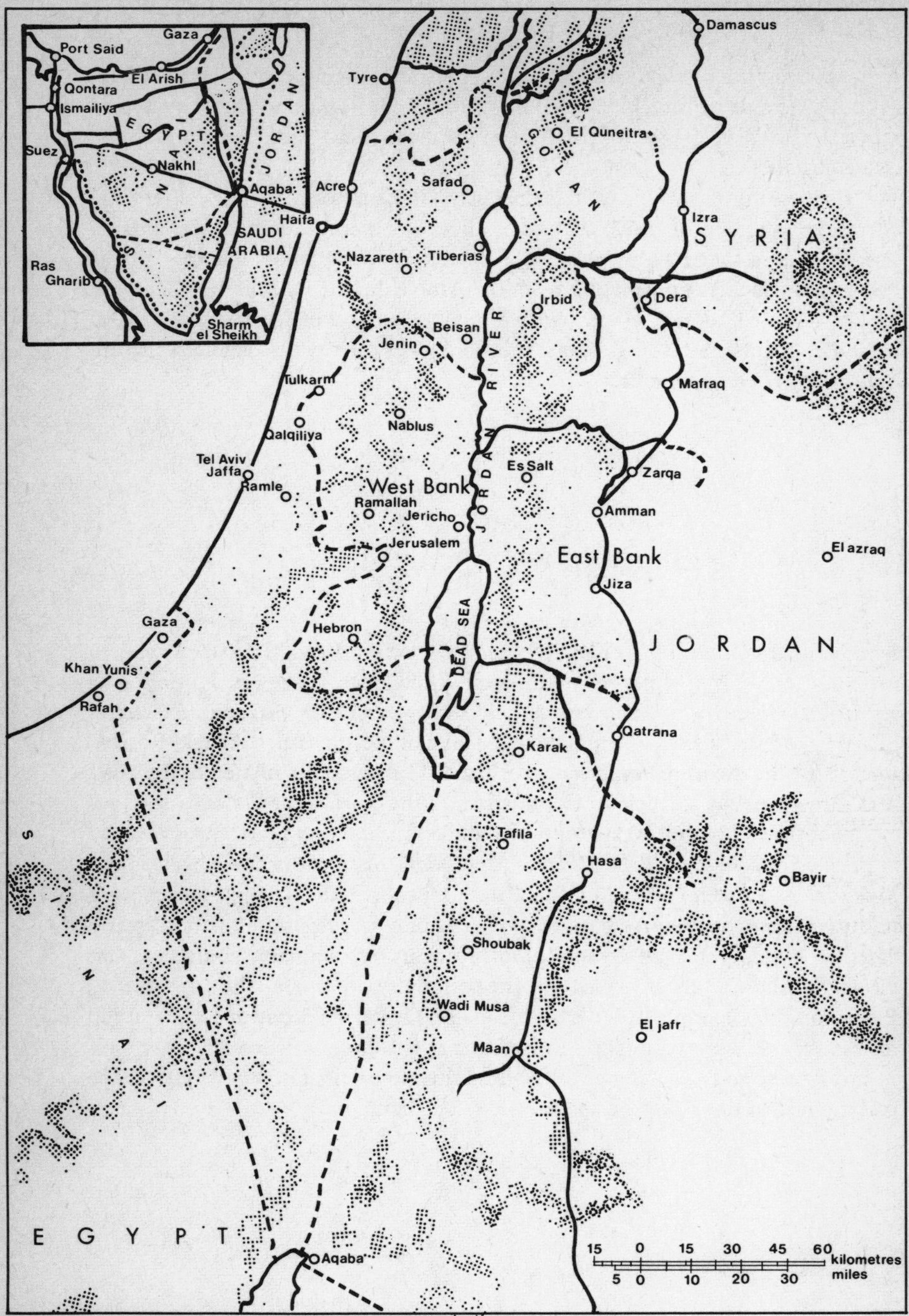

Map 1. The Hashemite Kingdom of Jordan.

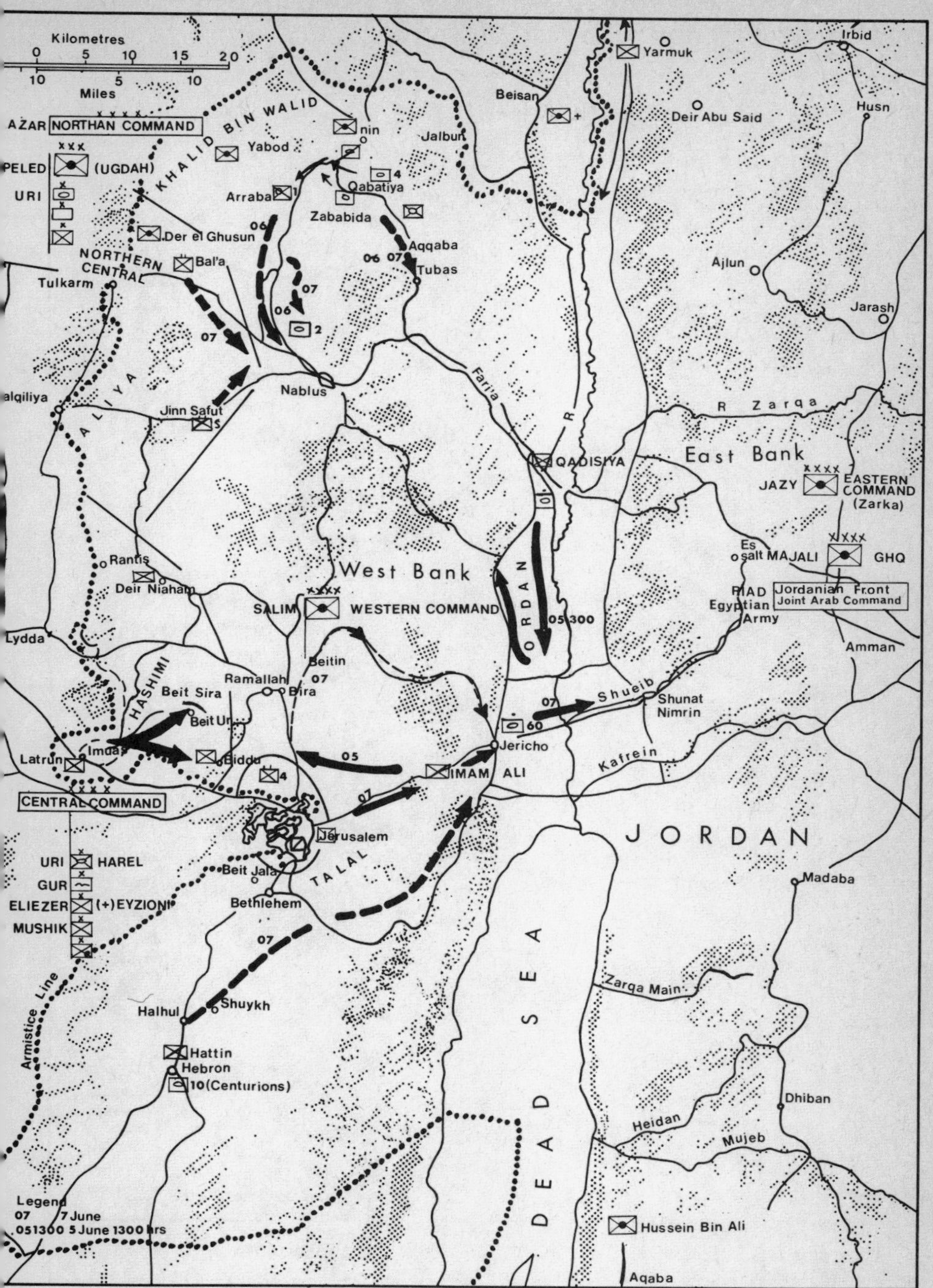

p 2. Operations on the Jordanian Front, 1400 hrs. 5 June – 2230 hrs. 7 June 1967.

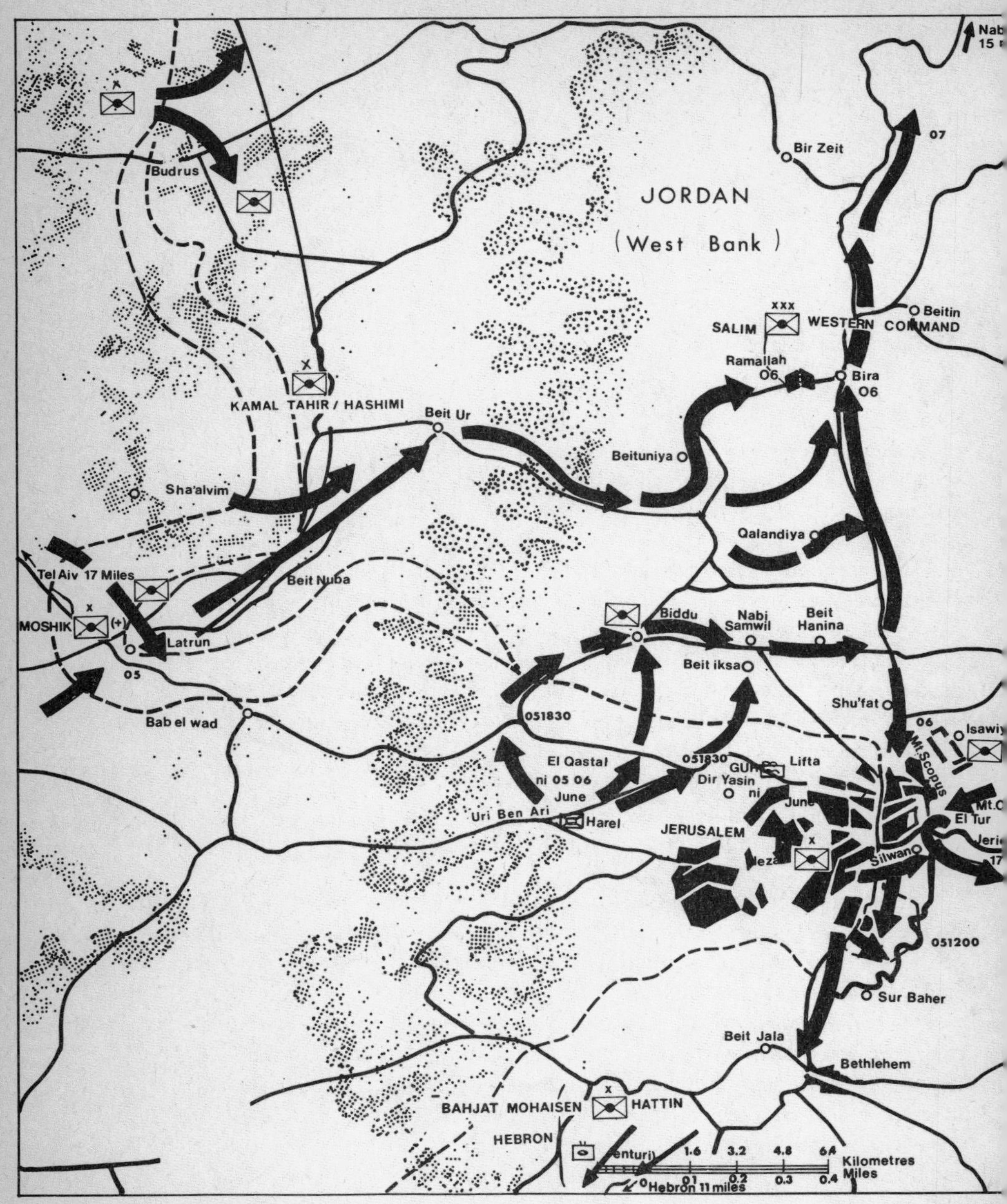

Map 3. The Campaign in Jerusalem, 1400 hrs. 5 June – 2200 hrs. 7 June 1967.

Chapter 1

The decision-making process in Jordan

The position of leader in the Arab world

In contrast with many Western nations where the political party plays a primary role in determining a nation's policies, in many Middle Eastern countries the personality of the leader is of over-riding importance. There are several reasons for the dominating role played by one individual, including the absence in the Middle East of a popular consensus on the nature of political processes, the close relationship between the ruler and the means of coercion, and the absence of a historical tradition of popular participation in political life. Historically, traditional Arab society has always reserved a place for a single dominating figure in social, political and religious affairs. Sharabi points out that the Arab world's tribal pattern of strong civil or political leadership was in existence before the birth of the Prophet Muhammad, who lived in the seventh century A.D.[1] The establishment of Islam strengthened this tradition through the institution of the Caliphate. The Caliph is the supreme leader of the Muslim umma or nation and combines in his person religious and political leadership. Even though the Caliphate died with the Ottoman Empire, the tradition of reverence surrounding the position of leader is still strong at every level of contemporary Arab society.

The assumption that there should be a leading figure in religious, civil and political affairs remains implicit in many Arab communities. In many countries of the Fertile Crescent, including Syria, Lebanon and Jordan, the mukhtar (village head) and tribal leader have positions of considerable authority.

This pattern of according a prominent role to religious and other leaders is not necessarily conducive to the development of nations. The Middle East is a patchwork of different ethnic and confessional communities, and the existence of parochial attachments is antagonistic to the development of loyalty to the state which transcends these. The tragic experience of Lebanon stands as an example of the destructive effect of numerous religious and ethnic groups, each with its own leader.

Although the position of leader in Muslim society is often the result of inheritance or descent from the Prophet, the influential leader must also prove that he possesses the necessary qualities. Hudson points out that 'the leader must demonstrate his personal competence if he is to earn the traditional oath of allegiance'. Equally important is the fact that in such societies 'personal leadership plays a legitimizing role'. Accordingly, in all Arab monarchies, 'the king, amir, shaykh or sultan does not merely reign but rules'.[2] This point is particularly relevant to Jordan where the monarch is the supreme arbiter and chief executive. King Hussein explains: 'To me, rule was not merely a crown or a mace but an honourable service.'[3] King Hussein sees his role as not merely titular but one of responsible decision-making. Ever since Jordan came into being, the main feature of Hashemite leadership has been its highly centralized character and the monarch's role as the nation's chief executive.

Although some political theorists have considered monarchies an anachronism in the modern world, they are forced to observe that 'those that have survived in the Arab world have proved more resourceful and adaptable than political theory would indicate'.[4] Hudson points out that the most legitimate form of monarchy in the Middle East is that of 'an Islamic theocracy governed by the ablest leaders of a tribe tracing its lineage to the Prophet'.

The ruler should adhere to the ethics of Islam and patriarchal consultative procedures of tribal decision-making.[5] To some extent the Hashemites of Jordan meet this ideal type. They are direct descendants of the Prophet Muhammad, they profess adherence to the ethics of Islam, and they allow for patriarchal consultative procedures of tribal decision-making through the institution of the Royal Hashemite Diwan. However, while the Hashemites are accepted as the legitimate rulers within Jordan, these factors have failed to provide them with legitimacy in the region as a whole. This can be attributed to the following factors: neither King Hussein nor King Abdullah attempted to establish an Islamic state whose laws are based on those of Islam; many sections of society no longer regard blood descent from the Prophet as an authentic criterion of leadership; and many regard tribal patterns of decision-making as obsolete, archaic and irrelevant to the needs of a modern nation-state.

The decision-making elite

A political elite is generally recognized as a group of people who either directly exercise or are in a strong position to influence the exercise of political power. In political theory the meaning of the term elite has been the subject of long debate. In this particular context the term refers to a small, identifiable group of people whose preference may sometimes prevail in cases of differences over key political issues. The share of power enjoyed by this group is considerably greater than that available to other groups within the state.[6]

The Jordanian political elite is made up of a principal decision-maker, a ruling elite and a peripheral elite.

The principal decision-maker

Jordan's principal decision-maker is indisputably the monarch, particularly in the spheres of inter-Arab affairs and foreign policy. This view is unanimously confirmed by Jordan's political leadership.[7] For example, Abdul Munim Rifai conceded 'without hesitation' that King Hussein dominates Jordan's foreign policy.[8] Since first ascending the throne the King's role as principal decision-maker has grown steadily. Nussaibah explains that 'up to 1957 and even beyond that to 1963–5 liberal democracy was developing and was extremely important. But then there was a definite shift in the location of decision-making in favour of the King'.[9] By 1967 the King's position as supreme decision-maker was a well-established fact. Before the departure of the British the King's role in the formulation of policy was limited. For example, King Hussein admits that until his Arabization of the army, every important decision taken by the ruler was made in close consultation with either Glubb Pasha, the British Ambassador or other British officials.[10] Nevertheless, even after the Arabization of the army, power was not concentrated in the hands of the King. Nussaibah describes how, during the Suez crisis of 1956, King Hussein ordered the army to march from Jenin into Israel in support of Egypt. However, 'the cabinet was then the centre of power and it refused to heed the King's order'.[11] The struggle between King Hussein and Prime Minister Nabulsi ended with the reins of power firmly in the grip of King Hussein, and by the 1960s he was involved in policy formulation at almost every level.

Hudson points out that while the office of monarch generates a certain structural legitimacy, where King Hussein is concerned, 'the performance of the incumbent is more important'.[12] In the Middle East the qualities which the leader should possess are an astute sense of the socio-political climate and a deductive capacity supported by an impeccable talent for synthesis and courage. Of these qualities the most prominent in King Hussein are those of courage and an ability to respond to the prevailing socio-economic climate.

From the start of his reign King Hussein has developed the image of a courageous leader who has no fear of death.[13] He frequently declares that since the timing of one's death is preordained there is no point in fearing it. For example, he explains that his grandfather taught him 'the unimportance of death and the inner peace granted to those who do not fear death'.[14] King Hussein demonstrated his willingness to place himself in physically dangerous situations by visiting the army camp of Zarqa in 1957, when rebellion was brewing, and by his many visits to the front-line during times of crisis. His love of exhilarating sports such as flying and racing adds to the impression that he is a courageous man. Such an image endears him to his subjects and has also impressed Westerners. Some of the decisions taken by King Hussein show that he also has the courage to make difficult decisions. His dismissal of Suleiman

Nabulsi's nationalist government in April 1957 and his confrontation with the PLO in September 1970 were actions which were bound to meet with fierce opposition from important sections of Arab society, but which the King felt had to be taken.

King Hussein's sensitivity to the demands of the prevailing socio-political climate is one of the factors which has helped him to stay in power. His desire to keep in touch with the prevailing popular mood has been particularly important. Nussaibah explains that throughout the King's rule 'even though public opinion and the factors that influence people are not formally included in the decision-making process, they are taken into account and are present. They have influenced every decision which King Hussein has taken'.[15] The King's willingness to respond to popular feeling was evident in his decision to dismiss Glubb Pasha and to Arabize the army in 1956; his recognition of the PLO in 1964; and his decision to form a military alliance with Nasser shortly before the June 1967 war. In each of these cases King Hussein recognized that failure to react positively to the popular mood would jeopardize the continued existence of the state.

Other factors have contributed to King Hussein's prominent position. He strives to make his rule appear as an expression of popular will by seeking to minimize the gap between himself and his subjects. For example, he prides himself on his close relationship with his soldiers[16] and does his best to appear as a person with few privileges. The title of one of his books, *My Profession as a King*, emphasizes that he regards himself as an ordinary man with a very special job. In it he describes how he makes his own tea and lives a life which is not so different from that of his subjects.[17]

King Hussein also used public speaking as a means of communicating with his subjects. Between January 1962 and December 1967 he delivered 154 speeches – an average of two per month. Of these only eleven were addressed to parliament; forty-six were delivered at public rallies and twenty-nine were broadcast on the radio. His speeches to the public generally seek to generate support and to reaffirm loyalty and allegiance to his person. They become significantly more frequent in times of crisis. For example, on average King Hussein speaks at public rallies about five times a year, but in 1963 and 1966 the number increased to twelve a year. These years saw the war of words against the Hashemites of Jordan by Syria, Egypt and the PLO. The increased number of speeches indicates that King Hussein responded by appealing directly to his people.

In these speeches King Hussein addresses the nation as 'his Jordanian family' and refers to himself as the custodian of the Jordanian people. This reflects his attempt to develop a populist ideology in which he portrays himself as the father of the nation who is responsible for the welfare of the Jordanian people. Hudson explains that, like other monarchs in the Arabian peninsula,

Table 1 *Speeches by King Hussein, January 1962–December 1967*

			Location			
Year of speech	Parliament	Rallies	Radio	Army	Foreign policy	Total
1962	1	5	8	4	3	21
1963	4	12	5	3	4	28
1964	1	5	2	1	9	18
1965	2	9	5	3	8	27
1966	1	12	4	4	10	31
1967	2	3	5	5	14	29
Total	11	46	29	20	48	154

King Hussein has sought to legitimize the monarchy through 'the tradition of Kingship ... and an ideology emphasizing religious rectitude and kingship obligation'.[18] His use of a patriarchal style of authority is congruent with a culture in which 'the family is so central and revered and in which the father enjoys a high degree of deference from other members'.[19]

It is useful to utilize the concept of three circles to describe the three major areas in which King Hussein is actively involved in the Jordanian decision-making process. These are the local circle, the Arab circle and the foreign circle. According to Abu Odeh the monarch is invariably involved in both the formulation and implementation of policy decisions in each of these areas.[20] The extent of his involvement in the pre-decisional and post-decisional stages varies with each of the spheres.

In addition to the three circles, figure 1 shows four institutions which together form the inner executive group. These are the Prime Minister's office, the Royal Hashemite Diwan, the Cabinet and the Foreign Ministry. They are classified on the basis of their position and influence in the ruling hierarchy. The army is a separate category and its position and influence will be dealt with in the discussion of the subordinate institutional structure of the ruling elite.

The local circle

This is the area of internal affairs where theoretically the Prime Minister and his Cabinet have full control over the formulation and execution of policy. However, from 1957 onwards King Hussein's influence over policy formulation in domestic affairs grew considerably. By the 1960s policy formulation in the local circle was the result of consultations between the King, the Prime Minister and the King's advisers. However, policy implementation remains the sphere of the government of the day. One way for the King to exercise his influence over policy formulation is his Letter of Royal Decree, which is issued

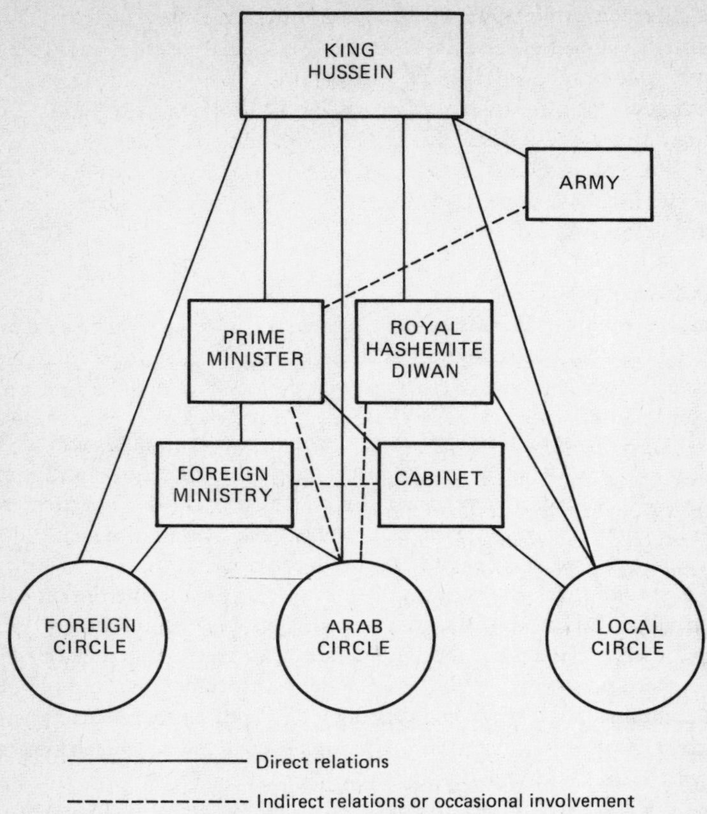

Figure 1. The three circles

by the Prime Minister at the beginning of each new government's period of office. This Letter is the result of consultations between the incoming government and the King and lays down policy guidelines. In moments of crisis the King may also take direct responsibility for decisions in the local circle. For example, he states: 'In 1966 I took into my own hands the personal responsibility of administering the Jordanian government. No one else but me decided to close down the PLO offices in all of Jordan's districts'.[21] However, even this decision was taken in consultation with the Prime Minister of the time, Wasfi Tal. Thus, it would be true to say that in the local circle policy formulation is the result of a liaison between the King and his government. The extent to which each side predominates depends on the personality of the Prime Minister and the importance of the decision. Responsibility for policy implementation usually lies exclusively with the government.

The influence of the Prime Minister and his Cabinet over the army is almost negligible.[22] They have no institutionalized authority over it and are not permitted to interfere in its affairs in questions of policy, training or strategy. For example, the decision to allow an Egyptian General to command the Jordanian forces a few days before the June was entirely King Hussein's. A similar situation prevails in relation to the security policy, although the executive is involved in the implementation of the King's decisions through the Ministry of the Interior.

The Arab circle

The nature of King Hussein's involvement in inter-Arab affairs is closely related to his status as a Hashemite. He sees himself as standing at the vanguard of 'the Arabs' great march in their sacred revolution under the leadership of their knight and pioneer Hussein Ben Ali'. He believes that 'from the minute that the martyr-builder King Abdullah raised his standard high in the sky this country became the focus of the aspirations and dreams for which the hearts of the Arabs have beaten over the years'.[23]

An Arab leader with such a strong sense of identity and such a belief in his heroic role must inevitably find himself and his regime actively involved in regional Arab affairs. This is reflected in the active role King Hussein took at the meetings of the Arab League and the summit meetings, which were the main forums for Arab affairs in the period between 1963 and 1967.

The extent to which King Hussein participates in the Arab circles depends on several factors. Abu Odeh points out that it is 'subject to variation depending on the nature of the issue with which he is dealing'. It also depends on the 'particular Prime Minister in power and the nature of his relationship with the King'.[24] According to Abu Odeh, in affairs relating to the Arab circle, the relationship between the King and his Prime Minister is 'more of an interaction than a one-way system' at both the pre-decisional and post-decisional stages. For example, while the decision to attend the summits initiated by Nasser in 1963 was exclusively the King's it was of direct concern to the Prime Minister and his Cabinet at the post-decisional stage. The summits saw Jordan's acceptance of the creation of a Palestinian entity (the PLO) and the Prime Minister, Bahjat Talhouni, became Jordan's representative at the follow-up committee formed to implement this and other summit decisions. Where policy decisions in the Arab circle relate to bilateral relations, the role of the Prime Minister and the Cabinet at the pre-decisional and post-decisional stages is generally greater.

The relationship between King Hussein and his executive in the Arab circle is highlighted by the experience of Wasfi Tal. In March 1967, as Arab–Israeli tension grew, King Hussein found it imperative to move closer to Egypt. At that time Tal was again Prime Minister. Since he represented an obstacle to the rapprochement with Nasser, King Hussein removed him from office, replacing him with Saad Juma'a who was more likely to be able to effect the required reconciliation. This example illustrates that if the Prime Minister is a strong figure he is allowed considerable influence over the Arab circle. However, at time of crisis it is the King who is the final arbiter.

The foreign circle

According to Abu Odeh the area of foreign policy decision-making is 'almost entirely dominated by the King'.[25] The extent of his activity in this sphere from the 1960s onwards is illustrated by the fact that the monarch's foreign policy speeches between 1962 and 1967 outnumbered those of every other category (table 1).[26] One of the most important reasons for the emphasis King Hussein gives to the formulation of foreign policy is that as the head of the state his foremost concern is its survival. Since Jordan has always been heavily dependent on other nations, the survival of the Kingdom is closely tied to foreign affairs. Throughout his reign King Hussein has strived to maintain a dialogue with both Western and Arab nations, and to establish good relations with them. Since coming to the throne he has developed his role as a diplomat, and by the mid-1960s the international press referred to him as 'the official spokesman of the Arab world'.[27]

A second reason for the King's domination of the foreign circle is that his position as head of state since 1953 has allowed him to establish direct contact with leaders throughout the world. His long rule has resulted in an expert knowledge of foreign affairs and he is therefore in a better position than any Jordanian politician to pursue Jordan's foreign policy aims. Numerous foreign policy decisions stem directly from the King, including the decision to support Nasser in the 1956 Arab–Israeli war; the acceptance of American military aid in 1957; the calling in of British troops in 1958 following the revolution in Iraq; the decision to sever relations with the Federal Republic of Germany in 1965; and the acceptance of United Nations Resolution 242 in November 1967.

The period after the 1967 war saw King Hussein's foreign policy activity at its height. At that time the King believed that the only way in which he could hope to regain the West Bank was through diplomacy. Accordingly he visited twenty countries between the end of June and November 1967, travelling twice to Europe, twice to America, and three times to Egypt[28] with the aim of establishing a Jordanian foreign policy which would take into account the post-June war situation. His visits resulted in the formulation of five principles that constituted the basis of Jordan's foreign policy and played an influential part in the eventual formulation of United Nations Security Council Resolution 242.

The ruling elite

Zaid Rifai explains that 'Jordan has a highly personalized system of government in which decisions are made by the King, through the influence of the King's advisers and in some cases by the Prime Minister and his Cabinet. It is not an institutionalized process. It is a fact of political life in Jordan that we do not have an institutionalized process of decision-making'.[29] One of the reasons for this is that, in general, Jordan's ruling elite has been composed of the King's most trusted friends and aides. The influence of the Jordanian elite is based not on office but on the personal influence its members have on the King. In Abu Odeh's view 'the Jordanian elite exercises the constraints that are usually exercised by institutions'.[30] Its members operate as advisers and thus have a constraining effect on the Jordanian decision-making process which is comparable to that exercised by parliament, pressure groups and Governmental agencies in the West. In Jordan the main institutions in which these people are found are the Prime Ministership, the Cabinet, the Royal Hashemite Diwan, the Foreign Ministry and the army. Each of these institutions is considered in turn below. The Crown Prince, the King's shrewd and well-educated brother, who belongs to this category since he is considered responsible for the country's economic and social development policies, is also regularly consulted by King Hussein and acts as Regent in the King's absence.

In Jordan the participation of the subordinate authority (the state organs) in the decision-making process is limited to providing information and advice in the pre-decisional stage and implementation in the post-decisional stage. Aides who are close to the King are generally influential at the pre-decisional stage. According to Marwan Al-Kassem, King Hussein debates the issue in question with his advisers, then gathers together the various points of view, evaluates them and finally decides what course of action to take.[31] The final and ultimate authority remains, all the time, with the central and dominant figure. King Hussein has initiated all of Jordan's major policies. Demands on the political system have been made directly to him and in general he has also fulfilled them.

Nevertheless, the ruling elite has considerable importance as an instrument of the state because of its ability to modify decisional outcomes through the control of information, its advisory role to the monarch and its influence as a result of a particular method of decision-implementation.

The Prime Minister

When King Hussein first came to the throne the Prime Minister had considerable influence over Jordanian decision-making. Prime Ministers such as Tawfiq Abul Huda, Samir Rifai, Ibrahim Hashim and Said Al-Mufti influenced the decision-making process at pre- and post-decisional stages. Since they played a vital part in the consolidation and preservation of Hashemite rule following the assassination of King Abdullah, they were highly regarded by King Hussein. However, in the late 1950s the situation changed and the King played an increasingly influential role. By the 1960s key decisions were invariably made by him. This is not to say that from this time the Prime Minister's role was reduced to that of executor but that his influence varied according to his personality, expertise and the importance of the decision. There is little doubt that when Tal was Prime Minister his strong personality had a powerful impact on the decision-making process. In the 1970s and 1980s a number of people who had been the King's political advisers became Prime Ministers, including Zaid Rifai and Sharif Abdul Hamid Sharaf. Both these men had extensive experience in foreign affairs and consequently exercised considerable influence over policy formulation at the pre-decisional stage. For example, the close relations with Syria which were forged following the formation of Zaid Rifai's second Cabinet in November 1974 culminated in formal negotiations for union between the two countries. King Hussein and President Assad met several times and the two states decided to form a unified political leadership which would co-ordinate political, economic and military affairs. This development was strongly influenced by Zaid Rifai who sought to maintain the Hashemite's traditional role of promoting Arab unity.

One of the principal means by which the Prime Minister exerts his influence is the Cabinet Statement, which he delivers before parliament and which outlines the policies with which the government will concern itself. The more vital the decision the more likely it is that the influence of the King will be paramount. For example, in the spring of 1967 King Hussein became increasingly concerned that the Arabs were heading for a military confrontation with Israel. Accordingly, in April 1967 he placed in power a man who would pursue the foreign policy aims he desired. In a sense Juma'a gained office because of his willingness to implement the King's desire to bring Jordan back into the mainstream of Arab politics, which at that time meant aligning the nation with Egypt.

The Cabinet

The paramount role of the King in the formulation of policy means that the role of the Cabinet is essentially executive. Its function is particularly curtailed in the sphere of inter-Arab affairs. This is illustrated by the decision that Jordan should join forces with Egypt at the end of May 1967. Nussaibah explains that in reaching this vital decision 'constitutional institutions played a minimal – almost negligible – role. If I remember correctly, the Cabinet accepted whatever was said to it without much questioning. Its members thought they were doing the right thing because they themselves were not properly briefed about the military situation or had perhaps been misled by false information, either deliberately or out of ignorance.'[32]

In the past, recruitment into the Cabinet was based on tradition. Apart from a brief period between 1956–7 and the early 1960s Cabinet members tended to be drawn from families which had always been prominent in the political, tribal and social spheres, and which had a tradition of loyalty to the monarch. At the time of Tal's first Cabinet in January 1962 this pattern changed to one based on merit rather than inheritance. Tal began to initiate into political life a number of young, specialized technocrats who often lacked political experience. They were brought directly into political life at the level of Minister by virtue of their specialized knowledge and skill. Their role was not one of policy formulation, which they had little control over, but one of policy execution. 'While they lacked the political expertise needed to formulate policy, King Hussein's directions to the Prime Minister were sufficient to set them on the right trail.'[33] Tal was particularly demanding and those who did not meet his requirements soon found themselves out of office. In August 1962 he reshuffled his Cabinet and four out of the ten newly appointed ministers were replaced by six different men. Both King Hussein and Tal showed a willingness to try out fresh personnel and their impatience with the pace of development in the departments of the outgoing ministers illustrates the emphasis they placed on achievement. Qualities of specialized knowledge and proven administrative ability were required, although candidates still had to demonstrate loyalty to the throne.

In the absence of political parties, those who are recruited into the executive branch of the government stay there because they accept their muted function in the formulation of policy. This ensures that at the level of the executive there is little conflict over broad policy outlines since its membership is not involved in their creation.

The relationship between the Cabinet and the Prime Minister varies according to the personality and status of the latter. The experience and strong leadership qualities of Prime Ministers such as Ibrahim Hashim, Tawfiq Abul Huda and Samir Rifai meant that their Cabinets enjoyed considerable influence over all aspects of policy formulation. This was accepted as normal by the monarch from the time of King Abdullah to the early years of King Hussein's rule. The new generation of Cabinet Ministers lacked the same experience in the field of foreign affairs, particularly when compared with that enjoyed by King Hussein. Consequently, from the early 1960s Prime Ministers tended to limit the role of their Ministers at the pre-decisional stage and instead concentrated on their executive function. This trend has helped to create a special relationship between the King and the Prime Minister on the basis of the latter's ability to offer the King advice at the pre-decisional stage in his individual capacity as a close adviser rather than as the representative of a collective body. This was the case with most Prime Ministers of the 1960s and 1970s, including Bahjat Talhouni, Sharif Hussein Ben Nasser, Wasfi Tal, Saad Juma'a, Zaid Rifai and Sharif Abdul Hamid Sharaf.

The Royal Hashemite Diwan

Political observers of Jordan usually fail to examine the Royal Hashemite Diwan, although it can be as influential as the Cabinet. No comparable institution exists in the West. The principal function of the Diwan is to monitor policy implementation in the local circle. It also plays an important 'mediating role between [the monarch] and the Cabinet'[34] and has an advisory function which is similar to that of the office of the White House Chief of Staff in America. Depending on the personality and experience of the Chief of the Diwan, advice may be offered on domestic and foreign affairs at the pre-decisional stage.

The role of the Diwan as an executive council in a vital sector of domestic affairs is one of its most important functions. The key personalities in the Diwan tend to belong to Jordan's traditional ruling families and are often drawn from prominent bedouin clans and tribes and social groups which ensures that the Diwan is an important source of support for the throne. Amongst the bedouin, King Hussein's image as patron-ruler has penetrated deeply and he continues to fulfil the role established by his grandfather as a 'super-tribal' leader, particularly over the tribal inhabitants of the East Bank. This is illustrated by the example of Talhouni who was Chief of the Diwan in the late 1950s. When Nabulsi's government challenged the status quo Talhouni brought together those groups which remained loyal to the throne in order to reaffirm their fealty to the King and to express their opposition to the nationalist pro-Nasser trend led by Nabulsi.

In order to facilitate this function the Diwan contains a department called the Tribal Council whose task it is to liaise between the monarchy and the bedouin. Its importance is reflected in the fact that for many years it was led by the King's brother, Prince Muhammad. Tribal leaders consult its officials as often as once a week and King Hussein pays many visits to the tribal districts. The Council serves to promote the loyalty of the bedouin and ensures that the Crown is in constant touch with events in the rural areas of the East Bank. Leaders of bedouin tribes also make frequent visits to the Diwan for various reasons. For example, they may want to reaffirm their allegiance to the King or make requests for assistance or greater government attention to their tribe or district.

The Diwan also allows the monarch to keep in touch with events taking place in rural areas and with the mood of important sections of the population. Ordinary people are also able to visit the Chief of the Diwan in order to talk about their problems, and they may even request an audience with the King. Generally, the Chief of the Diwan is available to anyone who wants to see him. Such people include individuals from all walks of life who may wish to talk about events in their sect, tribe or kin-group. As a result of this liaison the King has succeeded in establishing a special relationship with the rural population to the extent that the inhabitants have an almost personal affection for him. This is reflected in the fact that many do not call the King by his name or title but by an endearing adaptation of the Islamic sobriquet 'Sayyidna', which may be translated into English as 'Sir'.

It is obvious from this that the position of Chief of the Royal Hashemite Diwan is influential since the incumbent is the main aide to the King. According to Abu Odeh 'the Chief of the Diwan acts as a bridge between the King and the Prime Minister'.[35] This means that he is in close contact with both men and forms a close relationship with them. He also gains insight into the role played by the Prime Minister. Consequently the Chief of the Diwan is always a potential candidate for the Premiership. Since the early 1960s most of those who have been Chiefs of the Diwan have gone on to become Prime Ministers and vice versa. This was the case with Bahjat Talhouni, Wasfi Tal, Saad Juma'a, Sharif Hussein Ben Nasser, Ahmed Louzi, Zaid Rifai, Sharif Abdul Hamid Sharaf and others. Each of these men played an influential role in the formulation of policy at the pre-decisional stage, particularly in domestic affairs. In some cases the Chief of the Diwan has extended his role into foreign affairs if he is particularly well qualified in that sphere. This was the case with Marwan Al-Kassem who had been Foreign Minister and Sharif Abdul Hamid Sharaf who had been Jordan's Permanent Representative at the UN.

It should be noted that the framework of the Diwan also includes the post of the Minister of the Royal Court. The occupant of this post is usually a member of the ruling elite who acts as a trusted and senior aide to the King. In this capacity he serves as the main political adviser to the King and carries out a certain amount of diplomacy as his delegate. He may carry important letters or messages to other heads of state. He is therefore an influential figure at the pre-decisional stage of policy formulation and is often concerned with foreign affairs.

The Foreign Ministry

The Foreign Ministry of Jordan does not function as an advisory institution in the formulation of foreign policy but as an executive organ of the Government and the King. Zaid Rifai explains that Jordan depends on diplomacy for the formulation of its foreign policy and 'this is done through the person of the King. He is our chief diplomat and our foreign policy is dominated by him'.[36] According to Abdul Munim Rifai, who was Foreign Minister for a number of years, 'at the pre-decisional stage the King directs the Minister in the formulation of policy and the Minister then implements it'.[37]

The Foreign Ministry's limited role is reflected in the fact that in the critical years of the summits between 1964 and 1966 it barely participated in the major decisions. King Hussein was the most active participant and formulator of foreign policy. Many of his decisions were not the result of consultations with his advisers but were made on-the-spot at the summit conference table. Such decisions included recognition of the PLO, recognition of the republican regime of Yemen, and Jordan's participation in the Unified Arab Command. The same pattern occurred after the 1967 war when King Hussein travelled the world in search of a peace formula which would result in the return of the West Bank to Jordan.

Unlike many developed nations where the appointment of Ambassador is the responsibility of the Foreign Minister, in Jordan they are appointed by King Hussein. This weakens the influence of the Foreign Minister and increases that of the King. Ambassadors' reports are sometimes sent directly to the King rather than to the Foreign Ministry, which further dilutes its influence. Although the King does not necessarily examine these reports himself, they fall out of the orbit of the Foreign Ministry.

A large proportion of Jordan's information gathering activity is conducted by agencies other than the Foreign Ministry. Nussaibah explains that the Foreign Ministry 'competes with other agencies as a specialized institution for the dissemination of information'.[38] These include the General Intelligence Department, which is concerned with security, the monitoring service of Radio Jordan, the reports of Ambassadors and army commanders, and the daily bulletins of the information service of the Royal Hashemite Diwan. The existence of these diverse sources of information dilutes a fundamental function of a foreign ministry – the research, analysis and distribution of information.

One of the most important of these rival institutions is the Ministry of Information. Abu Odeh explains its role:

> The Ministry of Information deals with public information and public material. Any information reflecting new political trends or indications relating to Jordan or the region in general is reported by the Ministry through the Minister of Information to the Prime Minister, the Cabinet, the Royal Hashemite Diwan, and in some cases, directly to the King. At the Ministry there are direct telephone communications to Government institutions, the Royal Hashemite Diwan and Army GHQs. If the matter is not very urgent than it may be reported through a written report to some or all of the above. For this reason, the role played by the Ministry and the Minister has an important political content.[39]

King Hussein appoints personnel outside the Foreign Ministry to engage in diplomacy or other activity which is normally the domain of the Foreign Ministry. For example, when the King was anxious to effect a reconciliation with Nasser in May 1967 he did not send his Foreign Minister to Cairo but his Chief of Staff. The King may sometimes use the Chief of the Royal Hashemite Diwan or the Minister of the Royal Court to conduct similar diplomatic tasks.

It is important to note that the role of the Foreign Minister in Jordan depends on the personality of the Foreign Minister and his relationship with the King as well as the policy objectives of the period. If the Foreign Minister is highly respected by the King or possesses certain qualities he may have considerable influence on the formulation and implementation of foreign policy. Abdul Munim Rifai explains that these qualities may be those of 'special knowledge, expertise or experience, which are highly regarded by the King who at times seeks the advice of the Foreign Minister'.[40]

Abdul Munim Rifai's experience as Foreign Minister between 1967 and 1970 provides an example of the way in which the Foreign Minister sometimes influences the formulation of foreign policy. Rifai explains that in this period in which negotiations with the UN Mediator, Gunar Jarring, over the implementation of Security Council Resolution 242 were taking place, the Foreign Minister and the Prime Minister 'had full authority and exercised considerable influence over the formulation of policy. The King used to be informed of what was happening and we reported to him or asked for his directions, but we did not refer to him for the details'.[41] This illustrates that the influence of the Foreign Ministry is subject to three factors: the issue at hand, the status of the incumbent and the trend prevailing at the time.

Zaid Rifai points out that 'The Minister has access to the King who listens to him. He can argue his case. But the degree of influence he has depends on his calibre. This is why the success or failure of Governments here is a highly personal matter'.[42] One of the reasons why the system works is that the Foreign Minister is almost invariably drawn from the top levels of Jordanian society and therefore tends to share the same outlook as King Hussein. This means that there is often a strong coincidence of views.

The role of the Foreign Minister also depends on the political requirements of the day. For example, in 1966 when Jordan was in need of friends in the Arab world Akram Zu'aiter was chosen for the post of Foreign Minister. His task was to carry the King's messages and to establish closer links with Arab nations, particularly those in North Africa.

The army

In systems where elites, ideologies, institutions and social processes have been institutionalized over a long period of time, the oscillation between legitimate authority and coercive control is limited. In democratic, constitutional and pluralistic states the possibility that the state will have to revert to the use of force to impose its authority is remote. Dekmejian explains that 'in constitutional systems such as the USA and Britain the likelihood of a major decline in the legitimacy variable in relation to that of force is almost negligible, except in rare moments of great crisis'.[43] On the other hand, the frequency, magnitude and consequences of a fall in elite legitimacy in many developing nations are more common occurrences because of the weakness of new or imported ideologies, institutions and social processes. Some of these weaknesses can be related to problems of poverty; class and racial divisions; ethnic differences;

regional variations; poor communications; and the absence of an efficient civil service, which hamper the process of social integration necessary for the building of a nation in the Third World.[44] For this reason in such countries force is often used as a means of controlling and in many cases, maintaining, the integrity of the state. A case in point is Jordan's experience of the civil war in 1970. Dekmejian points out that 'the force component is held in reserve to put down marginal opposition elements if the need arises'.[45] This has occurred a number of times in Jordan, for example, after the Nabulsi Cabinet crisis of 1957 and after the Israeli raid on the village of Samu in 1966.

Because of its critical role in the maintenance of the state, Jordan's rulers have always ensured that members of the army enjoy privileged status.[46] By the 1960s the army had an extensive welfare service, including education, housing and medical facilities and the provision of generous financial allowances. 'The army ... receives generous patronage, salaries and other benefits and the regime makes a special effort to emphasise [its] potential status by giving [its] representatives privileged access to the palace'.[47] King Hussein has always taken a special interest in the army and had made every effort to build on the pre-existing loyalty of its troops. Lt General Amer Khammash points out that the King displays 'a large degree of camaraderie and addresses every soldier by his first name as if he knows them all'.[48] In return the soldiers address him as 'Sayyidna'. King Hussein makes frequent visits to army units where he meets many of the soldiers. He is also in close contact with senior army personnel through visits to army GHQs, where he is kept informed of all relevant developments.

As Supreme Commander King Hussein has complete control over the army. In domestic affairs this control is exercised in consultation with his General Staff, but in foreign affairs decisions affecting the army are made by him alone. The most striking example of this was at the end of May 1967 when King Hussein agreed to place the army under the command of the Egyptian General Abdul Munim Riad. Although the army is the mainstay of the government its officers do not determine policy. This coalescence of political leadership and control of the means of coercion is one of the reasons for the stability of Hashemite rule in Jordan. Army officers may act as executors of government policy but they do not formulate it.

Recruitment into the army and promotion of senior personnel up its hierarchy may be subject to the approval of the monarch. The Hashemites of Jordan have generally favoured bedouins because of their loyalty to the King and they form the hard core of the army. Even in the 1960s loyalty was a key qualification of recruitment and promotion, and if a candidate was exceptionally competent but his loyalty was in doubt he found his path blocked. Promotion to the highest echelons of the army has always been dependent on the will of the King. Thus, the rise to power of Ali Abu Nuwar from Major to

Major General and his appointment as Chief of Staff was at King Hussein's instigation. The importance of loyalty is also reflected in the fact that some of the King's most senior and highly trusted army Generals never retire from public service, except for reasons of age. A number have been absorbed into political service through the Royal Hashemite Diwan or the House of Notables (The Senate). For example, in 1967 Habes Majali was appointed Minister of Defence and later became a member of the House of Notables. After the 1967 war Sharif Nasser Ben Jamil and (in 1979) Lt General Muhammad Idriss were appointed military advisers to the King in the Diwan. Others serve the King as his close advisers. For example, Khammash was Minister of the Royal Court for many years. Because the King's relatives are assumed to be loyal supporters of the throne they tend to rise in the army's hierarchy swiftly. Sharif Nasser Ben Jamil, the uncle of the King, was Commander-in-Chief of the army for many years, and the present Commander-in-Chief, his cousin Sharif Zeid Ben Shaker, is considered to be one of his close advisers.

The political elite (the peripheral elite)

The influence of the political elite is exercised either individually or collectively in a consultative capacity and frequently expresses trends in public opinion. This group includes members of the House of Deputies (Parliament), the House of Notables (the Senate) and religious, social and tribal leaders.

Although the parliamentary system of Jordan appears to be structurally similar to those of Western democracies, the power of the Jordanian parliament is limited by the power of the monarch to summon, prorogue and dissolve parliament, and to rule by decree for limited periods. The existence of the Upper House (the House of Notables) also enhances the power of the King since its members are appointed by him. Its members are generally the leaders of tribal, social and religious communities as well as ex-Prime Ministers, ex-Ministers, retired army commanders and civil servants. Their duties include participating in ceremonial occasions, such as welcoming visiting dignitaries, and travelling as representatives of the Jordanian parliament to foreign nations. They also debate issues and policies of the day, although they have no institutionalized power to implement their conclusions.

The abolition of political parties in 1957 has also meant that most members of the House of Deputies who are elected are already members of the establishment who support the status quo. They are elected on the basis of their tribal, family, sect or ethnic allegiance or on their prominent economic, social or academic position. Their interests are therefore tied to those of the ruling elite to which they either belong or with which they have extensive ties. For these reasons the influence of the Jordanian parliament on the formulation and implementation of foreign policy is limited. Instead it operates as a platform for the discussion of important issues and presents opinions which tend to reflect public feeling and by this means influences the nation's leaders.

Within these limitations, the Jordanian parliament has certain spheres of influence. The Jordanian Constitution enables parliament to conduct votes of confidence in the Government and provides for the impeachment of Ministers. Thus, on 20 April 1963 Samir Rifai's new Cabinet failed to gain a vote of confidence and was forced to resign the following day. There have also been occasions when the King and his Prime Minister have had difficulty in implementing their policies. For example, Wasfi Tal's support of the deposed Imam of Yemen against the Egyptian-supported republican regime was opposed by the majority of parliamentarians. Parliament's view reflected that of public opinion and Tal had considerable difficulty in gaining parliamentary confidence. Accordingly, on 1 October 1962, less than eight months after the formation of his first Cabinet, Tal was forced to ask the King to dissolve parliament because of non-co-operation between the legislature and the Government. Parliamentary opposition was one of the factors behind King Hussein's apparently abrupt reversal of Jordan's policy in Yemen in 1964.

Parliament also possesses some financial control over the Government's fiscal policies. All appropriations of Government Ministries and Departments are strictly controlled by parliament through its specialized finance committee. It should also be noted that in spite of parliament's limited control of the executive the fact that the monarch and his ruling elite have gone so far in giving the country a constitutional and parliamentary system is an indication of the importance attached to democratic values. The ideology of popular participation is strong in Jordan and cannot be ignored. King Hussein's attempt to liberalize the political system soon after he came to the throne reflects his recognition of the need to democratize it as much as possible, although this proved impossible without threatening the survival of the state. This is particularly the case in domestic affairs as the issue of Samu was to show at the end of 1966. Popular sentiment expressed through parliament and public disturbances played a significant role in influencing the decision that Jordan should participate in the 1967 war.

Chapter 2

The principles and practice of Jordanian foreign policy

King Hussein's values and images and their relationship with Jordan's foreign policy aims

In view of the central role played by King Hussein in the formulation of Jordan's foreign policy throughout the period leading up to the 1967 war it is useful to examine the values and images which influence him. These are: his Hashemite heritage; his commitment to Arabism; his commitment to Arab solidarity and co-operation; his commitment to the cause of Palestine; his commitment to the West and antagonism to communism. A further point examines Jordan's foreign policy aim of survival, which at times overrides all others because without the survival of the state all the other values are meaningless.

King Hussein's Hashemite heritage

In a sense all King Hussein's values can be seen to be rooted in his Hashemite heritage. The Hashemites have stood for, *inter alia*, Arab unity and co-operation, commitment to the needs of the Palestinian people and commitment to the West. All of these have been central elements of Jordan's foreign policy aims from the time of King Hussein's accession to the throne until the present day. King Hussein's image of himself as a Hashemite and great-grandson of the man who instigated and led the Great Arab Revolt is therefore one of the keys to understanding the objectives behind Jordan's attitude to other Arab countries.

King Hussein was strongly influenced by his grandfather King Abdullah and was 'brought up to believe in the manifest destiny of the Hashemite family'.[1] Prime Minister Zaid Rifai and Nussaibah confirm that the King is acutely aware that his heritage has imposed on him a total commitment to the ideals for which his family has struggled.[2] According to Zaid Rifai the King believes his task 'is not limited to the service of his Jordanian people but encompasses a larger Arab role'.[3] Abu Odeh also points out that King Hussein's awareness of his Hashemite heritage is coloured by a sense of his family's tragic misfortune. Sharif Hussein was driven out of the Hijaz, King Faisal was executed in Iraq and King Abdullah was assassinated in Jerusalem. The King feels that as the last ruling Hashemite the burden of fulfilling the values they stood for rests on his shoulders.[4]

Despite his Hashemite heritage King Hussein has not automatically received legitimacy as a ruler, particularly in relation to other Arab states, nor has it guaranteed the survival of his regime. On the contrary, it has been the cause of considerable criticism and suspicion by radical Arab states and was a major factor behind political instability from which Jordan suffered in the period prior to the 1967 war. King Hussein came to power at a time when Arab nationalist feeling and antagonism to Western imperialism was becoming an increasingly potent force. He found himself in a position of dependency on the West yet a vociferous element of his population demanded an end to that dependency. It was an age of revolution in which the Jordanian regime was in opposition to the mood of the time.

The Hashemites have traditionally stressed the need for moderation in the political arena and this is something that has been continued by King Hussein. At Arab political meetings, particularly at summits, he has exercised a moderating and stabilizing influence that helped shape final decisions and served to temper calls from radical Arab states for sharp provocative action against Israel. King Hussein has maintained that this attitude of moderation is essential if the Arab world is to maintain its integrity.[5]

In the 1950s and early 1960s the King's moderate stand, his regime's dependency on the West and the rebellious mood of the times, together with the claim that Jordan was unviable as a state, were used by the Ba'ath regime in Syria and Nasser in Egypt as the basis of their propaganda campaign against King Hussein. Certain Arab leaders even went so far as to regard the overthrow of King Hussein as a necessary preliminary step before the liberation of Palestine could be contemplated.[6] This acted as a major constraint on the ability of the King to implement Jordan's foreign policy.

Commitment to Arabism

The concept of Arab unity covers many different forms and although most Arab leaders shared a commitment to the ideal, they differed over the method by which it should be realized. King Hussein believed that the Arab world has 'as its objective a broader nationalism which, while preserving the integrity of the various Arab states, looks towards the eventual amalgamation of them into a large whole',[7] but he saw this as a slow evolution in which political unity was the last step.

The King envisaged an initial period of close co-operation in the cultural, economic and military fields between the four Arab geographical units of the Fertile Crescent, the Arabian peninsula, the Nile valley and the Maghreb. His idealism was mingled with a conviction that his regime could not exist in isolation from the Arab world; this gave him a realism that was not always acceptable to the more radical Arab leaders, who advocated an immediate organic unity at the political, social and economic levels.

King Hussein believed that all activities aimed at achieving this goal should be undertaken 'through an active, respected Arab League in which equality and sincerity of joint purpose would be assured and in which danger of domination by any member of the family would be eliminated'.[8] His belief that the Arab League was the anvil on which Arab nationalism must be forged reflects his pragmatic approach as much as his desire to preserve his regime in the face of the revolutionary tide.

Until the early 1970s Arab differences over how Arab unity should be achieved were the cause of considerable strife in Jordan. Radical states such as Egypt, Syria and Iraq argued that Jordan's dependency on the West was incompatible with King Hussein's commitment to Arab unity, and he was accused of being 'a force actively working to undermine radical Arab nationalist causes'.[9] This claim formed one of the major constraints on Jordan's foreign policy activity in the period leading up to the 1967 war, even though it conflicted with the way in which King Hussein quickly accepted Nasser's call for an Arab summit in 1963.

Arab solidarity and co-operation

As a short-term foreign policy objective King Hussein has always regarded Arab solidarity as the best means of serving the interests of the Arab people. Jordan's vulnerable geographical position has made its ruling elite acutely aware of the dangerous effects of inter-Arab conflict. Jordan has the longest border with Israel and its military capability is considerably weaker than Israel's (see table 6). For this reason, under King Hussein the ruling elite tried to follow a policy of relying on 'joint Arab action and on being part of a larger regional body to enable [Jordan] to survive'.[10]

However, Jordan's ability to implement this policy was limited. Although virtually every Arab leader in the 1950s and 1960s professed his commitment to the ideal of Arab unity the reality was different. The Arab world was split not only between radical and reactionary camps, but within those camps themselves. No genuine movement of regional co-operation emerged and on the whole Jordan remained isolated.

In spite of these problems King Hussein continued to emphasize the need to pursue the ideal of Arab co-operation and his foreign policy activities constantly demonstrated his desire to achieve this. This is illustrated by his response to Nasser's appeal that Arab nations should sever diplomatic relations with the Federal Republic of Germany in retaliation for its arms deal with Israel in 1965. Nussaibah, who was Foreign Minister at the time, explains that although the King was 'vehemently opposed' to such a move his desire to co-operate with his Arab brethren eventually led to his decision to agree to Nasser's request.[11] The same pattern occurred at the Arab summits of 1964 and 1966 when King Hussein accepted many changes in Jordan's foreign policy.

More than anything else, inter-Arab co-operation through the summit concept came as a total vindication of King Hussein's evolutionary view of achieving the ultimate goal of Arab unity. He sought to achieve fraternal relations, full Arab co-operation, support for the Arab League and to safeguard the right of every Arab country to organize its internal affairs and choose the social system that suits its own circumstances and national interests. The *Guardian* newspaper went so far as to describe the King as the 'most diligent apostle of the spirit of inter-Arab co-operation to which [the Cairo summit] gave birth'.[12]

The King's commitment to inter-Arab co-operation was well rewarded by the establishment of the Unified Arab Command to which Jordan subscribed with enthusiasm. This was part of a programme for the mobilization and intensification of Arab efforts to arrive at the necessary position of strength for decisive action on the question of Arab rights in Palestine. To Jordan the main benefit resulting from the establishment of the UAC was the plan which gave Jordan the opportunity to build up its military capability and the power to enable the Jordanian armed forces to resist armed aggression.

Commitment to the cause of Palestine

The creation of the state of Israel at the expense of the Palestinian people ran directly against the Hashemite call for Arab self-determination and unity. To Sharif Hussein and his descendants, Palestine and Transjordan were one entity which together constituted part of Greater Syria. In King Hussein's view the Sharif 'practically abdicated his throne . . . because he could not bring himself to accept an alienation of Palestine from the rest of the Arab homeland'.[13] From an early age King Hussein learnt to view the issue of Palestine as one of the most important and serious of his concerns. The search for a solution favourable to the Palestinians became an integral part of his value system.

The King's intense involvement with the issue of Palestine was also the result of the incorporation of the West Bank into Jordan. This had far-reaching repercussions on Jordanian society which could not be ignored. The refugee problem was enormous. In May 1967 there were 722,687 registered refugees in Jordan. While the United Nations Relief and Works Agency (UNRWA) provided them with some of their needs, it was far from adequate. The Agency's 1965–6 report candidly states that its ration scales 'provide about two-thirds of the normal intake of a poor Middle Easterner'.[14] Consequently the refugees became dependent on Jordan's meagre economic resources. There were also many refugees without refugee status whose plight was even more desperate. In the two decades following the Arab–Israeli war of 1948 the Jordanian Kingdom's failure to integrate fully the Palestinian refugees into the nation resulted in an insoluble problem for the government. Their miserable state and subsequent bitterness made them susceptible to the propaganda of radical Arab states such as Egypt and Syria, with resulting sporadic civil unrest.

There were also important ideological differences between King Hussein's interpretation of a just solution to the problem and that of other factions in the Arab world. The Hashemites' espousal of the Palestinians had been based not on *Palestinian* self-determination but on *Arab* self-determination. It therefore did not preclude the absorption of Palestine into a larger Arab entity such as Jordan. This view was in contrast with that of the radical Arab states and some elements of the Palestinian people who were dedicated to establishing a Palestinian state.

Despite these disagreements, from the start of his reign King Hussein made considerable efforts to help the Palestinian people living in Jordan. Upon taking up his constitutional duties in 1953 he carried out an extensive programme of visits to all parts of the country, including refugee centres, particularly on the West Bank. The purpose of these visits was to meet his Palestinian subjects and to learn about their needs and aspirations. Abdul Raouf Fares, the late MP for Nablus, recalls that the King was appalled at the plight of the Palestinian refugees and was determined to help them as much as he could. He remembers that at almost all meetings with West Bank leaders and refugee representatives at the Royal Palace and elsewhere the King made a point of hearing about the problems the refugees faced and how the various government bodies were dealing with them.[15] Where possible he tried to find an immediate solution to problems that had appeared intractable. For example, at that time Palestinians wanting to travel to other Arab countries, such as Saudi Arabia, had difficulty in obtaining visas, particularly when they were either known as, or suspected of being, political activists. When the King learnt of this he instructed the Minister of the Interior to make it possible for Palestinians to obtain work abroad with the minimum of bureaucratic procedure.

Fares also confirms that King Hussein's visits to Gulf states have helped to facilitate and ease recruitment procedures for his subjects who have sought employment there.[16] For example, before the King's intervention, Jordanians of Palestinian origin had to include in their applications for employment a 'Certificate of Good Conduct and Behaviour' as a precondition for being granted a residence or work permit. In effect this amounted to the screening of all Palestinians who wished to travel to the Gulf states. As a result of the King's efforts, the General Intelligence Department, whose task it was to issue these certificates, limited its strict control procedures to those Palestinians who were known to be a security risk.

However, these attempts to ease the lot of the Palestinians were overshadowed by the conflict that resulted from their desire to fight for their homeland. The fact that many of the refugees were within striking distance of their usurped homes and land made raids on Israeli territory inevitable. Israel responded with a policy of massive retaliation which caused deep distress to the inhabitants of Jordan. There was also the ever-present fear that Israel would invade the West Bank if it felt that these incursions had reached an intolerable level.

For these reasons King Hussein was sometimes forced to take a repressive stand against his Palestinian subjects. This happened in 1955, 1957, 1963 and 1966 when he used the army to impose law and order by force.[17] Despite this, his desire to find a just solution to the Palestine problem continued and was one of the reasons for his acceptance of the creation of the PLO at the Cairo summit in 1964.

Anti-communist and pro-Western stance

King Hussein has demonstrated his commitment to the West many times during his reign. His antagonism to communism has been as pronounced as his commitment to the West. In his open letter to Prime Minister Nabulsi in February 1957 the King issued a warning that he would not tolerate pro-communist activity. It was followed shortly afterwards by a ban on all forms of communist literature. King Hussein believed that the communist bloc had a long-term strategy to destroy small and vulnerable countries such as Jordan because of their strategic value to the West.

The Hashemites' tendency to lean towards the West has its roots in Sharif Hussein's battle against the Ottomans on the side of the Allied Forces in the First World War. This pattern was continued by his sons. Both King Faisal and King Abdullah were allies of Britain and generally co-operated with the Western powers. Although the collapse of the Ottoman Empire led to a struggle for power in the Middle East which brought the Hashemites into conflict with the British, they eventually compromised with them and were ultimately supported by them in Transjordan and Iraq.

The second reason for King Hussein's positive attitude to the free world is his adherence to the religion of Islam. His faith in Islam makes him antagonistic to communism because of communism's denial of the existence of God. He argues that 'there can be no life for Arabism under the alternative to freedom – local or world-wide communism' because 'communism denies all faiths and thus the very principle on which Arab nationalism is based'.[18] Sharif Hussein's fervent belief in the teachings of Islam formed the foundation of his leadership of the Great Arab Revolt and of his refusal to accept the Ottomans as the rightful heirs to the Caliphate. As the Sharif's direct descendant it is only natural that King Hussein should believe that the future of Arabism cannot be isolated from the values and teachings of Islam.

Finally, King Hussein's pro-Western attitude has been reinforced by the poor state of Jordan's economy, its vulnerability to Israeli attack and its isolation from its powerful Syrian and Egyptian neighbours. These factors have made it dependent on external military and financial support. Because the Arab world has never been able to provide Jordan with the support it needed, the Hashemites' traditional association with the West made King Hussein turn to it for aid.

Survival

Jordan's vulnerable position is such that its survival is the principal foreign policy objective to which all the above aims are subject. Many of the values enshrined in its foreign policy aims have been forced aside at various points as a result of threats to Jordan's existence. For example, Jordan's alliance with the West in defiance of the King's commitment to Arab solidarity was the result of the state's need for financial and military support. Even at the height of anti-British feeling King Hussein was reluctant to end the treaty with Britain because he feared that it would deprive him of the British subsidy at a time when no alternative was available.

The same principles of Arab unity and co-operation were cast aside in favour of Western support when King Hussein called in the British in 1958. With the destruction of the Hashemite regime in Iraq, King Hussein was left without an ally in the Arab world. In the circumstances he had no choice but to turn to the West for support. In 1964 King Hussein's antagonism to communism was overlooked when he joined the non-aligned movement. Support for the West was cast aside when Jordan formed a military alliance with Egypt at the end of May 1967. In September 1970 King Hussein's opposition to the PLO led to civil war when radical Palestinian organizations began to threaten the existence of his regime. It is apparent from these examples that survival lies at the heart of King Hussein's foreign policy objectives and the weight given to each one is juggled according to the realities of the situation.

The underlying reason for this unfortunate situation is Jordan's precarious position. This was particularly the case before the June war. Until 1967, in addition to its financial problems, Jordan was hemmed in by hostile neighbours. In the 1950s and 1960s it was threatened by Israel, Egypt and Syria. After 1958 it was threatened by Iraq and prior to that by Saudi Arabia. If the Jordanian government allowed raids into Israel to take place, it risked massive retaliation and the possibility of invasion. If it weighed too heavily on the

Palestinians and failed to respond aggressively to Israel's threats it was subject to violent propaganda campaigns by radical Arab states which were designed to undermine its leadership and lead to revolution. If it failed to co-operate with the Arab world the risk of revolution increased, yet if it did co-operate the risk of Israeli invasion increased. Heavily dependent for its survival on subsidies from the Western world Jordan could not afford to align itself too closely with the revolutionary Arab regimes, yet neither could it afford to alienate them. Such has been Jordan's position and it is against these conflicting, contradictory and tempestuous forces that its foreign policy activities should be placed.

The pursuit of Jordan's foreign policy aims

Among the instruments used by countries to pursue their foreign policy aims are those of diplomacy, clandestine activities, propaganda, the threat of force and the use of force. This section examines Jordan's use of these mechanisms between 1955 and 1967.

Diplomacy

Diplomacy is a central instrument used by countries to implement their foreign policy. It is particularly important to Jordan because the nation's impoverished state means that it has few alternative instruments of foreign policy implementation. In many cases, for example, when seeking financial aid, diplomacy has been the only instrument available to it. For this reason King Hussein has always laid great emphasis on diplomacy and over the years has developed his diplomatic role to the full. Zaid Rifai remarks that 'because of the constraints upon our country and geographical position, because of the relative weakness of the country compared to most of its neighbours, we depend mostly on diplomacy and this is done through the person of the King'.[19]

King Hussein has consistently sought to keep open the channels of communication between himself and his critics within the Arab world. His willingness to meet other Arab leaders and to attend conferences has been demonstrated throughout his reign and has contributed to the survival of his regime because it has minimized the extent to which Jordan is isolated. As the King's behaviour at the summits of 1962–6 illustrated, his diplomatic activity displays a flexibility which has enabled him to effect radical policy changes when failure to do so might have resulted in a serious threat to Jordan's political stability.

King Hussein's diplomatic activities have become increasingly important over the years. In 1964 the *Guardian* described the monarch as the 'diplomatist extraordinary of Arab brotherhood – and on the international as well as the

Arab front'.[20] By developing his diplomatic role to the full the King has pursued his desire to serve as an advocate for the Arab cause.

Since his first visit to America in 1959 King Hussein has dealt with eight American Presidents and he visits the USA at least once a year. Zaid Rifai believes that in the 1960s the King 'appeared to the Americans as the young, courageous, sporting, and what was most important – moderate – King, surrounded by an ocean of extremism, radicalism and hostility to the West. This made him the odd-man-out in the Arab world and the Americans could identify with that'. However, Rifai goes on to argue that 'when it came to the crunch and Jordan sought support against Israel, for example, all these factors simply vanished'.[21]

In the previous chapter it was explained that although the role of Jordan's ambassadors is often limited to routine bureaucratic work and the gathering of information, they are sometimes of vital importance in bilateral relations. For example, in the mid-1970s the then-ambassador to Syria, Nabih Nimr, was instrumental in implementing Zaid Rifai's policy of re-establishing cordial relations between the Jordanian and Syrian governments. Nimr's efforts played an important part in terminating the long-running feud between the two countries and in the establishment of an unprecedented level of co-operation. As a result King Hussein paid several visits to Damascus and also received President Assad of Syria in Amman.

Jordanian ambassadors to the United Nations have also made important contributions. As Foreign Minister, Abdul Munim Rifai played a vital role in the negotiations initiated by Ambassador Gunar Jarring for finding a formula for solving the Arab–Israeli conflict on the lines of UN Security Council Resolution 242. Rifai's successor, Abdul Hamid Sharaf, was delegated a number of times to conduct talks with the US State Department and with senior officials of the White House. Hazem Nussaibah was active in achieving Jordan's reconciliation with representatives of radical Arab states at the UN, thereby enabling the Arabs to present a united front over the issue of Palestine after the 1967 war. This was a considerable achievement in view of the enormous differences of opinion that existed between the various Arab governments.

Clandestine activities

Although Jordan has been the target of much clandestine activity by other nations,[22] its own activities in this field have been limited. The General Intelligence Department, which is concerned with gathering intelligence data relating to state security, is not involved in clandestine activity to a significant extent and no other organization exists to utilize this technique of foreign policy implementation. There are several reasons for this.

First, clandestine activities require a degree of solvency which Jordan has never enjoyed. Unlike its wealthier Arab neighbours, Jordan's military requirements have left little money available for subversive activity.

Secondly, Jordan's dependence on Western military and economic support has made the development of clandestine activity difficult. The most suitable countries to teach the Jordanians subversive techniques were America and Britain, but the potential threat this would have presented to Israel eliminated this possibility.

Thirdly, the presence of a large number of dissatisfied Palestinians within Jordan meant that Jordan's enemies had no difficulty in recruiting anti-monarchical elements who could be used to counter any Jordanian subversive activity.

This is not to say that Jordan has not been suspected of clandestine activity. Nasser accused Jordan of being involved in the Syrian coup which ended the union between Egypt and Syria in 1961. In 1960 the Jordanian intelligence service was accused of supporting and financing the attempted coup in Lebanon by military elements of the National Syrian Party, a political organization which sought the union of the countries comprising the geographical area of Syria. It is also rumoured that, prior to the 1967 war, Jordanian intelligence liaised with Syrian dissidents who attempted to overthrow the Ba'ath regime in a military coup.

Propaganda

Although in the 1950s and early 1960s Egypt and Syria mounted a massive propaganda campaign against the Jordanian regime, Jordan did not retaliate to the same extent. Instead King Hussein concentrated on defending himself against these accusations, rather than on attacking the Egyptian and Syrian regimes. As with clandestine activities, Jordan's failure to indulge in this kind of propaganda was due to financial and technical constraints.

Prime Minister Wasfi Tal's campaign against Nasser which lasted from late 1966 until April the following year was the exception to the rule. In this campaign Nasser was accused of being too frightened to confront Israel and of hiding behind the United Nations Emergency Force in Sinai. It was also pointed out that by failing to stop Israeli shipping passing through the Gulf of Aqaba he was helping Israel to survive. On the whole this campaign was effective and was one of the factors which led to Nasser's closure of the Straits of Tiran to Israeli shipping on 23 May 1967.

In general, King Hussein's good relations with the West have enabled him to present himself and his nation positively in the eyes of the Western media. This is due to his generally moderate and pro-Western stance and to his readiness to make himself available to the media, rather than the result of conscious government policy.[23]

The threat of force

The threat of force is a powerful instrument available to any strong country in the pursuit of its foreign policy aims. To a small and militarily weak country such as Jordan the value of such an instrument is limited, because the threat of force makes no impact if the country lacks the military power to carry out its threats. This has always been the case with Jordan in relation to Israel.

In the 1960s Jordan's position in relation to Arab countries was slightly better and although small, the Jordanian Army had a reputation for efficiency. When Syria announced that it was going to close its borders with Jordan in 1966 Prime Minister Wasfi Tal responded by threatening to open it by force. In the same way, when King Hussein learnt of the coup in Iraq in 1958 and the murder of his cousin, his first response was that he would revenge King Faisal's death and restore the Arab Union (the federation between Iraq and Jordan) by force. However, it quickly became apparent that such a course of action was not feasible.

The use of force

Just as Jordan was limited in its ability to threaten forceful imposition of its foreign policy aims, so it was limited in its ability to use force. However, there were occasions when force was the only available option. This was evident when, for example, dissent within Jordan – which was often related to Jordan's foreign policy activity – was repressed by the military. The three occasions when Jordan used its army as a means of implementing its foreign policy aims in the Arab world were in the early years of the Yemeni civil war, in Kuwait at the time of independence and in Oman when it helped to crush the revolt in Zufar at the request of Sultan Qaboos. The most important area where the use of force has served as a means of implementing Jordan's foreign policy is over the issue of Palestine. Jordan's determination to play a role in this field resulted in its entry into the Arab–Israeli wars of 1948 and 1967.

Capabilities and Constraints

This section examines Jordan's ability to implement its foreign policy aims in terms of the social, economic and political factors which affect it. It includes a discussion of the Jordanian economy, Jordan's relationship with external

Table 2 *Population increase by region 1943–63*

Region	1949	1952	1961	1963	% increase or decrease
East	**400,000**	**586,885**	**885,143**	**985,389**	68.00
Settled Nomads		386,885	729,618	932,460	
Nomads		200,000	55,525	52,929	−75.00
West	**850,000**	**742,289**	**805,980**	**875,094**	7.90
Settled	400,000				
Refugees	450,000		578,547		
Abroad			62,863		
Total:	**2,100,000**	**1,329,174**	**1,691,123**	**1,860,483**	

Source: N. Aruri, *Jordan: A Study in Political Development* The Hague, Martin Nijhoff, 1972, p. 67.

powers, the Palestinians living within Jordan and the capability of the army as a means of enforcing government policy.

Social considerations

Urbanization

Jordan shared with many developing countries the problem of rapid urbanization accompanied by a high level of unemployment and under-employment. Urbanization occurred at an increasingly rapid rate between 1952 and 1963, particularly in the East Bank.[24] Amman's population increased by 156 per cent and Zarqa grew from virtually nothing to a population of 109,274.

Growth figures for West Bank cities were much lower. As table 2 shows, a considerable amount of East Bank urbanization was the result of rural migration and Palestinian immigration. Both of the groups had been forced off the land, one mainly by the mechanization of agriculture and the other by Israeli territorial expansion. The economy was unable to absorb this pool of often unskilled labour and the cities became crowded with a pauperized mass of unemployed who were susceptible to the anti-Jordanian propaganda of radical Arab forces.

Although the radicalization of new urban migrants was not carried over into rural Jordan in the period following Nabulsi's resignation and throughout the late 1950s and early 1960s, the urbanization of rural and even bedouin elements of Jordanian society continued to carry with it the potential of civil unrest. In their often pauperized state many of these people were quick to criticize the Jordanian regime and were therefore easily influenced by the propaganda of

Egypt and Syria. This pattern may be regarded as one of the principal reasons for the attempted coups d'état which occurred in this period. The failed attempts to overthrow the King which took place in 1960, 1961 and 1963 were all inspired and led by army commanders of rural origin such as Mahmoud Al-Rousan and Sadek Al-Share'.

The bedouin

The bedouin have always been a bedrock of support for the Hashemite regime in Jordan. By 1967 the bedouin had ceased to be nomadic warriors and had settled on new agricultural land or found work in Jordan's urban centres. Nevertheless the impact of nomadic traditions is, even now, of much greater significance than the figures would suggest, in view of the tenacity of desert culture and the cohesive organization of nomadic tribes. It is still common practice, even for urbanized groups (and more so for villagers), to identify themselves as tribes and clans, more or less as they did when still in a tribal, nomadic state.

King Abdullah and King Hussein cultivated the loyalty of the bedouin by integrating them into the state-apparatus through service in the army. Their loyalty has acted as a counterbalance to the instability caused by the dissatisfied Palestinians. The role of bedouins in the army has been crucial to the maintenance of the power of the monarch. For example, in 1957, during the conflict between King Hussein and the Nationalists, the King turned to the bedouins, inside and outside the army, for support. In 1957, after Abu Nuwar's attempted coup, 200 bedouin chieftains went to the palace to assure the King of their loyalty. Important army units were also placed under the leadership of bedouin officers. As a result, the King was able to form a new government, crush the opposition and ally the country with America. Thus, bedouin support has enhanced King Hussein's ability to deal with domestic problems which had frequently been instigated by external powers.

Minority groups – Christians and Circassians

In comparison with Syria and Lebanon, Jordan is homogenous as far as religious adherence and language are concerned. The majority of its inhabitants are Arabic-speaking Sunni Muslims. The exceptions to this are the Circassians[25] and the Christians.[26] The Christians are Arabic speaking and the Circassians are Sunnis. However, even these differences are tempered by other factors.

The absence of significant religious divisions within Jordan, together with the strong nationalist feeling of many members of minority religions, meant that religious adherence did not constitute a constraint on the state's foreign policy decision-making. Both Christians and Circassians are given greater political representation than their numbers warrant. The position of the

Circassians is further enhanced by their use in the state apparatus. They hold key positions in the armed forces, particularly the air force. Like the bedouin they are generally loyal to the King.

Economic considerations

From 1948 until 1967 Jordan had an enviable economic record amongst developing countries. According to the Central Bank of Jordan its economy prior to June 1967 witnessed higher rates of growth than any other developing country.[27] However, while a sound economic base obviously enhances a country's ability to implement its foreign policy aims, Jordan's economy was also faced with problems which restricted freedom of action at the political level. These problems are considered below.

Agriculture and water

Jordan is essentially a desert country and in 1964 only 13.4 per cent of its land was cultivable. Yet, as table 3 illustrates, the agricultural sector was the single most important source of employment. A planned development of the agricultural sector was therefore vital to Jordan's economic development. This was also seen as a necessary step on the path to political stability because of the need to provide employment for the large number of unemployed and underemployed Palestinians. The main obstacle in the way of agricultural development in Jordan is lack of water.

For this reason the development of irrigation systems was regarded by Jordan's decision-makers as vital for the future of the agricultural sector,[28] yet the potential for irrigation was never realized, principally because of conflict with Israel over the right to use the waters of the River Jordan.

Jordan's failure to develop its agricultural sector resulted in an underdeveloped economy which produced the constraining effects of dependence on foreign powers, a restless, dissatisfied population and an inability to maintain an army powerful enough to provide protection for any Jordanian attempt to carry out irrigation schemes.

Manufacturing and mining

Industrial development in the early 1960s posed a number of problems. One of these was the need for foreign capital. The poorly developed economy and shortage of domestic investors made Jordan anxious to encourage foreign investment. In 1955 the government passed the Law for Encouragement of Foreign Capital Investment. This placed foreign investors on an equal footing with newly established local industries, allowing them important financial exemptions and protection from competition. At the same time, foreign investment in Jordan was not without its problems: it resulted in a dependence on the West which King Hussein was anxious to avoid because it led to

Table 3 *Distribution of economically active population*

Occupation	Number	Percentage
Agriculture	137,757	35.3
Manufacturing, mining	41,932	10.8
Trade and services	84,881	21.7
Administration, professions, army and public security	73,350	18.8
Construction	40,159	10.3
Transport	11,899	3.1
Total	389,978	100.0

Source: Hashemite Kingdom of Jordan, Department of Statistics, Economic Characteristics of the Population, Amman, 1964, pp. 10–11.

criticism within Jordan that the country was being forced into a relationship of submission to the West in a new form of colonial exploitation. There was also the fear that such dependence made Jordan vulnerable to Western pressure in the political arena.

A second problem in the way of industrial development was that of transport. Within Jordan there was only one railroad and although major roads connected the cities within each Bank only two connected the East Bank with the West Bank. Jordan had only one port, Aqaba, situated in the south-west, far from the main urban centres. The lack of transport facilities made the cost of fuel extremely high, thus further discouraging industrial development.

Thirdly, there was the problem of the small size and relative poverty of the domestic market. It was not merely that the majority of the population had little spending power, but that many of these people were refugees whose income came from outside Jordan's economy and was exceedingly low. For this reason, Jordan was forced to seek markets abroad. Since this necessitated the development of good relations with other countries it acted as a constraint on Jordan's freedom of political action. This was particularly the case in relation to Syria who, by 1967, had become Jordan's most important trading partner.

Fourthly, there were the difficulties caused by the West Bank's precarious stability. Most of Jordan's minerals were located in this area but its vulnerability to Israeli attack made it unattractive to domestic and foreign investors.

Government anxiety to encourage industrial development resulted in the 1955 Law for Encouragement and Guidance of Industries. This law gave new industries many privileges and, together with the Law for Encouragement of Foreign Capital Investment, was an important contribution to the rise of new industries in the following years.

As a result of these measures, the period 1959–66 saw enormous growth in real terms in the industrial and mining sectors of the Jordanian economy. As with agricultural development, industrial development was directed towards reducing dependence on foreign aid and increasing employment. Under the Seven Year Plan of 1964 the manufacturing and mining sectors of Jordan grew rapidly. By 1967 Jordan had an industrial capacity that was beginning to make a considerable impact on the dual constraints of unemployed refugees and dependence on foreign aid.

Ports

The arbitrary lines drawn up by Britain and France after 1919 left Jordan with access to the sea only at the small, undeveloped port of Aqaba in the south-west corner. This situation was made worse after the 1948 war because the creation of Israel cut off the West Bank from the natural outlets it had used for thousands of years.

The importance of Aqaba led the government to undertake an extensive modernization programme in the early 1960s, making it suitable for international shipping, and constructing a road linking it to Amman. However, Jordan's exclusive reliance on Aqaba continued to act as a constraint on the country because its shipping lines to the Mediterranean passed through the Suez Canal. This meant that Egypt controlled the flow of trade out of the port and was able seriously to threaten Jordan's trade with Europe and North America. Although the replacement of UN troops with Egyptian ones at Sharm Al-Sheikh in southern Sinai in 1967 was directed against Israel, Jordan's poor relationship with the UAR at that time meant that Nasser could attempt to threaten Jordan's trade to the East as well.

The only other trade routes open to Jordan were through the Mediterranean ports in Syria and Lebanon. This meant at least high tariffs and the possibility of a complete Syrian refusal to co-operate. It was only after the 1967 war that Jordan's vulnerability in this regard was eased because of the improvement in its relationship with Syria.

The budget: trade and aid

Although it has been shown that developments in agriculture, industry and mining helped to reduce Jordan's dependence on foreign aid the balance of trade remained precarious. Jordan's chronic budget deficit has existed as long as Jordan itself and has resulted in a need for budget support from foreign sources. The bulk of foreign aid originally came from the UK. From 1957 the USA took over as the principal donor of aid and therefore as an important influence on Jordan's foreign policy. Reliance on budget support represented a crucial constraint on Jordan's ability to implement its foreign policy objectives and acted as a major factor influencing decision-making in this period. This is illustrated by the fact that after Jordan abrogated its treaty with Britain in 1957 there were rumours that the government could not pay the salaries of army personnel and was only able to do so because of the speed with which America provided aid.

Although King Hussein's pro-Western policies produced revenue for his regime it did not provide a stable income because it was at the mercy of changes in US foreign policy and in the regional balance of power. It was also a cause of domestic instability because of Palestinian antagonism towards the USA, Israel's most important ally. The riots of 1963 in support of Jordan joining the proposed union between Egypt, Syria and Iraq were an expression of resentment against Jordan's position as an American dependency and were actively encouraged by Egypt and Syria. Even though these riots failed to make Jordan's decision-makers favour the country's radical Arab neighbours, this pressure, together with other restrictions caused by Jordan's dependence on the West, led King Hussein to attempt to diversify his sources of budget support. This had an important effect on Jordan's foreign policy since the Jordanian government was forced to look to the Arab world for aid. The summits of 1964 increased this potential and revealed that while Jordan's relationship with its Arab neighbours often acted as a constraint on its foreign policy, it always held the potential of adding to the military and economic capabilities of the nation. As it turned out, Jordan received very little of the money it had been promised and dependence on the West continued.

Jordan's endeavour to move away from reliance on Western aid was influenced by other economic factors. Sixty-one per cent of Jordan's trade was intra-regional, dependent on Arab good-will.

Between 1961 and 1965 the average export value to countries within the region was as follows: (in US$ millions)[29]

Iraq	Kuwait	Lebanon	Syria	Saudi Arabia	U.A.R.	Total
1.6	2.3	3.1	2.4	1.8	—	11.2

By 1963 Arab influence on Jordan was becoming increasingly important. Although it remained hostile to Jordan, Syria was developing into the country's most important trading partner. Kuwait and Saudi Arabia not only became significant trading partners but were also important donors of aid. This affected Jordan's foreign policy activities and was one of the reasons for King Hussein's support of the Saudi-supported royalists in the Yemen in the early 1960s.

However, since aid from Arab countries proved as erratic as American aid, King Hussein became even more determined to build a stronger domestic economy in order not to be constrained at the political level nor to be subject to the vagaries of the foreign policies of other countries. Contrary to the

Table 4 *Imports and Exports ranked in order of value*

Export to Jordan	Imports from Jordan
United Kingdom	Syria
United States	Yugoslavia
German Federal Republic	Lebanon
Syria	Kuwait
Japan	Saudi Arabia
Italy	Czechoslovakia
Lebanon	India
Saudi Arabia	Poland
Turkey	Iraq
France	United States
Belgium	Greece
Netherlands	Italy
United Arab Republic	Germany
Iraq	
India	

Sources: A Directory of Jordanian Industrial Firms, pp. 26–7; Jordan, Ministry of Information, Al-Iqtisad Al-Urduni, pp. 16–20.

pessimistic predictions of the 1950s, by 1967 Jordan had succeeded in decreasing its dependence on foreign aid, reducing it from an average of 17 per cent of GNP between 1959 and 1962, to 13 per cent between 1963 and 1966. This was due to an increase in agricultural production, tourism and the remittances of Jordanians living abroad.

By the end of 1966 Jordan had begun to generate its own capital for investment and the main aim of the 1964–70 Seven Year Plan for economic self-sufficiency looked within reach. This offered Jordan the possibility of decreasing its dependence on Arab and Western nations, thereby increasing its ability to implement its foreign policy objectives. However, the intervention of the 1967 war shattered this hope.

Political considerations

Jordan's relationship with the USA

Since the Second World War the USA had viewed the Middle East as crucial to the balance of power between East and West. From that time until the early 1960s developments in the area were seen from the point of view of a policy of containment of Soviet influence. With this aim in mind America tried to maintain a chain of pro-Western governments, for example, in Greece, Turkey and Iran.

By the mid-1950s many countries which had previously allied themselves with Western powers had either turned towards Soviet Russia or were seeking to become independent of any superpower. Jordan was one of the few Arab countries which maintained its alliance with the West because of King Hussein's belief that this was the only way by which he could ensure adequate defence of his country. The irony was that whilst Jordan paid a heavy price for its alignment with the USA in terms of internal instability and the criticism of anti-Western Arab countries, the advantages it gained were limited because from the early 1960s American Middle East policy became increasingly weighted in Israel's favour.

Official United States policy in the Middle East between 1950 and 1965 was expressed in the Tripartite agreement of 1950 in which Britain, France and the USA agreed to support the political independence and territorial integrity of all Middle Eastern nations. However, the threat of Soviet influence in the area made Israel increasingly important to America as a bastion of Western power and influence, and this was used by Israel to gain American support.[30] While King Hussein's pro-Western regime was important to America, Jordan did not have the power, influence or strategic importance of Israel; when it came to taking sides, America invariably sided with the latter. The Jewish lobby in America was also numerous, well-organized and vociferous. By the time of the Presidency of Johnson the influence of Israel on the American government was supreme. King Hussein notes that whilst Eisenhower adopted a 'very courageous position' in relation to Israel in 1956 'since then there has been a change of emphasis in the US as far as the Israelis and the Zionist movement was concerned and we felt that in the sixties . . . [the influence of the latter] grew'.[31]

This had a powerful impact on King Hussein's ability to implement his foreign policy objectives, particularly those relating to the question of Palestine and Israel since, in his own words, 'nothing could be done or achieved without US participation'.[32] Nussaibah echoes this feeling: 'There is no doubt whatsoever that the Americans, who are unreservedly committed to Israeli designs, were always an important influence on policy-making and the decision-making process.'[33] Although Nussaibah adds the rider that 'this does not mean that the King invariably or even generally accepted their restraints' there were many occasions when King Hussein had little choice.[34] This was reflected in the domestic environment in 1952 when Jordan was forced to back down over its plans to irrigate the area of the Ghor because of the withdrawal of American and UN financial aid.

These constraints on Jordan's freedom were eased in the latter 1950s and 1960s as a result of changes in the international situation. In the early 1960s official American Middle East policy changed from one of containment to one of non-interference. This was reflected in the fact that the USA offered no military support to Kuwait when Iraq attempted to annex it. Similarily, the USA stayed out of the Yemeni conflict and refrained from reacting to the 1963 Union between Syria, Egypt and Iraq. Jordan was able to enter limited alliances with Arab states that either were or had been hostile to America, which culminated in the formation of the Unified Arab Command at the first Arab summit conference.

The same period witnessed a deterioration in Soviet Russia's relationship with Egypt. The USA was invited to trade with Egypt and a substantial shipment of American grain was sent to Egypt. This made it difficult for Egypt to criticize Jordan for being a client-state of the USA. Thus the constraint imposed by Arab propaganda against King Hussein's pro-Western policies eased considerably. However, in 1966 it was to resurface in even more violent form.

The superpowers – their common and conflicting objectives

Despite Soviet hostility to Israel, both superpowers had an interest in the continued existence of Israel. The reasons for this in the case of the USA have already been noted. In the case of Russia, Israel was important in so far as it maintained the polarization of East and West in the Middle East and therefore ensured the continuation of a Soviet role in the region.

The USA and the USSR wanted to avoid being drawn into a war in the Middle East and for this reason both sought to maintain the status quo. Their interests in the region were limited to the supply of arms, military training and economic aid. By these means they ensured that the countries in the region were dependent on them to a greater or lesser extent. However, until 1967 such involvement by either side did not extend to either overt or covert offers of active military support.

Inter-Arab relations

Inter-Arab relations in the period preceding the 1967 Arab–Israeli war are examined in the following chapter. This section seeks to provide a brief description of how inter-Arab relations affected Jordan's ability to implement its foreign policy objectives.

Jordan faced an insoluble dilemma in its relationship with the Arab world. Its vulnerable position made it imperative that it align itself with its Arab neighbours. Zaid Rifai points this out when he says: 'Our geographical position has forced us to rely on joint Arab action – on belonging to a larger body to be able to survive.'[35] The Jordanians knew that if Israel invaded the West Bank they could not depend on American military aid and that since they could not defend themselves on their own they would have to look to the Arab world for support.

While Jordan's dependence on America made it difficult for King Hussein to fulfil his ideal of inter-Arab co-operation there were times when this did occur. Under these circumstances, Jordan's relationship with its Arab neighbours acted as an enhancing rather than a constraining factor on Jordan's foreign policy activity. For example, Egypt's relationship with Jordan varied considerably over the years. In the early fifties the relationship between the two had been good, and it was with hurt surprise that King Hussein learnt of Nasser's rejection of the Baghdad Pact and the commencement of his campaign against the Hashemite regime in the mid-fifties.

This situation altered in 1958 when the Iraqi Prime Minister, Abdul Karim Kassem, started to suppress Iraqi Nasserists and Nasser turned to Jordan for support at the Arab League in an attempt to isolate Iraq. The same pattern occurred in 1964 when both Egypt and Jordan wished to resist Syrian pressure for a war with Israel.

The plans for the diversion of the River Jordan drawn up at the 1964 summit were partly designed to control and in the immediate future delay, any potential war with Israel. This development was of considerable benefit to Jordan which had always sought to be part of an Arab regional defence system. However, this alliance proved precarious and by 1966 each country had resumed its propaganda war. This situation prevailed until Saad Juma'a became Prime Minister of Jordan, barely six weeks before the June war. In general, apart from a brief period during the summit era when Jordan received financial aid to help it to develop its army through the Unified Arab Command, inter-Arab co-operation acted more as a restraining than an enhancing factor on Jordan's ability to implement its foreign policy.

Jordan's relationship with Israel

Although Israel constantly emphasized its fear of annihilation by hostile Arab states, it was widely recognized by all parties that even a united Arab world could not hope to defeat Israel in a military confrontation.[36] On occasion this was openly recognized by Israel itself. In the 1960s Prime Minister Eshkol stated that 'the firm and persistent stand we have taken on behalf of our rights has strengthened the awareness among our neighbours that they will not be able to prevail against us in open combat'.[37] If anything, it was Israel's Arab neighbours who were anxious about what Israel might do. King Hussein's perception of the threat represented by Israel is apparent when he says: 'Always in our minds, and in my mind in particular, was the fact that the West Bank was the most important target as far as Israel was concerned'.[38] The same fear is echoed by Tal, Saad Juma'a and many other Jordanian politicians.[39] Jordan's incorporation of the West Bank gave it the longest border of any country adjoining Israel. This created a number of security problems for the Jordanian government. First, it increased the possibility of Palestinian terrorist infiltration into Israel; secondly, it meant that Israeli retaliation raids were equally difficult to prevent (and the history of Jordan between 1948 and 1967 includes an endless saga of border violence); thirdly, because of this problem Jordan was forced to deploy a large proportion of its military strength to attempt to guard the border.

Israel followed a policy of massive retaliation to Arab attacks and, in the early 1950s, had a special military unit called force 101, whose purpose was to conduct raids into neighbouring Arab countries. Jordan was the most frequent target, because it was the least capable of defending itself.

Since Jordan was constrained by its military weakness in relation to Israel, it sought to preserve the status quo; King Hussein pursued a policy of minimal belligerence towards Israel. He believed that it was foolish to attempt to fight Israel since neither Jordan nor a united Arab force could hope to win. Every action against Israel merely provided it with the excuse to enter Jordanian territory and ultimately to seize it. However, this policy brought Jordan into conflict with its Arab neighbours and constrained its ability to fulfil its foreign policy objective of Arab co-operation, because Egypt and Syria condemned Jordan for its failure to support guerrilla attacks on Israel. It also conflicted with Jordan's support of the Palestinian people. This had far-reaching implications for the nation's foreign policy activity as the riots that followed in the wake of Israel's raid on the Jordanian border village of Samu in 1966 were to demonstrate.

The Palestinian problem

The presence of the Palestinians in Jordan has been one of the most crucial constraints on Jordan's ability to implement its foreign policy objectives.

The Israeli victory over the Arabs in 1948 caused more than 800,000 Palestinians to flee from their homes and lands, and most went to the West Bank and Transjordan. When King Abdullah united the West Bank with Transjordan he more than doubled the number of his subjects.

Although non-West Bank Palestinians are not homogenous in terms of rank and status, and not all supported the PLO or other political groups, some felt unhappy about their absorption into the Jordanian state because they felt that this signified their acceptance of Israel's seizure of their homeland. For this reason, many 'focused less on integration than on the creation of a political atmosphere conducive to the restoration of Palestine'.[40] No matter what their social status, government efforts to create economic prosperity in order to persuade these Palestinians to accept their identity as Jordanians have failed. Even though, by 1964, the Jordanian government had succeeded in creating a relatively high degree of employment and prosperity, some Palestinians did 'not cease to be Palestinian Nationalists. For an ever-increasing number of refugees the problem [was] not lack of a place to live or lack of food or insufficient shelter; it [was] political homelessness'.[41]

The initial reluctance of the Palestinians to identify themselves as Jordanians was strengthened with the absorption of Western political ideas. Contact with concepts of trade unionism and democracy made them critical of a monarchy which they believed relied on traditional groups and the military as its ultimate source of power. Although King Hussein presented an image of 'one Jordanian family' and Jordan was the only host Arab state to offer full citizenship to the refugees, most were reluctant to accept the new situation for fear of losing their Palestinian identity which in turn could result in giving up all hope of returning to Palestine. Aruri describes the impact of the Palestinians on Jordan's foreign policy aims: 'Important issues such as the Anglo–Jordanian treaty, rejection of the Baghdad Pact, the dismissal of Glubb and the ultimate victory of the opposition in late 1956 are directly traceable to the influx of the Palestinians into the political system of Jordan'.[42]

The recognition of the Palestine Liberation Organization (PLO) by the majority of Arab states in 1964 heightened these problems. Until that time the Palestinians had no widely recognized organizations which enabled them to express their political aspirations. Soon after its creation the PLO was infiltrated by radical elements and was used against the Jordanian government by hostile Arab states. The PLO and similar organizations threatened King Hussein's sovereignty. First, its leaders sought to establish a Palestinian state within the state by, for example, seeking the right to conscript and tax Palestinians living in Jordan and secondly, because the PLO conducted raids into Israel which were not authorized by the government. Both of these factors heightened the possibility of massive retaliation by Israel and its potential invasion of the West Bank. Criticism of King Hussein by the Palestinians, encouraged by Syria and Egypt, mounted in the 1960s and was one of the major reasons for Jordan's entry into the 1967 war.[43]

For these reasons, while King Hussein could claim that he and his country had lost the least ground to Israel in 1948, had offered the Palestinians more equal opportunities and participation in political life than any other Arab country, and had tried to create prosperity for all Jordanian citizens, it often appeared that the Palestinians provided the most fertile ground for King Hussein's enemies in Jordan and in other Arab countries. As a result of this, his foreign policy options became even more limited and his choices even more tortuous.

The army

Three broad areas of the role of the military in politics can be discerned: the internal cohesion of the army; the role of the army in the maintenance of internal security; and the role of the army in the maintenance of external

Table 5 *The growth of the Jordanian armed forces 1939–67*

1939	Total strength 1,500: gendarmerie
1948	Total strength 6,000: 400 vehicles
1949–50	Total strength 12,000
1953	Total strength 17,000–20,000, plus 30,000 in the National Guard; Base Technical Organization 2,300; 4,000 vehicles.
1956	Total strength 25,000: this figure includes 1,500 officers. The command and control structure included a GHQ with a General Staff headed by a CGS composed of Operations and Intelligence, Personnel and Logistics. Operational armed forces were divided into infantry, armour, artillery and supporting services.
1967	Total strength 55,000.

By 1967 the structure and organization of the Jordanian Armed Forces had become more sophisticated and was based on the structure of a modern army. The command structure was headed by a Commander-in-Chief, a Deputy Commander-in-Chief and a Chief of Staff. Field troops were divided into nine infantry brigades, two armoured brigades and two independent tank regiments, as well as an airforce of twenty-one Hawker Hunters.
Source: S. El-Edroos, *The Hashemite Arab Army: 1908–1979*, Amman: Publishing Committee, 1980, pp. 396–7.

security. Each of these areas is examined in relation to Jordan in the late 1950s and early 1960s.

Table 5 illustrates the growth of the Jordanian Armed Forces between 1939 and 1967. In that period it grew from a gendarmerie composed of 1,500 men, whose concerns were limited to the maintenance of law and order and whose commanders were British, to a fully fledged army of 55,000 men, entirely staffed by Jordanians and possessing all the support organizations required by a modern army.

The internal cohesion of the armed forces

The most important factor influencing the role played by the army in Jordan is the recruitment of bedouin tribesmen into its ranks. This had initially occurred in the late 1930s when General Glubb used bedouin in the Desert Patrol (later the Arab Legion) as a means of curbing unruly tribesmen. Vatikiotis describes the process that occurred: ‘The army civilized the tribesman towards a measure of modernity by diverting his sense of tribal collectivity and esprit-de-corps into a sense of loyalty and a feeling of allegiance for a paramount chief – the monarch. From an occasional raider of other tribes or of settled agricultural communities for pillage and plunder, the tribesman has been transformed in the Legion into an expert professional in the organized and disciplined use of force for purposes determined and ordered by a central government’.[44]

The role of the bedouin as the pillar of the newly established Hashemite Kingdom continued after independence. King Hussein maintained Britain's policy of encouraging bedouin recruitment so that bedouin representation in the army was considerably higher than their number in the population warranted. As late as 1967 30–40 per cent of army personnel were bedouin.[45]

King Hussein built on this foundation by forging intimate links with the army. He knows most of the officers by name as well as those of many of the ordinary recruits. El-Edroos describes how the familiarity of recruits is such that a private soldier thinks nothing of approaching the King and tugging his sleeve for attention.[46]

Two factors have threatened the internal stability of the army. One was the incorporation of the Palestinian National Guard and the other was the dilution of the bedouin element that occurred in the mid-1950s at a time of domestic conflict.

Because the army plays such a key role in the maintenance and survival of the Hashemite regime, recruits to it are carefully screened and promotion is only proffered to those who are assessed as loyal. Incorporation of the Palestinians into the army was a sensitive subject and when Glubb suggested the creation of a National Guard using Palestinians from the villages bordering Israeli-occupied territory he was opposed by both the government and West Bank leaders. Eventually a compromise was reached: the National Guard was established in 1951 but kept separate from the army until 1956, by which time it had reached a strength of 30,000.

The process of merging the National Guard with the Arab Legion, which began in 1956, was one of the factors which contributed to what was arguably the most important incident of internal disruption that has occurred in the history of the army. In the mid-fifties the army underwent a period of expansion and reorganization which included the dismissal of its British officers, the complete Arabization of army personnel and an influx of townsmen into what had been a corps d'elite composed of villagers and tribesmen. This dilution of bedouin representation in the army coincided with the conflict between King Hussein and the nationalist government of Nabulsi.

The newly appointed army Chief of Staff, Major General Ali Abu Nuwar, was an urban Transjordanian[47] who had received military training in Britain and had served as military attaché in Paris. He was influenced by the Egyptians and the Syrians and liaised with Nabulsi's government and other army officers in plotting to overthrow the King. When the attempted coup d'état on 8 April 1957 failed and led King Hussein to dismiss the Government, clashes in the military camp of Zarqa, between troops loyal to the King and those influenced by Abu Nuwar, erupted. Since there were rumours that he had been killed the King went to Zarqa where he was received by jubilant troops. Realizing that his role in the conspiracy would inevitably be revealed, Abu Nuwar left Jordan for

Syria and was followed by some of the leaders of the deposed nationalist coalition. Shortly afterwards, army units were reorganized and many of their officers dismissed.

These events provide an excellent illustration of the importance of the bedouins. Abu Nuwar's failure to influence them made it impossible for him and his Syrian-backed political supporters to carry out an effective coup d'état.

The role of the army in domestic politics

In the Middle East and many underdeveloped nations the instrument of coercion is often closely allied to the government. This is true of Jordan, where the Hashemite monarch is also the Supreme Commander of the armed forces. However, Jordan differs from many underdeveloped nations in the remarkable stability of the army which in turn has heightened the stability of the state.

There have been a number of occasions in the history of Jordan when internal disruption threatened the existence of the Hashemite regime. On these occasions Jordan's rulers have turned to the army to maintain law and order. Following Israel's raid on Samu in 1966 riots occurred in many Jordanian cities and the government instituted martial law. In this extremely tense period the loyalty of the troops was tested to the utmost and stood the regime in good stead. Similar domestic disturbances occurred: in 1955 upon Jordan's attempt to join the Baghdad Pact; in 1958 after the Iraqi revolution; and in 1963 when popular pressure for Jordan to join the proposed union between Syria, Iraq and Egypt was repressed by the military. These examples illustrate that the loyalty of the Jordanian Army has been a major factor behind the survival of the Government and has allowed it a measure of freedom from the constraint of public opinion.

The role of the army in foreign affairs

The major problem affecting the Jordanian army has been finding sufficient finance to maintain an efficient military capability. The army which had swallowed up the nation's resources has proved inadequate to implement Jordan's foreign policy objectives at regional and international levels. The need for a strong army is dictated by the presence of Israel but, as illustrated in table 6, Jordan has never been able to match the military might of Israel. Nor does this raw demonstration of quantitative difference take into account the qualitative difference. Israel's weapons were supplied by France and America and were generally superior to those supplied by America to Jordan because America was anxious that no Arab country should match Israel's military prowess. Not being hampered by problems of domestic political instability Israel, unlike Jordan, followed a policy of conscription and every able Israeli spent a period of a few months a year in the army. The level of education of Israeli troops was superior to their Jordanian counterparts and the quality of

Table 6 *A comparison of Jordanian and Israeli armed forces in 1967*

	Jordan	Israel
Troops		
Infantry and mechanized brigades	7	23
Armoured brigades	2	8
Artillery brigades		12
Artillery	200	
Armour		
Tank and self-propelled guns	200	1,050
Armoured personnel carriers	250	
Armoured fighting vehicles		1,000
Air force		
Fighters	22	
Fighter-bombers		200–30
Bombers		25
Helicopters	3	25
Transport	6	20
Trainers/ground attack planes		60
Naval units		
Destroyers and frigates		4
Submarines		2
Motor torpedo boats		12

Source: Based on Brecher, 1980, pp. 415–516.

leadership was also higher. In view of this disparity Jordan was forced to ally itself with other Arab nations and this operated against Jordan's freedom of political action.

The same pattern of military inferiority is also evident if Jordan's military capability is compared with other Arab nations. In 1967 Egypt's army consisted of 210,000 men, Syria's of 63,000 and Iraq's of 56,000. Each of these countries also had air forces which were vastly superior to Jordan's minuscule force. An objective assessment of Jordan's chances of defeating any of its neighbours must have concluded that this was most unlikely. For this reason, foreign policy decision-making had to be taken in the context of a military capability which could not use either the threat or use of force in a convincing manner.

Chapter 3

Friends and enemies: Jordan in inter-Arab affairs

Jordan and the Arabs

Despite strong ties of culture, religion and language the period after the Second World War saw the Arab world deeply divided. Different ethnic groupings, different religious sects, a variety of political parties, disputes over national boundaries, competition between political leaders and the issue of Palestine, led to friction between the nations that made up the area of the Middle East. These divisions, which existed within nations as well as between nations, can be divided into two main blocs: revolutionaries and conservatives. Syria and Egypt belonged to the revolutionary bloc, while Jordan and Saudi Arabia were regarded as conservatives. Following the 1958 revolution Iraq was generally regarded as revolutionary although the rival faction of the Ba'ath Party that ruled Ba'athist Syria denied this.

One of the key issues which divided the conservative and revolutionary states was their attitude towards the West. The revolutionary Arab states condemned association with the West on the grounds that in the past Western countries had exploited the Arab world and continued to do so. The more radical Arab states regarded the destruction of imperialism in all its forms as one of the key objectives of the Arab revolution. This attitude to the West was in contrast with Jordan's and Saudi Arabia's who maintained friendly relations with Western countries, particularly America and Britain, whom they regarded as allies. They did not feel that there was any contradiction between association with Western nations and the advancement of the Arab world.

The issue of Israel was closely bound up with this dichotomy of views. The revolutionary Arab states identified the fight against Israel with the fight against imperialism. They regarded Israel as an imperialist outpost and a weapon of imperialist expansion. For this reason they regarded co-operation with the West as virtually equivalent to co-operation with Israel. This view of Israel was not shared by the conservative Arab states, who did not see any contradiction between their association with the West and their condemnation of Israel. While they feared Israel's expansionist designs and growing power, they did not regard this as a manifestation of Western imperialism. Nor did they feel that their conservative policies stood in the way of Arab co-operation, Arab unity or the fight for the rights of the Palestinian people.

The gulf between these different perceptions was one of the factors which, in the early 1960s, divided the Arab world. Jordan was isolated from many of its more radical Arab states who regarded its government with suspicion. Faddah explains that 'Arab nationalists argued that Jordan could not be relied upon because it benefited most from the Palestine conflict with minimum military operations; that it was basically opposed to the revival of Palestinian nationalism as well as to any changes in the territorial status quo which had existed since the Rhodes Agreement of 1949'.[1] Furthermore some claimed that since Jordan was dependent on Western financial, military and diplomatic support it was subject to Western pressure. Left-wing Arabs believed that this dependence on the West constricted Jordan's ability to participate in any serious action against Israel. Despite King Hussein's frequent protestations of commitment to the cause of Palestine, his radical opponents argued that there was a contradiction between Jordan's policies and Arab nationalism which could only be resolved by a revolution in Jordan.

Jordan's most active opponent was Syria which had a history of antipathy to the Hashemites and which regarded Jordan as a competing neighbour. The Syrian government maintained an almost uninterrupted campaign of vilification against the Hashemite regime. It accused Jordan's rulers of being allies of Israel and urged the Jordanian people to rise up and overthrow them. According to the Syrians, the liberation of Palestine could only take place after the Hashemites of Jordan had been destroyed.

One of the reasons behind Syria's antagonism towards Jordan was its different policy towards Israel. Jordan pursued a policy of avoiding confrontation with Israel because of its inability to provide adequate defence against Israeli raids and its fear of providing Israel with an excuse to invade the West Bank. Syria, on the other hand, actively sought to bring about a confrontation with Israel. To this end it encouraged guerrilla raids into Israeli territory. Since these raids were often carried out from the areas of Jordan's northern border, Jordanian villages were subjected to Israeli retaliation raids. Naturally this was a source of considerable friction between the Syrian and Jordanian governments.

Although equally stormy, Jordan's relationship with Egypt was more ambiguous than its relationship with Syria. Whilst Nasser claimed to stand at the vanguard of the Arab revolution he possessed a strong pragmatic streak which modified his actions. On the one hand Nasser argued that since imperialism and zionism were two sides of the same coin it was necessary to purify the Arab world of all traces of imperialism before zionism could be tackled. He declared: 'We cannot liberate ourselves from imperialism and zionism before we get rid of reaction and exploitation';[2] 'We shall restore

Palestine after organizing our internal front and after we get rid of the reactionary partners of Zionism and imperialism; ... How can we enter Palestine leaving behind us the reactionary Fifth Column ... I expect the Arab people to liberate themselves and purify themselves from the Fifth Column; only then will the hour of Palestine come'.[3] On the other hand, Nasser treated Jordan with a degree of circumspection because he knew that Israel had threatened to invade Jordan if its moderate regime was overthrown and a more radical one installed. Consequently Nasser was hesitant to call for the overthrow of King Hussein,[4] although this did not stop him from allowing Palestinian opponents of the King to operate from Cairo. However, Nasser's preoccupation with his conception of the liberation of the Arab people meant that no nation escaped his criticisms. According to Abu Odeh, 'Nasser's speeches about reactionary forces in the Arab world were part of the struggle between his concept of pan-Arabism and those Arab states that opposed his interpretation of it. He therefore used every tool at his disposal against his opponents. When he referred to reactionary regimes he was generally addressing Saudi Arabia and by implication Jordan. When he was not happy with the Syrians, he even called them other names, such as the Ba'athists. After Syria's secession, this word carried with it connotations of ridicule. He often described the Ba'athists as petty intelligentsia, empty-headed, etc. Nasser's rhetoric was not only directed at those he called reactionaries, including Jordan, but was also addressed to competitor regimes. The criterion was: whoever stood in the way of his interpretation of pan-Arabism, which depended on his belief in the support the Arab masses gave his policies'.[5] For this reason Nasser's Arab policy was subject to considerable variation.

As a force in the Arab world Nasser could not be ignored. His ability to capture the mood of the Arab people and to act as the embodiment of their aspirations placed him in a unique position. To the masses Nasser was somehow the embodiment of Arab nationalist aspirations. His decisions were always accepted by the masses as correct. From the time of Suez in 1956 until his death in 1970, changes in inter-Arab relationships were in part due to shifts in Nasser's foreign policy. To the Arab masses Nasser expressed their resentment against the yoke of Western imperialism and was the incarnation of their drive towards independence and modernization. His successful handling of the Suez crisis saw his star rise to its zenith, driven by his anti-imperialist policies which had begun with his attack on the Baghdad Pact, followed by the Czech arms-deal. As Badeau puts it, after Suez Nasser 'suddenly filled the Middle Eastern horizon becoming ... a regional hero. To restless and frustrated Arab nationalists he seemed a second Salahadin turning the table on Western imperialism'.[6]

Egyptian nationalism expanded to embrace Arab nationalism; outside Egypt, 'Nasserism became the most potent formula of Arab political salvation'.[7] Nasser declared that the movement which he spearheaded should be 'the result of a struggle in every Arab country'. He told his followers: 'It is not my responsibility to go to every Arab country and organize an Arab movement. Such is the responsibility of all the honest revolutionary elements in any Arab country'.[8] Nasser was therefore appealing to the masses over the heads of their rulers and King Hussein was only one of many Arab sovereigns who felt his disturbing influence.

Nasser's prominent position in the Arab world in the 1960s related to his manipulation of two basic issues: Arab unity and the Palestine cause. Arab unity was not a static concept for Nasser but could be redefined to reflect new circumstances. Dawisha identifies three major objectives of Arab unity which operated during Nasser's presidency: a maximum objective of comprehensive and constitutional unity; a minimum objective of Arab solidarity and an intermediate objective of revolutionary change.[9] The maximum objective was abandoned as a viable political objective some time after the Syrian secession. Between 1958 and 1967 Nasser's Arab policy fluctuated between the minimum and intermediate objectives in response to events in the Arab world. Nasser had claimed that Syria's breakaway from its union with Egypt had been the result of reactionary forces and an imperialist plot.[10] This policy altered when Israel's diversionary works of the River Jordan determined a return to Arab solidarity. This changed to a revolutionary policy after the failure to find a solution to the civil war in Yemen and King Faisal's proposal to create an Islamic Pact. Jordan's relationship with Egypt fluctuated according to these trends.

King Hussein's attitude to Nasser was, if anything, even more ambiguous than Nasser's attitude towards him. Even before Suez King Hussein had been aware of Nasser's charismatic qualities and political astuteness. He realized that Nasser 'had the required qualifications and circumstances were more favourable to him than to others, for him to serve the aspirations and aims of the Arab nation and to recover our rights'.[11] At the same time the King was not blind to Nasser's faults. He observed: 'I believe Nasser was a great Egyptian patriot. He believed in Egypt, he strove for it to be great. Unfortunately his approach was to destroy everything in the Arab world in the process of enhancing Egyptian control rather than approaching it in the sense of creating a unity of equals. This is part of a trend that some people have in our part of the world – they believe that the world begins and ends with them and they feel that they have to destroy everything that went before, which is tragic'.[12]

Although Nasser's revolutionary policies distanced him from King Hussein, this was modified by Nasser's realistic appraisal of Arab–Israeli relations. He was aware of the grip that the issue of Palestine had on the hearts of the Arab people but Nasser recognized that there was very little the Arabs could do. This realistic perception of Arab–Israeli relations was a source of considerable friction between Egypt and Syria. Nasser stated his views plainly: 'I do not agree with becoming involved in semi-military operations . . . Whoever says we should go to war without preparing for it is a traitor to his country and his people'.[13] The experience of 1956 had made Nasser aware of the strength of Israel and he realized that before the Arabs could confront Israel they would have to increase their capabilities. He told his people that 'the cause of Palestine requires preparation, development and power. The power required is not only military power but economic and industrial power as well'.[14] This perception was shared by King Hussein who stressed the vulnerability of the Arab world in relation to Israel and consequently sought to preserve the existing staus quo. Since the Suez war Egypt had joined Jordan in refusing to allow Arab guerrilla incursions into Israel. However, Nasser's policy of restraint towards Israel was concealed beneath an aggressive rhetoric which accused Israel of being 'an imperialist, racist aggressive base . . . created by force at the expense of the Arabs'.[15] This rhetoric made Egypt appear as bellicose towards Israel as Syria although, in reality, this was not the case.

The background to the summits

The main issue dominating the Arab world between 1964 and 1967 was Israel's diversion of the waters of the River Jordan. The River Jordan above Lake Tiberias was a major source of fresh water for the irrigation schemes of Israel and Jordan and could also be put to valuable use by Syria and Lebanon. The Johnston plan of 1955 had allotted to each state enough water to fulfil its estimated needs. But this plan had been rejected by the Arabs, partly because they feared anything which would increase Israel's prosperity and thereby strengthen its economy. Despite the absence of an agreement Israel began diversionary works with the intention of conveying water from Lake Tiberias to the Negev Desert. Jordan immediately expressed its concern about this. According to King Hussein, 'it was fairly obvious that the Israelis wanted to fulfil their dreams and plans of settling many more people in the area than they wanted water'.[16] The Jordanians also feared that by diminishing the volume of water the river's saline content would rise and cause catastrophic damage to Jordan's arable land. The Jordanian Ministry of Agriculture claimed that almost 50 per cent of Jordan's vegetable produce would be lost. Although the Israelis maintained that they would only draw off what had been allotted to them under the Johnston plan, the Arabs pointed out that the size of the works indicated an intention to exceed this. They feared that the Israelis would seize sufficient water to irrigate the Negev desert which they would then fill with millions of young Jewish immigrants who were trained to fight. This would make the Negev desert a Zionist military base and a threat to the safety of the Arab states.

Soon after Israel began its diversionary works Jordan called for a joint Arab response. It argued that the question of the waters of the River Jordan was part of the Palestine question and therefore concerned all Arabs. Syria issued a call for progressive Arab forces to oppose its activities by force.[17] As the most influential figure in the Arab world, Nasser could not afford to ignore the issue but he found himself in a difficult position because of Syria's demand for a military confrontation with Israel. At that time half of the Egyptian army was fighting in Yemen and Egypt was not in a position to challenge Israel. However, Nasser realized that if he ignored Syria's challenge he would appear to be dragging his heels on a vital issue. Although he could not hope to win a war against Israel he knew that if he stated this publicly he could be accused of cowardice in the way that Syria accused Jordan. By professing themselves to be ready to attack Israel and to defend the Arab people the Syrians would take the initiative away from Nasser and appear to be at the vanguard of the progressive forces in the Middle East.

Nasser's solution to this problem was to bring together all the Arab Kings and heads of state at a summit meeting to discuss Israel's diversionary works. He realized that by bringing together conservative and progressive forces Syria's belligerency would be rendered ineffective. He hoped that by creating a unified Arab front which recognized the need to act with caution the responsibility for putting off war with Israel would be a collective one rather than his alone. Abu Odeh explains:

> when Nasser first called for a summit meeting he did not really mean to pull the rug from under the feet of the Syrians so much as he wanted to avoid having to take full responsibility for the Palestinian problem. This was the task that had been entrusted to him by the Arab masses. Nasser, more than any other Arab, understood how dangerous Israel was and knew the full extent of its power. This was because he had faced them in 1956. The summit was Nasser's method of avoiding direct confrontation with Israel in which Israel was likely to invade Sinai. He chose to invite the Arab leaders to a summit so that they could share the responsibility with him to prepare for such a confrontation, while at the same time restraining the Syrian radicals who wanted an immediate confrontation. For when all the leaders meet together the Syrians would not be able to impose their will on the others.[18]

There were other reasons why Nasser wished for reconciliation with the conservative Arab regimes. By 1963 he had begun to realize that his efforts to unseat or influence the governments of conservative Arab states through propaganda had proved unsuccessful. Consequently the notion emerged in Egypt's ruling circles that influence over other nations might be more easily achieved by conciliation and tolerance than by threats and abuse.

Nasser hoped to extricate himself honourably from the war in Yemen. The opposing forces of Saudi Arabia and Egypt were locked in a stalemate and the war was draining the Egyptian economy. By re-establishing cordial relations with Saudi Arabia, Nasser hoped to resolve the situation without any loss of prestige. He hoped to reassert his supremacy as the architect of Arab unity and the champion of the Palestinians; and to bring the Arab world together to examine the whole question of Palestine and Israel in a rational manner in order to find a satisfactory way of dealing with the problem.

The time was also ripe for the Arab world to gather together to discuss the issue of Israel. Many Arab leaders, including Nasser and King Hussein, recognized that their position in relation to Israel was weak and that for this reason they needed to develop a new strategy towards it. Any attempt to confront Israel was undermined by many areas of Arab weakness. Vatikiotis[19] points out four of these:

No single Arab state had the economic, military or political power to deal with Israel. Collectively, the Arab states had never been willing or able to devise a stable common policy that could serve as the basis of sustained action against their adversary. No Arab state had been able to concentrate its efforts and acquire overwhelming, or at least significant, diplomatic and political influence over the policies of the Great Powers involved in the region. Every attempt at unified Arab action had been paralysed by domestic dissensions, inter-Arab divisions and mutual distrust.

On 23 December 1963 Nasser announced his wish to invite Arab Kings and heads of state to Cairo for a summit meeting. In his speech he made it plain that the summit was intended to be a forum which cut across the boundaries of conservative and progressive ideologies. He declared: 'Those with whom we are in strife we are prepared to meet; those with whom we have a quarrel we are ready, for the sake of Palestine, to sit with ... The battle of Palestine can continue and the battle of the Jordan is part of the battle of Palestine.'[20]

King Hussein's enthusiasm for reconciliation

King Hussein was deeply preoccupied with, and determined to demonstrate his commitment to, the Palestine cause. One of the most bitter events experienced by the Palestinians had been the loss of Lydda and Ramallah to Israel in 1948. Jordan's rulers argued that the loss of these areas was inevitable because of the small size and poorly equipped state of the Arab Legion at the time. However, the Palestinians blamed King Abdullah for failing to defend them adequately and accused him of betraying them.

As King Abdullah's grandson, King Hussein inherited this legacy of bitterness and suspicion. King Hussein explains that when he came to the throne in 1953 'the erroneous and tragic treatment of Jordan for its performance in 1948 dominated the minds of many Jordanians, particularly Palestinians. The facts were terribly distorted. Perhaps it was a fault or perhaps it was a virtue that the founder of the Kingdom and his government did not try to present their case as they should have done but instead relied on its strength.

However, it is a fact that the Jordanian army fought in Palestine and saved that part of Palestine which remained Arab until 1967. They did this with only 4,000 soldiers. It was the smallest, most badly equipped of the Arab armies yet this was not clear in the minds of Jordanians. They were not as proud of their army as one would have expected them to be'.[21] As a result of this legacy, King Hussein felt that he had to prove that the Arab accusations that the Hashemites only acted out of self-interest and cared nothing for the Palestinian people were unfounded.

King Hussein's desire to demonstrate his commitment to the cause of Palestine was also the result of his Hashemite heritage. Sharif Hussein had been at the vanguard of Arab unity and Palestine had been a central issue in his dealings with the Western powers. For this reason, King Hussein could not fail to participate in any action directed towards helping the Palestinians.

Jordan's Arab policy was also influenced by its proximity to Israel. Israel's existence was felt as a threat to Jordan's security but Jordan was ill-placed to defend itself because of its limited military capability. Its border with Israel was the longest of any Arab nation yet it possessed the smallest army. Throughout his reign King Hussein had sought to resolve this problem by bringing Jordan into a regional defence structure. King Hussein describes his attempts to improve Jordan's defence capability from the time he first came to the throne:

It was a turbulent period for this area. The Arab–Israeli issue was still there, the tragedy was before us. It seemed incredible that there was a ceasefire line which separated and split up villages and towns. Within a very short belt of only a few kilometres all along that line in the West Bank there were hundreds of villages. The army could not cope adequately with the defence of the entire front if the Israelis mounted an attack. The Israelis could always concentrate, always easily mount a raid on any position, achieve their objective and quickly withdraw before reinforcements could be brought in. Those who had the initiative had the advantage throughout . . . I tried to improve the condition of the armed forces, to increase our capabilities, but our economy was poor and undeveloped. Our means were limited except for the subsidy we received as a result of the Anglo–Jordanian treaty. This led us to examine the possibility of entering the Baghdad Pact. There was a period of confusion because we did not approach the question on our own but looked at the realities on the ground. We sought to bring with us not only Iraq but other Muslim states in the area and as a matter of fact we were in touch with Egypt at the time to consult on whether or not to join. Indeed, at the very beginning Egypt was involved in the negotiations as well over whether it should join the Pact itself. Always in our minds and in my mind in particular was the fact that the West Bank was the most important target as far as Israel was concerned. We were in the hills and close to the sea in some places. If the Israelis were to implement their plans and settle comfortably, and extend beyond the area of Palestine, then obviously the first objective would be Palestine itself. Therefore the most important area apart from Jerusalem was the West Bank. This is what drove us to try and find ways of improving our position and to ensure that we were safe, not in terms of individuals but in terms of territory. This territory was very precious territory, not only to Christians and Muslims but to us as well. Unfortunately the Pact did not come to very much . . . so we had to consolidate and look to ourselves once again. I continued to try and Arabize the army but that did not work very well and although I had great respect for Glubb Pasha there came a time when I felt very strongly that either we had to act to retrieve what I believed was our right and reshape our relations with Britain . . . or face the destruction of Jordan from within. So we took the step of Arabizing the army . . . We tried our best to give meaning, to give substance to being part of the Arab world in that we were true not only to our feelings but to those of our forefathers, the Arab League, its Charter, the Joint Defence agreements, to the concept that any threat to an Arab country was a threat to them all. If we expected help from others we had to prove that we were ready to stand by others if they were threatened. This was a principle that was part of adherence to the Arab League, the Charter and the Joint Defence agreement. Obviously what one wanted and tried to attain throughout the years was adequate preparations so that the threats would be minimized in the first place and so that we would not be so vulnerable. Unfortunately things did not turn out that way. Cairo and Baghdad were at opposite poles at that time. Then there was the 1956 war. Even then we were deployed on the West Bank ready to fulfil our obligations. Then there were a number of years in which we continued to try to build and cement our relations with our Arab brethren and to enhance the capabilities of Jordan.[22]

This long quotation describes King Hussein's fears of Israeli expansionism and his recognition that for this reason it was essential for Jordan to belong to a wider defence structure. His commitment to Arabism as well as geographical considerations made him anxious for that defence structure to be Arab. He describes how even when he considered joining the Baghdad Pact he wanted this to be part of an overall Arab strategy and not merely an alliance between Jordan and Britain. One of his motives in Arabizing the Arab Legion had been his recognition that it was impossible for Jordan to establish close ties with its Arab neighbours so long as Britain had a foothold in the Arab Legion. He describes how he constantly sought military alliances with other Arab nations. For example, when the Arab League organized a Pan–Arab Common Defence Treaty he had no hesitation in joining it. His short-lived union with Iraq and his later alliance with Saudi Arabia reflects a similar policy, as does his adherence to the Joint Defence Agreement. His readiness to participate in the 1956 war was the result of his recognition that if Jordan was to enjoy the support of its Arab neighbours it had to demonstrate its willingness to defend them.

There were also economic reasons behind King Hussein's desire to establish better relations with his Arab brethren. Although Jordan depended on the West for foreign aid this was undesirable since it alienated the Jordanian government from its Palestinian subjects, enabled radical Arab regimes to criticize it and prevented Jordan from maintaining a neutral political stance. However, while King Hussein had tried to replace Western aid with Arab aid, Arab financial support had proved so erratic that he had been forced to turn back to the West. Despite this, whenever an opportunity arose to free Jordan from dependence on the West and to tie it more closely to the Arab world King Hussein was quick to respond.

The Jordanian monarch was also concerned that Syria's aggressive policy towards Israel was heightening the chances of full-scale war. He was increasingly anxious about Israel's intentions, and felt that Israel might use Syria's activities as a pretext to invade Arab land. He believed that Arab unity was essential if the Arab world was to deal with Israel. Some years after the June war he wrote: 'It had become clearly evident since the last five years [before the June war] that if nothing was done we were heading straight for an armed conflict [with Israel]. With this in mind I published a "White Book" in the summer of 1962 entitled *Jordan, the Case of Palestine and Arab Relations*, in which Jordan's views on the necessity of establishing real [Arab] unity and stressing how urgent this was for the Arab world were explained. This unity seemed imperative to me.'[23] The summits offered the ideal forum for establishing this unity. Like Nasser, King Hussein hoped that Syria's provocative actions would be curtailed as a result of the pressure of collective Arab opinion which instead would establish a carefully formulated Arab–Israeli policy.

For these reasons, when Nasser offered Jordan the opportunity of mending its bridges with its Arab brethren Jordan responded with alacrity. No one had welcomed the era of summitry more than King Hussein because it had provided his country with a framework for peaceful co-existence and hence an assurance of security.

The summit issues

The first summit conference took place in Cairo in January 1964. Participants were composed of the thirteen Arab nations which formed the Arab League. The main purpose of the conference was to co-ordinate the Arabs' response to Israel's diversionary works on the River Jordan. Two further summit conferences were held: one in Alexandria in September 1964 and another in Casablanca in September 1965. The first summit conference resulted in the creation of three organizations:

The Jordan Diversion Authority (JDA)

The task of the JDA was the diversion of the River Jordan in Jordan, Lebanon and Syria. The Hasbani River in Lebanon was to be diverted west to the Litani River to irrigate Lebanon. The Banyas River in Syria was to be diverted south-east by a canal through Syrian territory into the River Yarmuk in Jordan. Since the proposed canal for the Banyas River ran close to Israel, military protection for the scheme was to be provided by the Unified Arab Command. (See below.)

Jordan was provided with financial support for its diversionary works and began to implement these after the summit. It set up the Regional Department for the Exploitation of Jordan Water and its Tributaries and planned to build the Mukhaiba Dam. Protection for its diversionary works was to be provided by the Jordanian army.

The Palestine Liberation Organization (PLO)

In the past, Jordan had resisted the creation of a Palestinian entity because of the fear that it would become a focus for subversive activities against the Hashemite regime and result in demands for the establishment of an independent Palestinian state on the West Bank. Despite this, at the first summit conference King Hussein agreed to the establishment of a Palestinian organization whose purpose would be to express the aspirations of the Palestinian people. Abu Odeh explains this sudden change in Jordan's policy in terms of its commitment to Arab co-operation:

> In view of Jordan's vulnerable location, its population and possession of Jerusalem, Jordan preferred to enjoy the umbrella of pan-Arab co-ordination and consensus. The Arab tide at the time was in favour of the establishment of a Palestinian entity. King Hussein therefore could not oppose the Arab consensus, which, essentially, is the cornerstone of his Arab policy. He accepted, subject to certain important procedural conditions in order to avoid any serious effect on the constitutional and social structure of the union of the two Banks.[24]

Nussaibah adds that King Hussein's decision to approve the creation of the PLO was taken 'to accommodate the almost unanimous Arab position that the Palestinian identity should be asserted because from the perspective at the time we felt that the Palestine problem had not been resolved and that the unity of the West Bank and the East Bank would not prejudice the ultimate solution to the Palestine problem. There was a tremendous pressure from all sides that this must be asserted'.[25]

If the Jordanian government failed to agree to a Palestinian entity, it risked isolating itself from other Arab nations and alienating its Palestinian population. For this reason Jordan gave the newly created Palestine Liberation Organization (PLO) its full support. At the same time, Jordan insisted that certain limitations should be placed on it. These included the following: it should place its military wing, the Palestine Liberation Army (PLA), under the direction of the UAC; undertake not to interfere in the internal affairs of any Arab state; undertake not to try and exercise territorial sovereignty in the West Bank. King Hussein explains his attitude to the newly established organization: 'we welcomed the principle behind the creation of the Palestine Liberation Organization and were ready to give it our unreserved support with only one condition: the PLO had to co-operate with Jordan without a trace of friction'.[26]

The decision in 1964 to establish the PLO was one of the most momentous made by the Arab world. Until then there had been no single body which represented the interests of all Palestinians and which was recognized throughout the Arab world. Without such an organization Palestinian nationalism could not have existed and flourished. The intention of the Arab leaders had been to create a political organization whose task was to gather support for the cause of Palestine and to act as the representative of the Palestinian people. King Hussein's acceptance of the creation of the PLO was rooted in his belief that its political aims were limited and that it would not constitute a threat to Jordanian sovereignty. He believed that since it was a creation of the summit conference it would be subject to the influence of Arab opinion. At the outset King Hussein spoke of the Palestinian entity as 'a new force to be added to and thereby reinforce the pan-Arab force. This entity would be a new weapon in the united Arab hand with which to open the way to the common goal'.[27] He believed that the PLO might actually support Jordan's role as the custodian of Palestinian aspirations so that the 'entire nation could support the Hashemite Kingdom of Jordan in shouldering the major burden of this sacred cause'.[28]

However, although the declaration issued at the end of the first summit conference in Cairo stated that 'organizing the Palestinian people to enable them to play their part in the liberation of their country and [to] attain self-determination' was 'essential to ward off the imminent Zionist menace',[29] many observers were of the opinion that in creating the PLO the Arabs were actually fobbing off demands for action. By creating a Palestinian organization but refraining from giving it any real power, the leaders of the Arab states were relieving themselves of some of the burden of solving the problem while appearing to further its solution. Stephens states that Nasser 'saw the PLO as a means of canalizing Palestinian national emotions and restraining any rash adventures into guerrilla warfare or more large-scale operations against Israel'.[30] Seale points out that the leader of the PLO, Ahmed Shukairy, was to be given 'a title, a radio station, an apparatus of propaganda to reassure the Palestinians that their cause was not forgotten, but no effective power'. He also points out that Shukairy was widely regarded as a vociferous but ineffectual demagogue.

This view of the motives behind the creation of the PLO is confirmed by Abu Odeh who explains that 'the establishment of the PLO was meant to dilute the process of Arab confrontation with Israel. My feeling is that the Arabs wanted – and I am certain this must have been on Nasser's mind all the time – to give the Palestinians the responsibility of their destiny should a political solution be reached some day, so that no Arab leader would find himself running against his own slogans. The fact that they elected Shukairy as leader meant that they wanted a political rather than a military organization'.[31]

Time was to show that if this was indeed the intention behind the establishment of the PLO it did not work. Instead the PLO became a radical force which affected all the nations in the area and was a major cause of the 1967 war.

The Unified Arab Command (UAC)

A Jordanian military paper presented at the Cairo summit set in motion the creation of a united Arab military organization. The establishment of the Unified Arab Command (UAC), whose head was the Egyptian General Ali Ali Amer, was one of the most important outcomes of the summits. The long-term objective of the UAC was the consolidation of 'Arab armed forces in the face of expansionist Zionism' and the protection of proposed Arab irrigation works. To this end it was provided with P Stg 154m. Each state was given the task of 'repulsing Israeli attacks on its own territory unless such attacks involved the occupation of Arab land'.

The UAC command drew up a detailed plan which described the measures the Arab world needed to take in order to improve its defences and eventually to progress from a defensive capability to an offensive one.[32] These measures included a programme for the development of the military strength of certain Arab countries such as Jordan. Some countries, such as Egypt and Saudi Arabia, were asked to provide financial support to enable this development. The UAC also laid down a number of requirements which needed to be fulfilled before the Arabs could contemplate war against Israel. These included the following:

Complete secrecy regarding all questions relating to the preparations of the UAC.

Unity and co-operation between the various Arab states.

A policy of non-belligerence towards Israel so that Israel would not be provided with any pretext to start a preventative war. This included the instruction that no Arab state bordering Israel should either encourage or tolerate commando raids into Israeli territory.[33]

A solution to the Yemen problem and the withdrawal of Egyptian troops from Yemen so that they would be available for combat against Israel.

A solution to the Kurdish nationalist movement in northern Iraq and the return of the Iraqi army from this area so that it could support the defence of the Eastern front.

The appointment of Syrian army officers on the basis of military competence rather than political allegiance.[34]

Jordan viewed this development with favour because in many respects the recommendations of the UAC were in keeping with its foreign policy aims. The creation of the UAC satisfied Jordan's desire to be part of a regional defence system and relieved King Hussein's anxiety about the vulnerability of the West Bank. Khammash states: 'Our plans for the defence of the West Bank were modified in 1965 in accordance with the UAC general plan; that is, that we should face the danger of Israel with a concerted Arab action whereby Israel should not be allowed to fight any Arab state on its own. Accordingly if we fought collectively we were supposed to expect the provision of air cover and the movement of Arab troops into Jordanian territory to augment our own defence.'[35]

Jordan's military establishment was also strengthened by the provision of funds from other Arab countries to develop its military capability. This was of great importance to King Hussein because it increased Jordan's ability to defend itself while decreasing its dependence on other states.

The recommendations of the UAC were also in keeping with Jordan's policy of non-belligerence towards Israel. The 'Heads of State had warned members of the conference against furnishing Israel with the slightest pretext for starting a premature war'.[36] This was in harmony with Jordan's policy of refusing to allow guerrilla raids into Israel and also acted as a brake on the desires of Syrian and Palestinian groups to conduct such raids. King Hussein was able to explain to his subjects that the Arab world had 'agreed that, at this stage, when we are working at building up our strength, it was only natural that the enemy should be watching us and waiting for us to provide him with a justification to force us into battle before we were ready. Clear and explicit instructions were issued [by the UAC] forbidding infiltration into the occupied area at this stage'.[37]

The same recommendation provided Jordan with a shield against any attempt by Palestinian organizations to gain sovereignty over the West Bank. The Arab leaders were aware that Israel had made it clear that it would regard Palestinian control of the West Bank as sufficient to warrant an invasion. For this reason, the summits supported King Hussein's resistance to the development of such tendencies.

At the same time, King Hussein could tell his subjects that he had embarked on a practical and realistic programme of action which promised that in the not-too-distant future the Arabs would be able to bargain from a position of strength and to use both the threat and the use of force to implement their desires. By this means King Hussein hoped to silence criticism that he was not living up to his commitment to the Palestine cause.

The Yemen

The civil war in Yemen had begun in 1962 as a result of the deposition of the ruling Imam and his replacement by a republican government. Egypt supported the republican regime and sent a substantial part of its army to Yemen.

Saudi Arabia supported the deposed Imam and responded to his fall from power by sending in troops. Jordan also supported the Imam. On 1 October 1962 Jordan's Chief of Staff was despatched to Yemen at the head of a military mission whose task was to contact Prince Hasan, the uncle of the deposed Imam. This was followed on 4 November by an official declaration of a military alliance of Jordan and Saudi Arabia in Yemen.

The Yemeni civil war was one of the factors dividing the Arab world, and nearly all the Arab states were anxious to resolve it. Although the issue of Yemen was not discussed at the summit meetings, they led to King Hussein's withdrawal of support for the deposed Imam in July 1964. This reversal of foreign policy may have appeared sudden, but it was influenced by factors which had existed before the first summit conference. King Hussein had been strongly criticized within Jordan for his policies in Yemen because they placed the Jordanian government in a reactionary light and allowed Egypt to accuse Jordan and Saudi Arabia of being the pawns of imperialism. According to Nussaibah many of the politicians in Jordan, particularly those from the West Bank, had never agreed with King Hussein's support of the Imam and 'there was an almost unanimous feeling that this was wrong'.[38]

Abu Odeh explains:

> King Hussein did not support the Imam as a system so much as he was trying to stem the tide of Nasserism beyond certain borders irrespective of who was deposed. This was one of Jordan's foreign policy objectives at the time and it coincided with the deposed Arab ruler being an Imam and was not the result of Jordan's support of the Imam himself. When it became evident that the republican regime in Yemen was in control of the country and that there was no way of changing the new status quo and the Nasserite movement was well established in Yemen, Jordan recognized the republican government right away.[39]

Another reason for King Hussein's decision was his desire to demonstrate his willingness to co-operate with the Arab mainstream, which on the whole was in favour of the new regime in Yemen. By acknowledging the republicans King Hussein showed that he was prepared to make considerable concessions for the sake of Arab unity. He also stood to gain practical help. In return for King Hussein's support Nasser offered to supply Jordan with surplus Russian arms. Although King Hussein preferred to buy Western arms the offer was valuable since it meant he could apply pressure on America to supply him with the arms he required.

King Hussein was also asked to act as an intermediary between Egypt and Saudi Arabia in an effort to solve the Yemen problem. In a speech made on 28 October 1965 the King stated that Jordan had 'persistently suggested constructive proposals to fellow Arabs for a solution to the Yemen problem and was quick to contact all parties to the dispute and to attempt, sincerely and honestly, to find a common basis for understanding in a manner which would serve the interests and dignity of all concerned'.[40] Some of these proposals were outlined in a newspaper article published on 22 June 1965.[41] This suggests that Jordan sought to achieve a compromise and to establish a dialogue between the parties. The proposal put forward by King Hussein had been a 'comprehensive reconstruction plan . . . which must be carried out by a government which is neither Imami nor Republican'. He also suggested to Nasser that an Arab security force should be stationed in Yemen to replace Egyptian troops.[42]

The collapse of the summits

According to Kerr 'what wrecked the spirit of the summits was a chain reaction, touched off by the obstinacy of an obscure group of politicians in the Republic of Yemen and carried forward by a combination of exaggerated Saudi ambitions, Egyptian sensitivities and Syrian proddings . . . By the end of the year the Arab world was once again sharply divided on ideological lines; this time with a Syrian-Egyptian axis confronting a Saudi–Jordanian one'.[43]

The UAC

Although Jordan had responded to the creation of the UAC with enthusiasm, it found it difficult to abide by all of its decisions. An essential part of the plan to protect Arab irrigation works and to defend Arab land had been the stationing of troops from other Arab nations on the soil of the countries concerned. However, three of the states bordering Israel (Jordan, Lebanon and Syria) refused to accept Egyptian troops onto their territory. Each of these nations felt that the threat represented by Israel was remote compared with the undesirable impact which the presence of such troops would make on the delicate balance of their internal politics. This fear was expressed by King Hussein: 'If these troops were to be sent from outside they would engage in activities intended to cause confusion with a certain aim in mind.' He even stated that 'the troops to be sent by a certain country would include saboteurs among them'.[44]

King Hussein was also concerned that if the Jordanian army was reinforced by troops from other Arab nations Israel would use this as an excuse to attack Jordan. He stated: 'Israel may exploit the entry of these troops . . . to justify their mounting a major operation'.[45] He explained: 'What concerns us is that our enemies . . . are preparing to outstrip us and impose on us an untimely battle. They have declared more than once that they might use the entry of these troops, which are small in number and resources and which are for defence purposes only, as a pretext to launch a large-scale operation. They cannot destroy us but they can perhaps create a situation in the Arab world whereby we enter a battle without being 100 per cent sure of the outcome.'[46] He argued instead that foreign troops should be allowed into Jordan only when war with Israel appeared inevitable. King Hussein claimed that the Jordanian army was strong enough to deal with any action taken by Israel and that it did not need token forces for defence purposes. He pointed out that until the Arab world had reached a point where it could equal Israel's military capability it should do its best to avoid providing Israel with an excuse to attack.

A third reason for Jordan's refusal to accept troops from other Arab countries onto its soil was that it believed that they would not be deployed in time to deal with Israeli action. King Hussein explains that 'there was always the question, "Why not have Iraqi troops in Jordan, why not have Arab troops in Jordan?" Our approach throughout has always been that you should first concentrate on building your own force so that you are able to withstand any Israeli action or any threat from any quarter and to give you time to receive the help that might come subsequently'.[47] Jordan regarded itself as the first line of defence against Israel and therefore sought to be capable of fending off an initial attack on its own while support from other Arab nations was brought in.

Another bone of contention between the UAC and Jordan was the latter's refusal to comply with the recommendation to buy Russian arms and jet fighters. King Hussein believed that the Eastern bloc's willingness to sell arms to Middle Eastern countries at low cost was because of its desire to acquire a foothold in the Arab world. King Hussein had always opposed communism and was reluctant to allow Eastern bloc countries to have such a powerful influence on Jordan. There were also cogent practical reasons for refusing arms from the communist world. King Hussein explained: 'everyone knows that our army had always, since it was first created, depended on the West as its source of supply'.[48] He believed that accepting arms from Russia would impose severe problems of compatibility with the existing Western-made equipment and for this reason refused to have them. He also believed that the Russian planes which he was offered were inferior to the American planes he proposed buying. He stated that an exhaustive study had demonstrated that the American planes had proved to be more effective 'than those advocated by the biased quarters which claim the contrary'.[49]

King Hussein was also disillusioned with the UAC because 'resources that were promised were not forthcoming ... We approved the planning decisions but there was no way of checking on an annual or regular basis what point we had reached and what inadequacies there were, how to deal with them and how to keep the process alive to achieve our objectives'.[50] Juma'a also describes how most of the wealthy Arab nations did not pay the contributions to Jordan that had been agreed at the summits. He writes: 'This was particularly painful as those states [to whom the money had been promised] had already concluded arms supply contracts which they then found they could not meet.'[51]

Syria

Although the process of reconciliation within the Arab world meant that Jordan had to face difficult decisions and compromise over important issues, it had welcomed the era of Arab co-operation because it alleviated some of Jordan's most pressing problems. However, this attitude was not shared by all the countries concerned. Syria was particularly unhappy with the policies resulting from the summits. Nasser had prevented Syria from dragging Egypt into a premature war with Israel or from exposing him as reluctant to take up arms. The Syrians were fully aware of this and regarded the summits as 'a formula for evading the issue and they urged, instead, for immediate action'.[52] For this reason the Syrians did their best to deepen divisions within the Arab world in order to destroy the spirit of the summits and to isolate Nasser from the influence of conservative states such as Jordan.

One of the ways in which the Syrians attempted to achieve this was by encouraging Palestinian fedayeen. A Palestinian guerrilla organization called Al-Fatah, which was financed, trained and supported by Syria, was of particular importance.[53] Abu Odeh comments that 'the Al-Fatah leaders understood the real reason for creating the PLO and therefore decided to work to eliminate the political organization the Arabs had created and to establish a military one to replace it, based on the Algerian model which they tried to copy'.[54] Realizing that the decisions taken at the summit conferences had tied their hands, the Syrians tried to radicalize the emerging Palestinian organizations and to transform the PLO from an essentially political organization to a military one which was bound to hamper the activity of the UAC and bring the PLO into conflict with Jordan. To this end they sponsored fedayeen attacks against Israel from Jordan. These were designed not only to upset Israel but also to shatter Arab unity and to make King Hussein and the Arab leaders in general appear to be antagonistic to the Palestinian cause since they would not allow the Palestinians to attack their enemy.

The Syrians persisted in their hostile campaign against Jordan and its King. Jordan was criticized for its reservations about the activities of the PLO and its tight surveillance of left-wing elements. The Syrians even offered to arm dissident Jordanian elements which plotted to overthrow the Jordanian government.[55] Jordan believed that Syria was actively conspiring to overthrow its Government and accused the Syrian authorities of sending saboteurs into Jordan to blow up government installations, bridges and military telephone lines.[56] The relationship between the two nations became so acrid that at one point the Syrians threatened to close the border with Jordan.

The PLO

The charter of the PLO had set out limitations on its freedom of action which were a source of dissatisfaction to many Palestinians. At an early stage at least four Palestinian organizations put forward more ambitious proposals which attempted to give the Palestinian organization a status closer to that of nationhood and which provided for greater freedom of action in the military field.

As time passed and the PLO failed to produce any significant results, some Palestinians became disillusioned with the efforts of Arab politicians. They began to feel that their cause was no more than a pawn in a game of Arab politics and that no solution to their plight was in sight. Consequently they rejected political action, ignored the promises of Arab leaders, and began to seek their own ways of dealing with their problem. At the second summit Palestinian organizations addressed a memo to the summit participants in which they claimed that 'the conditions necessary for the creation of a revolutionary Palestinian entity have not been fulfilled with the creation of the present entity [the PLO]. The Arabs have now come to doubt whether Arab leaders really cared to implement [the resolutions of the first summit conference] ... Continuous attempts are being made to keep the Palestinians away from the battle and to prevent them from playing a genuine role of leadership in liberating their homeland'.[57]

The role played by Shukairy, the leader of the PLO, also turned out to be different from that anticipated by those who had placed him in power. Although most political commentators observed then that Shukairy was unlikely to mobilize the Palestinians and upset the status quo, the reverse proved to be the case. Far from passively accepting the conditions laid down at the summits Shukairy demanded that the Palestinian people should be allowed to organize themselves independently. He insisted that the PLO should be allowed to tax the Palestinians, that they should be conscripted into the PLA and that arms should be distributed. King Hussein refused to accept these demands and argued that they were 'tantamount to the establishment of a dual authority over his Palestinian subjects, the beginning of a state within a state'.[58] This was something which the Arab leaders had expressly forbidden at the time of the creation of the PLO.

The Hashemites had always sought to keep the Palestinians integrated into the Jordanian nation-state and resisted efforts to establish a separate identity before a final solution to the Palestine problem could be found. However, while King Hussein declared that 'Jordan and Palestine were always one people and one country',[59] the majority of Palestinian refugees continued to hope that one day they would return to their homeland and create their own state. Failing that, some aspired to establish an independent Palestinian state on the West

Bank. This was something which King Hussein would not tolerate. He stated: 'No group which claims to work for Palestine should ever again attempt to disrupt this country's sacred unity . . . We are therefore fully determined to resist any such attempt with the same ferocity which we show towards Zionism and Israel.'[60] King Hussein was determined that any attempt by the PLO to gain independence from Jordan would meet with stiff opposition.

King Hussein's firm response to Palestinian demands was also influenced by his fear that giving way to them would result in intervention by Israel. He was particularly concerned about Palestinian guerrilla activity, which he believed was a challenge of principle well calculated to produce border violence or revolution or both. King Hussein's acceptance of Palestinian military organizations had been conditional on their operation within the framework of the UAC. When it appeared that the PLA was operating independently he refused to co-operate with it. He stated: 'We no longer believe in the efficacy of passionate displays and extemporaneous activities undertaken by any bodies or organizations outside the framework of the Unified Arab Command and Unified Arab Planning . . . Such unwarranted activities . . . serve only to impede Arab planning, weaken the mustering of Arab forces and allow our enemies to attack us or deprive us of the initiative so that we would be led unprepared into battle.'[61]

The Jordanian Government feared Palestinian guerrilla raids on Israeli settlements because the Israelis generally responded by attacking Jordanian border towns and villages, and because these attacks could be used by the Israelis to launch a full-scale attack on Jordan. Abu Odeh explains that 'the length of Jordan's border with Israel made it the bulwark against Israel not only in a military sense but also in terms of its political moderation. Miscalculation on the part of the Arabs would have meant the loss of Jordan because of Israel's superior strength. This explains the King's opposition to commando operations before 1967. He believes that these operations would provoke retaliation by Israel which neither Jordan nor other Arab states were capable of confronting'.[62] Indeed, King Hussein states that he did not think 'that the guerrillas contributed much to changing the situation on the ground, but they did provide Israel with an excuse for large-scale retaliation'.[63] These dangers were recognized by most Arab nations, including the UAR and Lebanon as well as the UAC. However, some Palestinian groups believed that guerrilla activity should be undertaken in order to force the Arabs into confrontration with Israel. Abu Odeh points out:

> one of the general misconceptions at present is that people tend to view Jordanian–Palestinian relations in the sixties or the past in general on the basis of present Palestinian realities in which powerful Palestinian nationalism found its expression through organizations founded after 1967. In the sixties this concept was not present. Palestinians were only calling for their return to Palestine and the implementation of UN

resolutions. They were not struggling in the name of Palestinian nationalism but were calling on the Arab nations to liberate Palestine for them . . . When the concept became clearly defined as a result of the PLO and later Al-Fatah, the call changed to a policy of forcing Arab involvement with Israel. In other words, it was based on what later turned out to be a mistaken belief of members of Al-Fatah which resulted from influence of Algeria – that the Arabs could fight and defeat Israel and that they were not doing this because they were cowards and traitors. They believed that by implicating the Arabs in a war with Israel the latter would be defeated. As a result they were dragged into the 1967 debacle.[64]

Al-Fatah's policy of direct confrontation with Israel was the reverse of that espoused by Jordan. Al-Fatah's communique of 1 January 1965 issued on the occasion of its first raid into Israel stated: 'The Asifa forces [of Al-Fatah] have been launched to reiterate to the enemy and the world in general that this people [of Palestine] did not die and that armed revolution is on the road to return and victory . . . Let us rise to the level of responsibility – the responsibility of an honourable battle – because this first operation is nothing but the beginning of a war of liberation with a carefully planned and studied programme'.[65] By 1966 fedayeen attacks on Israel from Jordan were a regular event. The Jordanian Government responded by condemning their activities and the army was instructed to intercept fedayeen attempting to penetrate their border. Palestinian guerrillas attempting to conduct raids on Israel were stopped and arrested.[66]

These developments escalated the conflict between Jordan and the Palestinians. Until this point, Shukairy had succeeded in holding back Palestinian desires to mount guerrilla attacks on Israel. However, the activities of Al-Fatah and other guerrilla groups made it necessary for him to follow their example or allow them to seize the initiative. Consequently, the PLA began to organize its own incursions into Israel, thereby increasing Jordanian–Palestinian tension.

Although the third summit conference rejected the PLO's demand to be allowed to recruit, train and arm Palestinians without reference to the local Jordanian Government, matters did not improve. Nasser tried to contain the conflict developing between Jordan and the PLO but his efforts to mediate between Shukairy and King Hussein were of no avail. Each side accused the other of wrecking the movement towards the recovery of Palestine. When Shukairy attacked King Hussein the latter replied: 'The continuation of this strange and suspect campaign which has been directed against us by the chairman of the PLO and his machine, can only be interpreted as designed to weaken conditions in Jordan, tear asunder the one community which is the heart of the Arab reorganization for Palestine.'[67] An attempt at conciliation in early 1966 collapsed after Jordan's purchase of American planes and Shukairy's subsequent criticism of the Jordanian Government. In April 1966, the Jordanian Government ordered the arrest of about 200 'subversive' elements, including most of the staff of the PLO office in Amman. This was followed two months later by the closure of the office. Wasfi Tal, who was Prime Minister at the time, explains his motives for this move: the PLO 'had begun to practise subversion on a grand scale. They were trying to divide the population of the East and West Banks of Jordan. They were taking into their ranks people who belonged to what we considered illegal parties ... Their goal was to replace Jordan's monarchy with some other political authority'.[68] Following this measure King Hussein declared that 'under the influence of communism the PLO was no longer a movement of liberation'.[69]

These developments destroyed any hope of co-operation between Shukairy and King Hussein and on 14 June the latter officially ruled this out. At the Jordanian House of Deputies (parliament) King Hussein explained that 'the Palestinian Liberation Organization was one of the organizations approved by Jordan and for which creation Jordan made a special effort. Regretfully, its leadership has deviated from its charter and saw fit to involve it in the labyrinth of disagreements and that Jordan should become a special target for subversive, instigatory campaigns launched by its leadership. This has prompted your esteemed House to adopt its unanimous decision to declare the deviation of that leadership'.[70]

The Islamic pact

Another factor which led to the collapse of the summits was the emergence of King Faisal as a potential rival to Nasser. King Faisal had succeeded his brother, Saud, to the throne of Saudi Arabia in November 1964. The relationship between King Faisal and Nasser was not good. Although Saudi Arabia's possession of vast oilfields made it one of the richest Arab states, to a large extent it remained a traditional desert society with a conservative, almost feudal, social structure. This was in contrast with Nasser's desire to modernize the Arab world by ridding it of all traces of traditional power-structures. Saudi Arabia also favoured the West rather then the countries of the Eastern bloc favoured by Nasser. These factors, together with the threat that Saudi Arabia's wealth would weaken Egypt's dominant position in the Arab world, led to rivalry between Nasser and Faisal. This rivalry reached new heights in 1966 as a result of Faisal's proposal to form an alliance of Muslim states.

When Faisal visited the Shah of Iran in December 1965 the two men announced their intention to hold an Islamic Conference in Mecca the following year. In a pointed reference to Nasser's socialist policies Faisal proposed that Saudi Arabia and Iran 'should unite in fighting elements and ideas which are alien to Islam'.[71] The following month Faisal visited Jordan and again proposed to hold an 'Islamic summit' in Mecca later that year. At a press conference in Amman, Faisal explained that the ties linking the Islamic world are much stronger than alliances and treaties since they are the ties of brotherhood. Faisal denied that he was setting up a forum for international Arab decision-making which rivalled that set up by Nasser. The fact remained that Faisal represented a rallying point for all those in the Arab world who opposed the revolutionary policies of countries such as Syria and Egypt. From the Egyptian point of view Faisal's initiative appeared to be calculated to isolate Egypt and other progressive camps from the mainstream of Arab politics.

King Hussein's first response to Faisal's initiative was favourable since he could not fail to answer a call which went out in the name of Islam. Like Faisal he may also have hoped to gather enough support within the moderate Arab world to put pressure on Nasser and prevent him from being influenced by Syria. However, Nasser's round condemnation of Faisal's proposals ensured that they were never fulfilled. Nasser stressed that far from being a spiritual forum the conference was a political one designed to produce a coalition of conservatives whose aim was to crush the Arab revolutionary forces. In an interview with Moscow's *Izvestia* Nasser declared: 'The forces of colonialism and reaction inside and outside the Arab world are launching a new offensive and therefore all progressive forces inside and outside the Arab world should close their ranks, solidify their unity, redouble their resistance and thus become effective.'[72] As a result of his support of the pact King Hussein found himself out of favour with Nasser, although he endeavoured to re-establish the relationship by espousing a policy of neutrality. Following his meeting in Cairo with Mahmoud Riad, the Egyptian Minister of Foreign Affairs, Jordan's permanent representative at the Arab League, Abdul Munim Rifai, stated: 'Jordan has informed the United Arab Republic that it will follow a policy of strict neutrality' concerning Arab differences over the Islamic Alliance between Saudi Arabia and the UAR.[73] However, these efforts proved to be in vain. One week after this meeting Nasser began to hint that the era of Arab summitry had come to an end since co-existence was being exploited by Arab reaction. On 23 July 1966 he officially declared that no more summits would be held and once more accused 'reactionary elements' of co-operating with imperialism against Arab nations. He went on: 'imperialism and those elements have taken advantage of the summit conferences ... We cannot sit together with such reactionary elements at future summit conferences'.[74]

Chapter 4

Samu

The road to Samu

In 1967 Glubb wrote that 'ever since her repulse by the Jordan army in 1948 Israel had longed for an opportunity to overrun the remaining Arab part of Palestine, but as long as Jordan was the friend of Britain and the United States and offered her no pretext, Israel could not move'.[1] This view of Israel was shared by Jordan's decision-makers who were convinced that Israel's leaders had never given up hope that one day the whole of historical Palestine would belong to the Jews. They recalled the fact that at the time of the Balfour Declaration in 1917 the Zionists had claimed the whole of mandatory Palestine, including present-day Jordan, as the territory on which the Jewish national home was to be established. According to Abu Odeh, 'Jordan's exclusion from the Balfour Declaration was decided in spite of Zionist opposition to this. Hence Jordan was always conscious of Zionist strategic ambitions over its territory. Accordingly it was constantly aware of the dangers posed by Zionist progress ... This historical point always remains alive in the Jordanian mind when treating the subject'.[2]

King Hussein had no doubts about Israel's desire to expand into the West Bank. In a speech made on 25 January 1967 King Hussein declared that 'the enemy's present objective is the West Bank; after that it will be the East Bank and after that they will expand throughout the Arab homeland to achieve their aims and ambitions'.[3] Shortly after the 1967 war King Hussein stated that 'the latest attack is not an isolated example but part of a deliberate Israeli expansionist policy, although they have somehow made it appear that they are a tiny unarmed country surrounded by Arab enemies'.[4] Nussaibah remarks that 'the Jordanian leadership was well aware that Israel had many plans to invade the West Bank. It was very much aware that Israel's plans were always there – hidden away – and that they were waiting for the opportune moment to carry them out'.[5]

The Jordanians' belief that Israel was anxious to capture the West Bank was accompanied by their knowledge that they could not defend it on their own. For this reason they wanted to belong to a regional defence system so that they shared the burden of defence with other nations.[6] The creation of the Unified Arab Command (UAC) in 1964 had met this requirement. It offered Jordan the security of belonging to a larger defence unit and the prospect of building up its own military capability. This was particularly important in the mid-1960s because the decisions taken at the Arab summits had resulted in developments which Jordan believed increased the likelihood of Israeli aggression.

One of these decisions was the co-ordination and strengthening of the Arab world's military capability with the aim of achieving parity with, and eventually superiority to, Israel's military power. The next step envisaged the restoration of Palestinian rights to the territory captured by Israel in 1948. This intention was widely publicized. For example, the Statement of the Arab Higher Committee for Palestine on the Resolutions of the Arab Summit Conference declared that 'the Committee hopes that implementation of the decision would lead to a massing of efforts and mobilization of Arab energy to tackle the very basis of the Palestine problem and to draw up a detailed plan aiming at the final destruction of the Zionist state which menaces the entire Arab world'.[7] Although Jordan welcomed the creation of the Unified Arab Command and the rapid growth of Arab military might, it was also conscious that Israel's Middle East policy was one of deterrence based on military superiority. It feared that if Israel felt that it could lose this superiority it might decide to launch a pre-emptive attack with the aim of destroying the Arabs' military capability. This view was expressed by Khammash: 'The Israelis were watching the development and expansion of our armed forces. New units were added, new equipment provided and the operational capability was increased and strengthened. We had done this largely in accordance with a programme proposed by the UAC. This was certainly not to the liking of the Israelis and we were indeed worried that they might do something to upset the programme'.[8]

A further cause of anxiety related to Arab irrigation schemes. The immediate reason for the Arab summits had been Israel's plan to irrigate the Negev with water drawn from the River Jordan. In response the Arabs produced a plan to divert tributaries of the river in Syria and Jordan. Although Jordan approved of this development, its leaders felt that Israel might use force to oppose Arab irrigation schemes and that the ensuing conflict could escalate and provide Israel with an excuse to launch a full-scale attack.

The summits had also witnessed the establishment of the PLO. This represented the first organized form of Palestinian resistance to Israel which was recognized and supported by all the Arab states. The aims behind its creation, as expressed in the summit's final statement,[9] were interpreted by Israeli leaders as an explicit threat to Israel's existence. The fact that the Palestinians became increasingly militant and began to implement measures which threatened to result in the creation of an independent West Bank state was also a cause of concern to Jordan. Israel had often stated that it would regard any change in Jordan's regime with disfavour. For example, Eban states that 'there had long been a paradox in [Israel's] relationship with Jordan. Israel had an interest in Jordanian stability'.[10] Even Nasser recognized that the downfall of the Hashemite regime in Jordan could lead to the country's seizure by Israel.

Anxiety about the impact of Palestinian organizations on Israeli foreign policy increased with the growth of Palestinian commando units, the most important of which was Al-Fatah. Its policy of violent confrontation with Israel conflicted with Jordan's desire not to alter the status quo. Jordan's policy had been consistently against guerrilla raids on Israel because, as Abu Odeh explains:

> Jordan was always aware that any provocation of Israel from Jordanian territory would attract retaliation. It is worth recalling that in 1956 when Israel occupied Sinai its excuse for launching the invasion was to put an end to guerrilla activities from Egypt. The Jordanians also knew that they were no match for Israel nor were they capable of taking retaliatory action as means of stemming Israeli aggression. For this reason their best course was to stop such commando operations. Jordan was quite clear on this matter and made its policy about such operations well-known in the Arab world.[11]

King Hussein felt that the solution to the problems described above lay in co-operation between Arab nations and for this reason he had regarded the summits as vitally important. With their collapse and the virtual demise of the UAC, Jordan was left to face Israel on its own. However, from July 1966 until May 1967 the Arabs were Jordan's most serious threat. In this period Arab propaganda against Jordan reached new heights. Syrian and Palestinian support of guerrilla activities along the Jordanian–Israeli border upset the delicate balance of Jordanian–Israeli relations and inflamed Palestinian feeling against the Jordanian Government.

In opposition to the recommendations of the UAC, Syria had continued to call for a 'popular pan-Arab war' against Israel, declaring that this was the only possible way of achieving the liberation of Palestine and the destruction of imperialist plans and alliances.[12] Although the Casablanca summit of 1965 had resulted in the Arab Solidarity Pact, in which the various Arab states agreed not to indulge in propaganda against each other, Jordan's suppression of Palestinian guerrilla activity was used by Syria to attack Jordan for its 'imperialist' policies. Syria joined the PLO in calling for the destruction of the Hashemite regime. In May 1966 the Syrian press charged the 'leaders of reaction' in Jordan with 'undermining the most sacred aspirations of our masses by abusing revolutionary and progressive principles'.[13] Syria called for an end to association with the reactionary Arab states and for a summit of progressive Arab nations.

Although Nasser had some sympathy with King Hussein's position[14] as the avowed enemy of imperialism in all its forms, he could not afford to identify himself with the policies of a country which the Syrians labelled an imperialist haven and King Hussein a traitor. Even if he had wanted to co-operate with King Hussein, public opinion made this impossible. He had no choice but to curtail the alliance and move closer to the Syrians. King Hussein had also angered Nasser by his support of the Islamic Alliance proposed by Faisal. Consequently a distance developed in the relationship between the two men while the relationship between Cairo and Damascus improved.

Although Nasser did not criticize King Hussein directly, he allowed Shukairy's 'Voice of Palestine' to broadcast from Cairo. Throughout the summer of 1966 Nasser's relationship with the King deteriorated. After his announcement on 23 July 1966 that he would have no further meetings with reactionaries,[15] the Egyptian media began to criticize the Jordanian regime. Jordan became increasingly isolated. This isolation intensified in November as the relationship between Egypt and Syria crystallized in the form of a defence treaty between the two countries. This development was of grave concern to Jordan. It spelt the end of the UAC and left Jordan once again painfully aware of its vulnerable position not only in relation to Israel but also to the radical Arab states and the PLO.

The Jordanian leadership interpreted these events in terms of a struggle between Nasser and Syria's ruling elite for leadership of the Arab world. Nasser had been consistently against taking militant action against Israel until the Arabs were ready to strike a decisive blow. Throughout the summit era he had demonstrated that he was fully alive to the realities of the situation and understood that the Arabs were not in a position to wage war. For example, at his public address shortly before the first summit in Cairo in January 1964 Nasser stated the matter plainly: 'We will sit and talk seriously at the meeting and it will be no shame if we come out and say that we cannot use force today . . . because our circumstances do not allow us . . . I would lead you to disaster if I were to proclaim that I would fight at a time when I was unable to do so. I would not lead my country to disaster and would not gamble with its destiny'.[16] The month prior to that the Cairo magazine *Rose Al-Yusuf* had stated that 'the United Arab Republic will not let itself be pushed into a battle with Israel before the attainment of unity among all the Arab countries'.[17]

The Cairo summit of 1964 had been a resounding success for Nasser, not because it had succeeded in drawing up a plan for the diversion of the waters of the River Jordan but because it had succeeded in diverting the Syrian government 'from any hope of immersing Gamal 'Abd Al-Nasir in war or embarrassment'.[18] It was for this reason that the Syrians found the summits detestable and were eager to end them. The problem faced by Nasser was that, as the leader of the Arab masses and self-proclaimed champion of the Palestinians, he was vulnerable to the Syrians' accusation that he was failing to act on their behalf. If he was to retain his dominant position Nasser had to prove that he was serious about confronting Israel. He could not allow himself to be outdone by the Syrians in this regard. Consequently, by calling into question Nasser's sincerity about the issue of Palestine, the Syrians were able to push him into an increasingly belligerent position towards Israel.

For this reason Jordan's decision-makers regarded the signing of a defence treaty between Egypt and Syria with dismay. They felt that the two nations were engaged in a perilous game of brinkmanship. Although they believed that Nasser hoped that by coming into a close alliance with the Syrians he would restrain Syria's aggressive attitude towards Israel, he had been, in fact, outmanoeuvred and had entered a volatile situation which was likely to get out of his control. According to Khammash, the Jordanians 'hoped . . . that by giving the Syrians his total support [Nasser] might have a restraining influence on them'. He goes on to say: 'the reverse was more correct'.[19] Jordan's leaders believed that Nasser had walked into a trap from which it would be difficult for him to extract himself. This belief is referred to by Abu Odeh: 'When Nasser signed the Syrian–Egyptian defence treaty we in Jordan realized that the Syrians had laid a trap for him.'[20]

The Jordanians feared that the Syrian–Egyptian defence treaty would increase the likelihood of Arab–Israeli war because it spelt the end of Nasser's moderate and cautious approach to Arab–Israeli relations. They believed that this played into the hands of Israel because it might result in a situation which would provide the Israelis with an excuse to attack the Arabs. This perception is reflected in Khammash's statement: 'Upon the signing of the Syrian–Egyptian defence treaty on 4 November 1966 we realized that the UAC was finished and that the prospect of war had definitely been increased. Indeed, we felt that the Arab radicals had played straight into the hands of the Israelis, particularly as Syria encouraged an increased wave of Palestinian commando raids into Israel'.[21]

Jordan's decision-makers believed that the Syrians were 'actively trying to involve Nasser in a war with Israel',[22] not to revenge the injustices done to the Palestinians but in order to gain supremacy over Nasser as the leader of the Arabs. The Jordanians were aware that the Syrians could not hope to defeat Israel. Kawash remarks: 'It always puzzled us as to why the Syrians boasted of their military preparedness and took such an uncompromising attitude towards Israel unless they over-estimated their strength and under-estimated Israel's.'[23] Jordan's elite believed that the answer to this puzzle lay in the fact that by forcing Nasser into a war with Israel the Syrians would be victorious no matter what the outcome was. If the Arabs inflicted defeat on Israel the Syrians could claim that the initiative had been theirs. If the war ended in defeat for the Arabs, Nasser could be held responsible and would be forced to resign. Even if he did not resign he would find his dominant position greatly reduced. King

Hussein's belief that they achieved their ambition is reflected in his bitter statement that 'following the war the people who had not checked Nasser [the Syrians] time and again as we did were the people who were most satisfied with the disaster. That was one of the ugliest things I experienced. I saw it before Khartoum [the summit], I saw it at Khartoum. They were almost gloating'.[24]

Jordan's leaders also felt that war with Israel would help the Syrians gain their objective of destroying the Jordanian regime, because such a war would embroil Jordan in a situation which left it with little room for manoeuvre. If Jordan failed to participate in the war King Hussein would find his subjects so antagonistic to his rule that his fall would be inevitable. If the war ended in an Arab defeat it would be attributed to his failure to participate. He would be branded as an imperialist tool and a traitor to the Arab cause. If the war was successful his failure to participate would have an equally destabilizing effect because he would be accused of failing to support the principle of Arab unity and the Palestinian cause. In either event public opinion would be so antagonistic to him that civil war would be inevitable. If Jordan entered the war Israel would almost certainly invade Jordan, thereby threatening its Hashemite regime. Thus, the Syrians stood to win whether or not there was an Arab victory and whether or not King Hussein participated in such a war.

Many Jordanians also believed that Russia played a significant role in these developments.[25] King Hussein frequently refers to his conviction that Russia was advising Syria and was plotting to gain control of the Arab world.[26] Shortly before the outbreak of hostilities the Jerusalem newspaper *Al-Quds* reported that it could be assumed that 'Communist hands were moving Syria and Syria in turn drags Egypt in a direction which is against Arab national interests, particularly to our occupied homeland of Palestine'.[27]

The same view is put forward by Juma'a who cites Glubb's *The Middle East Crisis* in which Glubb argues that it was the Russians who were responsible for the war. Glubb writes that it was the Russian claim that the Israelis were concentrating their troops on the border with Syria that led to an uncontrollable process of escalation. He believes that the Russians knew that the Arabs would suffer defeat but that this suited them because they believed that the Arab states would be in such a state of disarray that they would be forced to turn to the Soviet Union for aid. A war with Israel would also reveal to the Arabs the extent of Western support for Israel so that they would be filled with antagonism to the West. For the Soviet Union, as for Syria, an Arab–Israeli war would achieve their objectives no matter what the outcome. The effect of a war with Israel on Jordan's Hashemite regime would also suit Russia because of Jordan's pro-Western policies and antagonism to communism.[28] While Glubb provides us with no evidence to support his theories, and he and the Jordanian elite may exaggerate the extent to which Russia deliberately encouraged the Arabs to go to war and manipulated them to this end, there can be little doubt that their actions played an important part in bringing an already volatile situation to the boil.[29]

In order to achieve their objectives in Jordan, the Syrians embarked on activities designed to create instability there. These included a propaganda campaign against King Hussein in which the Syrians argued that the downfall of his regime was necessary before the issue of Palestine could be resolved. In June 1966 the Syrians announced their intention to close their border to Jordanian traffic. This was a serious threat to Jordan because it depended on Syria for much of its trade.[30] Jordan's Prime Minister, Wasfi Tal, responded by announcing that such an action would be prevented by force and that he was prepared to send in tanks to keep the border open.[31] Although the Syrians did not implement their threat they maintained their disruption of Jordanian traffic across the border which had a serious effect on Jordan's trade and tourist industry. They also maintained their efforts to topple Jordan's Government.

One of the ways in which the Syrians sought to subvert the Jordanian regime was through a campaign of terror. This included a plot to kill King Hussein and Tal as well as acts of sabotage. Another mechanism of subversion was the support of Palestinian commando raids into Israel from Jordanian territory. Such actions carried with them the threat of retaliation against Jordan by Israel and thus increased the tension between the two states.

The distressing experiences of many Palestinians living in Jordan had made them susceptible to Syrian attempts to radicalize them and turn them against Jordan's leadership. In recent years the fragile relationship between these Palestinians and Jordan's rulers had deteriorated. Many sections of Palestinian society regarded those West Bankers who were in office as power-seekers, not concerned either to represent or promote the interests of their fellow-nationals. Some also felt that Jordan's industrialization programme and taxation laws were designed to favour East Bankers over West Bankers.[32] Although the merging of the Palestinian National Guard with the Jordanian army in March 1965 had been regarded by the Jordanian leadership as the best opportunity for the PNG to defend their homes, this was interpreted in some quarters as an excuse to disarm them and to prevent the creation of an independent Palestinian military movement in the West Bank. The closure of the PLO office in Amman and the war of words between King Hussein and Shukairy further increased the alienation of important sections of the Palestinian population from the Jordanian leadership.

Although the appointment of Shukairy as leader of the PLO had been regarded with cynicism by many people he had considerable support from some Palestinians. His inflammatory remarks had an impact on the refugees and other Palestinians living in the West Bank.[33] Although in the past he had stood aloof from the activities of the Syrian-backed Palestinian organization, Al-Fatah, towards the end of 1966 he came closer to them and the Syrians supported him in his argument that the recovery of Palestine could only be accomplished after King Hussein had been ousted from his throne. By fermenting discontent in this way Shukairy and the Syrians hoped to impose their views on King Hussein's Government through the sheer force of Palestinian feeling, at the same time increasing the possibility of civil war. They felt that this was the best way of bringing about the downfall of King Hussein.

The Palestinians were not only used by Syria to isolate Jordan from Egypt but also to inflame the Arab–Israeli issue by providing them with a base for guerrilla activities. When Nasser announced the end of the summits in July 1966, Syria took the opportunity to increase its acts of aggression against Israel. The end of the summits meant that the muzzle of collective Arab opinion which had formerly restrained the Syrians was removed. The Syrians made their attitude to the activity of the Palestinian guerrillas clear. In order to promote their cause the Syrian Foreign Minister declared: 'In [the Palestinians'] legitimate struggle to liberate their usurped homeland they do not seek the permission of anyone. This right is guaranteed by principles of the UN and by all earthly laws. Consequently no Arab country can be held responsible for the struggle of the Palestinian Arab people'.[34]

From the middle of 1966 onwards, the expeditions of Al-Fatah became progressively more ambitious, efficient and frequent. Nor was Al-Fatah the only Palestinian guerrilla organization supported by the Syrians. Others added their fuel to the fire. Many of these raids took place by way of Jordanian territory. Between October and mid-November 1966 Syrian-backed Palestinian guerrillas carried out eleven raids into Israel. Six of these took place through Jordan.[35] This was a matter of grave concern to Jordan's leaders. Khammash states that it was this development that first alerted Jordan to the growing prospect of armed conflict with Israel because 'Syria was providing Israel with sufficient incentive to retaliate'.[36] The Jordanian Government knew that such activities carried with them the strong possibility of massive retaliation by the Israeli army on Jordan's border villages. This was precisely what happened in November 1966 when the Jordanian village of Samu was devastated by a brutal Israeli attack.

Samu

The village of Samu lies 16 km south of Hebron and 6.5 km from the border with Israel. In 1966 it was inhabited by a community of 4,000 peasants. At 5.30 a.m. on November 13 an Israeli force composed of one mechanized infantry brigade, supported by large formations of tanks, artillery and engineers, crossed the border separating Israel from Jordan. The operation was also provided with air-cover in the form of two Mirage squadrons. This was the largest engagement of the Israeli army since Suez. According to Wasfi Tal, the strength of the force concentrated on the Israeli side of the armistice line amounted to almost half of that deployed for the invasion of Sinai, including mechanized troops, armour and artillery.[37] The Israeli soldiers forced the inhabitants of the village out of their houses and, as the helpless villagers looked on, began systematically to blow up their homes and property, including their mosque. Forty buildings had been destroyed when a convoy of Jordanian army trucks appeared. The convoy had no chance of beating off the massive force of Israelis. In the ensuing battle, at least eighteen Jordanians were killed and many more were wounded.[38] According to the Israelis they lost only one soldier and a mere ten were wounded.[39] Fifteen Jordanian vehicles were destroyed and twenty-two Israeli vehicles were damaged.[40]

Israel's motive in attacking Samu was given various interpretations by Western and Arab observers. In general it was seen as a sign of weakness on the part of the Israeli government. Public opinion felt that Israel knew that its real enemy was Syria but that the Israeli government was frightened of taking action which might escalate into full-scale war and therefore struck at a country which was weak and unlikely to retaliate.[41] This was also the view of Syria and Egypt. They believed that the growth of the Egyptian army had made it a formidable foe which the Israelis were scared to confront. The fact that Jordan and not Syria had been the object of attack was seen by both Egypt and Syria as evidence of the success of their newly established defence treaty.[42]

One of the most important effects of the raid was to convince the Jordanians that the Israelis made no distinction between one Arab nation and another. Khammash states that 'this realization . . . became a determinating factor in our strategic view of Israel'.[43] Both King Hussein and Khammash point out that the attack was supposed to be a reprisal raid for activities undertaken not by Jordan, but by Syria. For this reason they concluded that one of the purposes behind the attack was to demonstrate to the Arab world that as far as the Israelis were concerned all Arabs were the enemy of Israel whether they were Syrians, Egyptians or Jordanians.[44] This interpretation of Samu is of the utmost importance in explaining later events. It made the Jordanians feel that the sheer logic of the situation demanded that they belong to an Arab regional defence system. King Hussein states that 'it helped enhance even more the idea we already had that collectively we faced an extremely serious threat'.[45] It also heightened the Jordanian leadership's awareness that Jordan's weak defences made the West Bank a prime target for Israel. Samu convinced them that sooner or later Israel would try to conquer the West Bank and that for this reason they needed to co-operate with the other Arab nations and seek to join them in a system of regional defence.

Secondly, the Jordanians felt that Samu was designed to provoke them to retaliate against Israel. This would provide it with an opportunity to invade Jordan, destroy its 'rapidly growing military capability'[46] and occupy the West

Bank. Tal claimed that at the time of the raid the Israelis had massed their force 'opposite the Jerusalem sector and a larger force in the north opposite the Jenin sector and in the Bissan area'.[47] He believed that this indicated that they were hoping that Samu would set off a retaliatory action. He said, 'It was clear to us at the time, as it is totally clear to the Arabs now [that is, after the June 1967 war], that the enemy was looking for an opportunity to launch a war against us'.[48]

Thirdly, the Jordanian leadership felt that Samu was designed to deepen the divisions within the Arab world. The Israeli attack led to charges from Syria and Egypt that the Jordanian government was incompetent, unable to defend its citizens and that its leaders were unfit to rule. Such charges hardened the rift between Arab nations and destroyed any possibility that the UAC would be an effective force. The Jordanians believed that the Israelis hoped that the Arabs would be so divided that they would be unable to mount a co-ordinated attack on Israel. Abu Odeh believes that this tactic was a standard policy of Israel and was designed to weaken the defences of the Arab nations.[49]

Fourthly, the Jordanians felt that Samu was designed to test the effectiveness of the UAC and its ability to provide rapid military support to the Jordanian front in terms of air-cover and possible action on other fronts.[50] At a press conference held on 21 November 1966 Tal pointed out that nothing had been done by the UAC, which demonstrated that it was totally ineffective.[51]

Fifthly, some of Jordan's leaders felt that Samu was designed to weaken their defences. Tal points out that the raid resulted in such a feeling of insecurity in the minds of the people living on the border with Israel[52] that it created pressure for the army to be spread even more thinly along it, thus decreasing its effectiveness. King Hussein confirms that this was one of the effects of Samu which forced the army to 'try and hold every inch [of the border with Israel] weakly'.[53]

Sixthly, the Jordanians believed that Samu was designed 'to provoke West Bank citizens to rebel against the government',[54] which Arab propaganda had already accused of being too soft on Israel. This increased the possibility that unrest in the West Bank would be so severe that it could be used as an excuse by the Israelis to invade. They could claim that the danger of the Palestinians gaining the upper hand in Jordan represented a threat which they could not tolerate. Tal pointed out that for this reason propaganda against Jordan by other Arab nations only served the purposes of the Israelis.[55]

The Jordanians also believed that the Israelis hoped that Samu would have an inflammatory effect on public opinion, which was already intoxicated by Egyptian, Syrian and PLO propaganda against King Hussein. This would make it extremely difficult for Jordan to 'stay out of any serious confrontation between the Arabs and Israel in the future'.[56]

This was seen, in broader terms, as part of a general Israeli strategy to draw the Arab world into a war for which it was not prepared. The Jordanians felt that the Israelis were using the Syrians and the PLO in order to lay a trap which would spell disaster for the Arabs. According to Khammash, shortly after Samu King Hussein 'met senior officers at the army GHQs and conveyed his thoughts to them ... The discussion ... reflected our fears that Israel was plotting something big and that it was provoking Arab radicals into providing it with the excuse to act. Later events were to confirm our perceptions beyond any doubt'.[57]

Indeed, King Hussein believed that Samu was 'the perfect psychological preparation which helped to set the trap' and that 'unfortunately we played into [Israel's] hands'.[58] It was felt that as well as forcing Jordan into the conflict, Samu was designed to provoke the Syrians and the Palestinians into more acts of border violence as a way of discrediting King Hussein in the eyes of his Palestinian subjects. The King believed that the Israelis felt that the existence of the Syrian–Egyptian defence pact meant that such activity would eventually embroil Nasser in a conflict which would ultimately result in full-scale confrontation with Israel. Since the Israelis were confident that they could defeat the Arabs this would result in Nasser's downfall – something which the Israelis were anxious to achieve.

The belief that the Israelis would only be too happy to engage in a military confrontation with Jordan prevented its rulers from taking retaliatory action. Tal writes: 'Fortunately, we concluded at the time that the enemy operation in Samu was an attempt to draw us into a battle which Israel could claim amounted to aggression against her. This, together with previous commando raids on her installations and military camps, would provide her with the excuse to invade the West Bank. At the time we had to face Arab wrath for that conclusion, although the events of June proved that we were correct.'[59] While some politicians, including many from the West Bank, pressed King Hussein to authorize retaliatory action, he and his Prime Minister felt that this was a luxury which Jordan could not afford. Both King Hussein and Tal were convinced that this was precisely what Israel wanted because Jordan's weak military capability and the ineffectiveness of the UAC made it an easy target for Israel. Tal writes: 'In my view we were not ready for war. Therefore we decided to enhance our defences, to defend the armistice line and to avoid giving Israel anything that might give it the excuse to drag us prematurely into armed conflict. Accordingly we refrained from taking any reprisal action for Samu and tried to prevent the commandos from carrying out any action along the armistice lines.'[60]

The aftermath of Samu

Throughout the summit era Jordan's strategy had conformed to the recommendations of the UAC. These had been based on three principles: the Arabs were not ready for war with Israel; for this reason they would have to exercise the utmost caution and restraint in order to deny Israel an excuse to draw any Arab country into an armed conflict; in order to alter this situation the armed forces of the confrontation states should be increased and strengthened. In particular, Jordan's forces should be enlarged, equipped and trained to bring them to a level sufficient to block an initial Israeli thrust, while military support from other Arab nations was brought in to deal with any prolonged fighting.

Although it had led to conflict with Syria and the PLO, Jordan had adhered to these principles very strictly. However, the developments that took place in the months after Samu made it almost impossible for it to continue to do so. Jordan found itself drawn into activities which were contrary to the advice of the UAC and became increasingly conscious that the chances of armed conflict with Israel were rising.

The fact that the Israelis had been so successful in destroying the village of Samu and killing and wounding a large number of Jordanian military and civilian personnel gave Jordan's enemies powerful ammunition with which to criticize the Government. Jordan was accused of neglecting the defence of its population. The dismantling of the Palestinian National Guard was a particularly sore point. Syrian and PLO propaganda declared that the inhabitants of Samu had been defenceless before the enemy. Riots broke out in Ramallah, Nablus, Jerusalem and other Jordanian cities.[61] The rioters demanded arms to fight Israel and expressed their support for the PLO. Criticism became even more intense when the government failed to take retaliatory action against Israel. A wave of protest swept through the cities of Jordan and was particularly powerful in the West Bank. The Palestinians were filled with a sense of betrayal, insecurity and anger. They felt that the government was insensitive to their needs and had callously stood by as their people and homes were destroyed by Israel. The force of their feelings was stimulated by Syrian, Egyptian and PLO propaganda which lost no time in fanning the flames. The Syrians accused the Jordanian government of being a traitor to the Arab cause and an imperialist stooge. They argued that, given the opportunity, King Hussein would betray the Palestinians in the way his grandfather was accused of doing. They claimed that the King was an agent of Israel which he was protecting by refusing to allow the Palestinian commandos to conduct raids against it. Egypt also accused Jordan of having come to an agreement with Israel to prevent further attacks. It claimed that the raid on Samu was part of an imperialist plot to bolster the Jordanian regime. Shukairy also claimed that Tal had been warned of the attack but had done nothing to prevent it.

On 24 November a PLO broadcast from Cairo called on the Jordanian army to join the people's rebellion and deal a crushing blow to King Hussein and Tal. In response refugees from two camps outside Ramallah marched to the city shouting slogans denouncing King Hussein, demanding arms and calling for the leadership of Shukairy. Troops were called in, the march was broken up and several hundred people were reported arrested. The following day the anti-King riots spread to Jerusalem where the rioters were only dispersed when the army fired at the demonstrators, reportedly wounding about forty of them. The same pattern occurred in other West Bank towns, and Nablus and Hebron were sealed off by troops. The citizens of Hebron, Jerusalem, Ramallah, Nablus and many other towns went on the rampage. Photographs of King Hussein were torn up or burnt by demonstrators. Government offices were stoned and members of the Jordanian army and the police were subjected to outbursts of hatred and violence by outraged crowds.

Although King Hussein sought to quell the riots by immediately agreeing to issue arms to villages on the Israeli border, authorizing the military conscription of all Jordanians between the ages of eighteen and forty and agreeing to the recommencement of previously halted training schemes, this did not alleviate the problem.[62] The propaganda of Egypt, Syria and the PLO had resulted in a war-fever which swept Jordan and other Arab countries. Radio broadcasts from Cairo and Damascus declared that nothing prevented the Arabs from revenging themselves on Israel but cowardice and complicity, and that the main obstacle was King Hussein.

So intense was Palestinian feeling that leading figures on the West Bank decided to declare the creation of an independent Palestinian state on the West Bank.[63] They believed that Egypt and Syria would not hesitate to recognize it and that in such circumstances the Jordanian government would find it difficult to resist such a movement. This was one of the reasons why Prime Minister Tal swiftly moved to dissolve Parliament and impose martial law. The wave of protest sweeping Jordan was crushed and the PLO was utterly suppressed. Nussaibah describes how 'leaders of the West Bank were called to the Royal Palace where they were given a stiff reprimand' by the King and Tal for their alleged support of Shukairy and their threat to break away from Jordan. When Nussaibah, who was unaware of the moves being made by the West Bank leaders, tried to see the King in order to express his objection to this action he was prevented by Wasfi Tal.[64] Thus, the Israeli attack on Samu created a deep rift between the Government and the Palestinians, including some of those in positions of influence.

On 22 December Tal resigned from his post as Prime Minister and formed a new cabinet the same day. On 23 December he asked for the dismissal of Parliament and the King granted his request the following day. This gave the Government a free hand to deal with the dangerous domestic situation. A strict watch was placed on all dissidents within Jordan and the army was charged with the task of preventing any commando raids into Israel from Jordanian territory.

The devastation caused by the Israeli raid on Samu also deepened the rift in the relationship between Jordan and other Arab nations because it resulted in intense speculation as to the causes of Jordan's failure to defend its citizens. Jordan argued that the blame lay with Egypt and Syria which had failed to respond to the needs of their ally. Tal argued that under the arrangements laid down by the UAC Egypt should have provided Jordan with air support. Since Egypt had failed to come to Jordan's aid he suggested that Egypt's troops should withdraw from Yemen and instead concentrate on the real enemy in Sinai.[65]

However, Syria and later Egypt responded by arguing that it was Jordan's failure to comply with the demands of the UAC that had resulted in Israel's victory. A special meeting of the Arab League Defence Council was held in the second week of December 1966 with the aim of examining the problem. At this meeting the Arab nations pressed Jordan to accept troops from Iraq and Saudi Arabia to help in its defence. Jordan was reluctant to agree, claiming that Israel could use this as an excuse to invade it. Jordan argued that acceptance of Arab troops should be dependent on two conditions. First, that Jordan should be faced with an immediate threat from Israel and secondly, that Egypt should demand the withdrawal of UNEF from Sinai and replace it with the Egyptian troops now fighting in Yemen.[66] Although Jordan eventually agreed to the proposal it demanded the fulfilment of two preconditions before it could be implemented. One was the fulfilment of the second of the two conditions described above and the other was the fulfilment of the financial commitments that had been promised to Jordan. In effect this amounted to a refusal of the recommendation since Egypt was not prepared to comply with Jordan's request and Saudi Arabia had already announced that it would not meet its financial commitments until the next summit was held. Jordan's refusal to implement the Arab League Defence Council resolution led to its condemnation by Syria, the PLO and Egypt, who accused it of failing to provide proper defence of the West Bank.

The antagonism towards Jordan increased when Shukairy, who attended the meeting as the representative of the PLO, accused Jordan of obstructing PLO operations[67] and argued that a PLA contingent should be allowed into the West Bank. Although this demand was not supported by the League, Jordan's adamant refusal to allow this led to its condemnation by Shukairy and the Jordanian representative's threat to walk out of the meetings,[68] as well as providing Syria and the PLO with more ammunition with which to attack the Jordanian regime.

Since Jordan had been the subject of such bitter attack at the previous Arab League Defence Council meeting, it was reluctant to attend any more. When another meeting was proposed Jordan refused to send a representative, stating that it would boycott all bodies instituted by the summits and also attended by Shukairy.[69] At the Council meeting Jordan was severely criticized and Syria strenuously tried to pass a motion condemning Jordan as a traitor to the cause.

Egypt also accused Jordan of 'deviating from the line of common Arab action' and proposed to withdraw the financial aid it had promised to Jordan or any other member state which did not implement the Council's decision.[70]

An Arab League Council Meeting was held on 14 March 1967. Once more Jordan was the subject of attack by the radical Arab states. A clash between Shukairy and the Jordanian delegation resulted in the latter walking out of the meeting. Consequently the Council passed a number of anti-Jordanian resolutions. Jordan now found itself completely isolated from its powerful Arab neighbours. Not only had it lost the support of the UAC but it had also lost the prospect of building up its military capability through donations from other Arab nations.

The propaganda campaign against Jordan conducted by Syria, the PLO and Egypt now reached new heights. Nasser declared that King Hussein 'was ready to sell the Arab nation in the same manner as Abdullah sold it in 1948'.[71] King Hussein was described as an imperialist agent,[72] a 'lackey of imperialism', and an 'ally of Zionism' among other, even more inglorious epithets. Every day Syria and the PLO called on the people of Jordan to rise against their King and to kill him.[73] They accused him of persecuting the Palestinians and the leaders of opposition movements and of protecting Israel by preventing Arab guerrilla raids into it. So vitriolic was this propaganda that in February 1967 King Hussein recalled his ambassador from Egypt and, just before the outbreak of the war in June, broke off diplomatic relations with Syria. Although inevitable, the Jordanians were concerned that this response also played into the hands of the Israelis whom they believed wanted the Arabs to be as divided as possible, and in particular, for Jordan to be isolated from its Arab neighbours. Zaid Rifai comments that 'the Syrian-backed PLO raids against Israel continued unabated and the Syrian–Egyptian propaganda campaign against Jordan intensified to the extent of calling on Jordanians to overthrow the monarchy. Thus, we were compelled to react by calling our ambassador from Cairo and severing diplomatic relations with Syria. Nevertheless, deep in our hearts we knew that this was precisely what Israel wanted us to do'.[74]

The relationship between Egypt and Jordan deteriorated further when Amman responded to the stream of anti-Jordanian propaganda that poured out of Cairo with an equally strident attack. The Jordanians claimed that Egypt, with the encouragement and connivance of Russia, 'was preparing to sell out the West Bank to Israel in return for a separate peace settlement'.[75] They declared that Nasser's war-like cries were no more than empty rhetoric and that he had no intention of actually going to war. They argued that the continued presence of UNEF in Sinai and Gaza made a mockery of Egypt's claims to be ready for war with Israel and accused Nasser of using it as a pretext for not confronting the enemy.[76] In a speech made on 25 January King Hussein declared: 'If UNEF remains there can be only one explanation for its presence –

that there is an agreement that this force stays until the Palestine question is settled or until reconciliation is reached.'[77]

By driving home these points to the Egyptian masses Jordan was calling into question Nasser's claim to be the champion of the Palestinians. At the third Arab summit in Casablanca Nasser had promised that the UN forces would not be allowed to stand in the way of offensive operations against Israel. By allowing the continued presence of UNEF in Sinai – something which the Israelis had refused to allow on their part of the border – Nasser's credibility was at stake. As the revolutionary champion of the Palestinians Nasser could not tolerate the accusation that he was failing to use every opportunity to correct the injustices they had suffered.

Although this barrage of criticism against Egypt conflicted with King Hussein's desire not to add to the already unstable situation, the Jordanian Government felt that it had to defend itself by pointing out that Egypt's actions contradicted its words. Unfortunately, Jordan's criticisms of Egypt pushed a volatile situation even closer to the brink because Jordan was goading Egypt into taking action which would undoubtedly increase the chances of armed conflict with Israel. Thus the Jordanian Government found itself engaged in activities which it felt were ultimately detrimental to the Arab cause but which were essential if it was to maintain its integrity in the eyes of its people.

Chapter 5

The gathering crisis

Prelude to war

An aerial dogfight between Syria and Israel in early April further divided the Arab world as well as increasing Arab–Israeli tension. It began with Israel's attempts to cultivate land in the Demilitarized Zone bordering Syria. The Syrians responded by firing on an Israeli tractor. This was answered by fire from the Israeli forces. Soon artillery, tanks and aircraft joined in. Six Syrian aircraft were shot down by Israeli fighter-planes, one of which went on to sweep over Damascus, triumphantly driving home Israel's victory over the Syrians.[1]

The ease with which the Israelis had defeated the Syrians aroused grave concern in Jordan.[2] It revealed the extent of Syria's military weakness and emphasized how hollow was its claim to be ready to fight a war of liberation on behalf of the Palestinian people.

At the same time, the Jordanians realized that the incident provided them with valuable ammunition against Egypt. They immediately grasped the opportunity to highlight what they saw as the hypocrisy of Egypt in failing to come to the aid of its ally, Syria. Radio Jordan condemned Nasser and pointed out that his boasts about the strength of his forces and his readiness to defend his Arab brethren were meaningless. The fight between the Syrians and the Israelis had lasted several hours yet Nasser had done nothing to help his ally.[3] Even the Syrians accused him of failing to come to their aid.[4] The Jordanians argued that for all his ranting Nasser was doing very little against his enemy. He condemned Jordan for repressing the activities of the PLO but seemed to forget that no Arab infiltrations into Israel had taken place from the Egyptian border for years.[5] Radio Jordan again pointed out that Nasser was in an ideal position to hit Israel where it hurt. The Straits of Tiran lay in Egyptian territory and Nasser could declare them out of bounds to the Israelis. Jordanian propaganda pointed out that by allowing Israeli ships to enter the Gulf of Aqaba, Egypt was helping Israel conduct trade and establish ties with Africa. The Jordanians claimed that Israel was receiving military supplies via the Gulf which were used to kill the Arabs whom Nasser had sworn to protect.[6] Although Nasser made some stinging replies to these criticisms they struck home and forced him into an increasingly offensive posture. If he was to maintain his position of power he not only had to speak about action, he had to demonstrate it.

The propaganda campaign against Nasser was masterminded by Wasfi Tal, who was known for his vehement opposition to Nasser. However, at the same time as this campaign, the current in favour of a rapprochement with Nasser, which had begun after Israel's raid on Samu, gathered strength. According to a number of Jordanian officials this development was associated with pressure from America. Tal states that after his resignation in December 1966 'a new Jordanian political current emerged which called for our patching up with Nasser'. He goes on to say that this pressure 'came from the King's aides, political aspirants and popular extremism. Also, I cannot forget manoeuvres exercised by the USA. I was not happy with the way matters were developing as I anticipated the outcome. Not for one moment did I hesitate to warn those directly responsible but they closed their ears to my advice'.[7]

Tal's statement sums up his perception of the dangerous situation into which Jordan was being pushed. When he refers to the internal aspect of this pressure, Tal is pointing his finger at his successor Saad Juma'a, who was then Minister of the Royal Court and close adviser to King Hussein. As such he was a serious contender for the position of Prime Minister. Tal believed that, in order to achieve his political ambitions, Juma'a was riding on the popular current which favoured Nasser's policies.

The most important point made by Tal is his belief that the combination of American pressure and popular extremism were leading the nation into a dangerous situation. Tal believed that those who called for Jordan to 'patch up with Nasser' were drawing the nation into a war which would almost certainly end in defeat and the loss of the West Bank.

Tal's claim that America suggested that Jordan ally itself with Nasser has also been expressed by other high-ranking observers. They claim that Richard Murphy, who was then a diplomat in Jordan (and later American Under-Secretary of State), approached politicians, including Suleiman Nabulsi, Akef Al-Fayez and Hazem Nussaibah, with this suggestion. Considering Nasser's profound expressions of antagonism towards America and his pro-Soviet leanings at that time this was extraordinary. It later led to the suspicion that America deliberately tried to draw Jordan onto the side of Egypt and Syria in the fatal war that was looming between the Arabs and Israel. Certain Jordanians concluded that elements within the American administration realized that Israel would take advantage of Syrian, Egyptian and PLO belligerency and engage the Arabs in a war which the Israelis would win. These Jordanians later felt that America had acquiesced with this and had done nothing to help Jordan because they believed it would lead to a peace settlement in Israel's favour.[8] As the summer of 1967 unfolded these Jordanians found that events confirmed their suspicions. By the end of the war they were in no doubt that their fears had been correct and that America had made it clear that its loyalties lay with Israel.

Despite these suspicions, the suggestion of a reconciliation with Nasser found fertile ground in Jordan. Tal was one of the few politicians who was adamant that such a move was too dangerous. He did not trust Nasser and believed that his game of brinkmanship with Syria would lead the Arabs to disaster. Abu Odeh explains that Tal 'was against joining the war because he believed the Arabs could not win it and that the outcome would be the loss of the West Bank. He was fully aware of the extent of the local constraint on the King but argued that this would not be as disastrous as losing the West Bank.'[9]

Whilst many people were deluded into believing Egyptian boasts of their immense military power Tal maintained that such a belief was tragically mistaken. He was an experienced military man and pointed out that the line-up of Jordan's forces was essentially defensive and gave the Israelis the initiative. They would therefore have considerable flexibility when it came to battle. The thinning of the Jordanian army along the border with Israel had placed it in a weak position and minimized its ability to stave off an Israeli attack in any one area.[10] The Jordanian air force was minuscule and the army had virtually no air cover. This meant relying on support from Egypt, Syria and Iraq who, even if they were prepared to offer Jordan their support, might prove to be ineffective when it came to the test. Samu had demonstrated that the UAC was defunct and the incident between the Syrian and Israeli air forces in April had revealed how ineffectual Egyptian support could be. Nor were there any co-ordinated Arab plans for dealing with either attack or defence against Israel. Most of the money promised to Jordan by the UAC had failed to materialize and Jordan had limited alternative resources. Egypt's troops were still heavily embroiled in the Yemen and Iraq's were in Kurdistan. Tal also believed that the Arab armies had been subjected to 'so many shake-ups, so many coups; and the introduction of politics into those armies meant that the position of officers or soldiers was based on their political affiliation rather than on their abilities. In a period of ten years more than 2,000 officers of three Arab countries had been dismissed for this reason'.[11]

Tal's view was shared by a few senior Jordanians. Zaid Rifai comments:

We knew a war was going to happen. We even knew generally that probably the war would start with an Israeli strike or perhaps an Israeli airstrike . . . At the point where matters had escalated to the degree where it was not possible to turn the clock back or to stop the countdown there was a war fever prevalent in Jordan and throughout the Arab world. I was not very happy about the direction of developments. There was in the country and all over the Arab world what you might call a mass euphoria about the possibility of war and that this was something we had been waiting for for a long time – we were going to defeat Israel once and for all. I knew better and so did some other

Jordanian officials. There were people in responsible positions who knew that we were going to lose the war. We were not prepared for it, nor did we know enough about Egyptian and Syrian preparedness, but as far as Jordan was concerned we knew we were not a match for Israel militarily. So when the war started it was no surprise.[12]

However, this view of the Arab world's military weakness was not shared by many people. Egyptian and Syrian propaganda was so powerful that few had a realistic conception of the military capability of the Arabs compared with the Israelis. From a purely quantitative point of view, in early 1967 Egypt appeared a formidable foe. It had been receiving arms from Russia for a number of years and seemed to have an impressive army. This was a source of pride to Egypt whose leaders frequently proclaimed its military might. The Egyptian Vice-President, Field-Marshal Amer, declared that Egypt was the most powerful military force in the Middle East.[13] In order to convince its inhabitants of its military prowess Egypt held regular displays of its military equipment. Included in these were the rockets 'Al-Kahir' (the Conqueror), 'Al-Zafir' (the Victorious) and 'Al-Nasser' (the Victory) which, it was claimed, could reach any part of Israeli territory. They carried warheads upwards of 1,000 lb and were said to have a striking distance of between 200 and 450 miles.[14] The Egyptian army consisted of 180,000 men, 60,000 reserves, 60,000 National Guardsmen and 30,000 members of the PLA. It was composed of two armoured divisions, with a third about to be formed, four motorized rifle divisions, one parachute brigade and twelve artillery regiments. Its armour consisted of 1,200 tanks and assault guns, including 350 Russian T-34, 500 T-54, a few British Centurions and French AMX tanks. Its navy consisted of 11,000 men with equipment which included 18 destroyers, 11 submarines as well as 6 escort vessels, 6 coastal escorts, 10 minesweepers, 18 missile patrol boats, submarine chasers and about 50 small patrol vessels. Its air force of 20,000 men was equipped with 500 combat aircraft and included at least 70 bombers, 120 MiG-21 interceptors with air-to-air missiles, 80 MiG-19 all-weather fighters and 200 MiG-15, MiG-17 and SU-7 fighter bombers in addition to transport aircraft.[15]

This was compared with Israel's military capability which was grossly underestimated.[16] The popular view was largely based on estimates provided by Arab propaganda and these were completely inaccurate. In May 1967 Radio Cairo described Israel's forces in the following way: 'Arabs, here are full and accurate details of Israel's military power obtained from sources which know the whole truth about Israel ... Israel has a number of old Sherman tanks which have been repaired and fitted with diesel engines and French 105mm guns ... In war Israel could mobilize within 48 hours 250,000 soldiers who could undertake home guard duties but who do not take part in battles involving regular armies ...' The broadcast concluded: 'We challenge you

Eshkol, to try all your weapons. Put them to the test; they will spell Israel's death and annihilation.'[17]

This assessment of Egyptian–Israeli strength was in stark contrast with the opinion of other observers.[18] The much vaunted Egyptian rockets were regarded as non-operational by the West and America argued that they constituted no more than a 'psychological threat'.[19] In May 1967 the Director of Central Intelligence reported to President Johnson that 'Israel would win a war against one or all of the Arab countries, whichever struck the first blow, in about a week'.[20] They were so certain of this that the Americans did not even bother to draw up contingency plans if the action went the other way.[21]

The mistaken view of the realities of Arab–Israeli military strength popularly held by the Arabs was extremely hard to dispel. Even members of the Jordanian Parliament were misled by Egyptian propaganda about the strength of its army. Jordan's former Speaker of Parliament, Hikmet Al-Masri, was one of a number of West Bank politicians who visited Cairo a few weeks before hostilities broke out. On his return he told Nussaibah that in the event of war with Israel, Egypt's prospects were 'more than excellent'.[22] Nussaibah commented that 'the leaders of the various sections of the population . . . never had any understanding of the balance of power between the two sides . . . We never realized we would experience the kind of defeat we received'.[23] The Egyptians' claims were so convincing that people of all ranks and hues became convinced that nothing prevented the Arabs from defeating Israel. When Nasser declared on 23 May that 'our armed forces and all our people are ready for war'[24] few people in his audience realized how wrong he was.

Even at the highest levels there was an over-estimate of Jordanian and Arab capabilities. Large quantities of British and American arms were procured by Jordan in early 1967 and some army commanders concluded that if war did develop the Jordanian troops would be capable of defending the West Bank for a few weeks at least.[25] King Hussein's understanding of the realities of Arab–Israeli strength was better than that popularly held because of his knowledge of the conclusions drawn by the UAC. He knew that the Arabs were not ready for war and hoped that it could be prevented. However, he believed that if war did break out the Arabs might at least prevent Israel from seizing their land if they acted in concert and forced Israel to fight a war on three fronts. Khammash explains this point of view: 'We had a fairly accurate estimate of Israel's power. What we failed to estimate or evaluate precisely was the Arab operational capability which we believed was sufficient to repel the initial Israeli strike and enable the joint Arab forces to put up a good show that might lead to a protracted battle.' He points out that 'given the excellent standard of the military training and preparedness of our troops and Arab infantry, armoured and air support promised to us following our defence pact with Egypt [of 30 May 1967] and the tremendous Egyptian and Syrian propaganda campaign which conveyed a gross over-estimate of Arab military power, particularly the Egyptian's claim to be the greatest striking force in the Middle East, it was difficult for any front-line commander to envisage a total collapse in a few days.'[26]

Many senior Jordanians also believed that the superpowers would not allow Israel to seize Arab territory.[27] According to Marwan Al-Kassem, they drew a comparison with the 1956 war in which American pressure prevented Israel from pressing home its advantage.[28] This point is made by Juma'a: 'We gambled with our destiny believing that it was a political game that would be ended by international interference on the assumption that the aim was to preserve peace in the area. The leaders would then gain popular adulation and applause as if the matter was a stupid entertainment.'[29]

Khammash makes a similarly revealing statement. He believed that once hostilities began it would only be a matter of time before 'international pressure would be brought to bear on both parties to halt military operations and perhaps resort to some sort of diplomacy as had been the case in 1948 and 1956'.[30]

For these reasons, with the notable exception of Tal and a few other politicians, all levels of Jordanian society were generally in favour of going to war.

Popular opinion also made a realignment of Jordan's loyalties necessary. It was becoming increasingly difficult for Jordan to maintain its position of isolation from the radical Arab nations which maintained a devastating campaign of subversion. The ordinary people, particularly the Palestinians, had been whipped up into such a state of frenzy against Israel and in favour of war that if Jordan stood aside while Egypt and Syria went into battle, discontent within Jordan would almost certainly reach a difficult level for Jordan's rulers to contain. There was a strong likelihood that if war with Israel erupted, many Palestinians and even Transjordanians would form militant groups of their own and would be aided in this by Syria and Egypt. In these circumstances King Hussein's regime would be seriously threatened. Abu Odeh observes: 'Nasser had reached the edge of political manoeuvring. We could not let him do it alone because that would have been at the expense of the country and the regime, because the alternative to it had already been established, namely, the PLO.'[31]

As a result of these factors Jordan attempted to improve its relationship with Syria and Egypt. One of the obstacles in the way of achieving reconcilation was Tal because of his long-standing antagonism to Nasser. As late as 26 May Nasser had declared that 'Wasfi Tal is a spy for the Americans and the British'.[32] Tal had also been strongly criticized by the Egyptian press and King Hussein realized that his presence at the helm of the government would make it difficult for Jordan to be received back into the Arab mainstream. Public opinion against Tal also made his removal necessary. Popular feeling was fiercely antagonistic to him. He was identified with a policy of the repression of Palestinian feeling, which was out of touch with the prevailing mood in favour of the militant assertion of Palestinian rights. Tal had also been the focal point for criticism of the Government's failure to prevent the Israeli raid on Samu and had been the object of extreme anger and condemnation for refusing to allow any attempt to avenge it.

In order to deal with this problem and to mark the change in Jordan's foreign policy, on 4 March 1967 Tal resigned from his post and Parliament was immediately dissolved. A caretaker Government took over until elections were held on 15 April. King Hussein appointed Tal Chief of the Royal Diwan. The position of Prime Minister was given to Saad Juma'a who, as Minister of the Royal Court, had been the King's closest adviser. Throughout his political career Juma'a had been strongly against Nasser. However, in 1967 he shifted his position in favour of Jordan joining forces with Egypt. As Tal suggests, this change may have been the result of the popular tide and American encouragement. On 23 April Juma'a formed a new Cabinet. One of the first actions he took was to call for a resumption of the summits,[33] although only three months earlier King Hussein had declared that meetings within the framework of organizations created at the summit meetings were 'useless'.[34] On 20 May 1967, shortly after the inauguration of the new Jordanian Parliament, a secret session was held which examined Jordan's policy in the face of the growing tension between Israel and the Arab states and considered the various measures Jordan was taking in support of its 'sister' Syria. The Speaker issued a statement supporting the Government in all its measures designed to aid Syria and affirming Jordan's call for a return to the Arab co-ordination that the summits had witnessed.[35]

Neither Syria nor Egypt responded to these overtures of friendship and they maintained their propaganda war against the Jordanian regime. Even though Tal was no longer Prime Minister Syria's terrorist campaign continued. Throughout 1967 Syria had sent small terrorist groups into Jordan to commit acts of sabotage there. On 21 May 1967 a truck loaded with dynamite exploded at the Jordanian border post of Ramtha, killing twenty-one Jordanian bystanders. Despite the tense Arab–Israeli situation and Jordan's desire to come closer to the Arab confrontation states, this act forced Jordan to break off diplomatic relations with Syria.

The fact that this act against an Arab regime had occurred at such a sensitive time in Arab–Israeli relations confirmed the Jordanian elite's belief that for the Syrians the enemy was not Israel but Jordan. It increased their conviction that Syria's real motive was to orchestrate the downfall of the Hashemite monarchy. They interpreted Syria's relationship with Nasser in a similar light, concluding that the Syrians were not trying to bring about the successful conclusion of the Palestinian issue, but were trying to promote themselves as the leaders of the Arab world. They believed that the primary objective of the Syrians was to bring about Nasser's defeat and disappearance from Arab politics, and that war or the threat of war with Israel was merely a tool towards this end.

Countdown to war

Throughout May the situation between Israel and the Arabs became increasingly tense. In the second week of May Israeli politicians made a series of declarations in which they stated that Israel would not tolerate Syria's continued support of guerrilla activity against it. On 11 May Israel had lodged a note with the UN Security Council warning that unless Syria altered its 'unrealistic and aggressive policy' Israel would 'regard itself as entitled to act in self-defence'.[36] The following day the Israeli Prime Minister, Eshkol, made a speech at a closed meeting of Mapai[37] leaders in which he said: 'In view of the fourteen incidents of sabotage and infiltration perpetrated in the past month alone Israel may have no other choice but to adopt suitable countermeasures against the focal points of sabotage. Israel will continue to take action to prevent any and all attempts to perpetrate sabotage within her territory. There will be no immunity for any state which aids or abets such acts.'[38] The implications of this statement were emphasized in Eshkol's broadcast to the nation on Remembrance Day: 'Any border which is tranquil on their side will be tranquil on our side as well. And if they try to sow unrest on our borders, unrest will come to theirs.'[39] On 14 May three Israeli newspapers carried interviews with the Israeli Chief of Staff, General Rabin, in which, like Eshkol, he warned Damascus that Israel would not tolerate its terrorist activities for much longer.[40]

Rabin's statements were widely reported in the press. For example, *The New York Times* of 12 May reported that 'some Israeli leaders have decided that the use of force against Syria may be the only way to curtail increasing terrorism. Any such Israeli action against continued infiltration would not be of considerable strength but of short duration and limited in area. This has become apparent in talks with highly qualified and informed Israelis who have spoken in recent days against a background of mounting border violence'.[41] The conclusion drawn by the Arabs and many other nations was that it would not be long before Israel attacked Syria with the aim of overthrowing the Syrian government. The prospect of an Israeli invasion seems to have been taken seriously by the Syrians and they conveyed their fears to Russia and their ally, Egypt. It is apparent that this had a profound impact on the Egyptian leadership. In his memoirs the Egyptian Foreign Minister, Mahmoud Riad, claims that Rabin had declared that Israel 'would carry out a lightning attack on Syria, occupy Damascus, overthrow the regime there and come back'.[42]

The Jordanian leadership interpreted Israel's warnings as a vindication of their policy of non-belligerence towards Israel. They had always claimed that tactics such as the 'popular liberation war' advocated by Syria and adopted by Palestinian organizations, such as Al-Fatah, would give Israel sufficient excuse to draw the Arabs into a war for which they were not ready. Unlike some Westerners who viewed Israel's threats as part of a general programme of deterrence,[43] they concluded that Israel was issuing warnings to the Arab world that Syria's support of terrorism had pushed it to a point where it felt free to take massive retaliatory action.

The Jordanians feared that the underlying motive behind such an action would be to put 'the Syrian–Egyptian defence pact to an agonizing test, that they were calling Nasser's bluff and provoking him to react'. This reaction would then spark off a war in which Israel would be able to 'unleash its real intention and seize Arab territory'.[44] They felt that the humiliation Nasser had received as a result of the aerial dogfight between Israel and Syria on 7 April had created a situation in which Nasser would be forced to provide an irrefutable demonstration of the validity of his image as the protector of the Arabs and champion of the Palestinians. They believed that Israel was deliberately provoking Nasser to act in a belligerent way and that this was part of an overall scheme of Arab provocation which had begun with the raid on Samu in November.

The situation entered a new phase with Russia's announcement to Syria and Egypt on 13 May that Israeli troops were massing on the Syrian border and intended to attack on 16/17 May with a force of eleven to thirteen brigades.[45] This evoked an immediate response in Nasser who now had an ideal opportunity to demonstrate his readiness to come to the defence of his ally and the strength of his commitment to the Palestinian cause. Ignoring all protestations from Israel and the UN[46] that the Russian report was mistaken, the following day he announced the mobilization of the Egyptian army. Two divisions were ordered into Sinai to support the reinforced division already there. This was followed two days later by his demand that UNEF withdraw its forces from Sinai. Three days later UNEF had vanished and Egyptian troops faced the Israeli army on the other side of the border. As UNEF troops left Sharm Al-Sheikh overlooking the Straits of Tiran Egyptian paratroops were flown in to occupy it.

Although Eshkol denounced the Egyptians, his response to this development was a model of moderation. His speech on 21 May demanded that Nasser withdraw his forces from Sinai but made no mention of the removal of UNEF from the Straits nor of what Israel would do if they were closed to Israeli shipping.[47] The next day Nasser announced to an astonished world that henceforth the Straits were, indeed, closed to all Israeli ships. Nasser had replied to Radio Jordan's argument of 19 May that 'if Egypt fails to [close the Straits] what value would there be in military demonstrations?'[48]

Nasser's actions have been regarded as part of a political manoeuvre to demonstrate his readiness to challenge Israel while having no intention of carrying out his threats. The mobilization of the Egyptian army had been conducted under conditions of wide publicity, with troops and equipment marching through the capital instead of taking a secret route to their destination. Such publicity is not usually sought by those about to engage in war. Moreover, the force confronting Israel in Sinai was not large enough to launch a full-scale assault.[49] Consequently, most observers concluded that Nasser was merely enacting an impressive display of strength and was not really threatening Israel.[50]

This perception was confirmed by some of Nasser's statements. As late as 2 June, when asked by the British MP Christopher Mayhew: 'And if they do not attack will you let them alone?' he replied, 'Yes, we will leave them alone. We have no intention of attacking Israel.' Similar assurances were repeatedly given to the USA by the highest Egyptian authorities.[51]

Nasser had also waited three days after taking direct control of the Straits before declaring it closed to Israeli shipping. Many observers believe that he did this in order to gauge the reaction his activity was producing in Israel. They argue that Israel's weak response convinced him that he might succeed in closing the Straits without embroiling Egypt in war.

The belief that Nasser was only bluffing was shared by the Jordanians. King Hussein wrote: 'I don't think the Egyptian President wanted it to come to actual war. I even suspect that he didn't really believe war would break out. In my view it was inescapable.'[52] Abu Odeh also remarked that 'Nasser intended to bluff the world, never believing for a moment back in May 1967 that confrontation with Israel was going to take place. He genuinely thought that he could outmanoeuvre the Israelis, make political gains and avoid war.'[53]

The Jordanian intelligence service drew the same conclusion. Abu Odeh confirmed that it 'was aware of all Arab political manoeuvring and what this implied. It was also watching and observing the implications to Jordan of various Arab moves. The [Intelligence] department managed to evaluate, assess and analyse all these moves, particularly those by Egypt and Syria. Hence they were well aware that Nasser was not really intending to go to war'.[54]

Nevertheless, as May drew to a close Nasser's declarations against Israel became increasingly extravagant and he taunted Israel to open hostilities. In his speech of 22 May at the UAR Advanced Airforce Headquarters Nasser cried, 'The Jews threaten us with war and we say to them, "ahlan wa sahlan" [welcome!] – we are ready!' He argued that the Israelis now had to take into account the power of Egypt and that 'there is a great difference between yesterday and today, between 1956 and 1967'. 'At that time we had a few Ilyushin bombers . . . Today we have many Ilyushins and other aircraft.' He declared that although Egyptian troops were still in Yemen this did not matter because 'we are capable of carrying out our duties in Yemen and at the same time doing our national duty here in Egypt'.[55]

On 26 May he declared, 'The battle will be a general one and our basic objective will be to destroy Israel'.[56] The same day Hasanayn Heikal, a close associate of Nasser, wrote an article in *Al-Ahram* explaining why war with Israel was inevitable: 'The closure of the Gulf of Aqaba . . . means first and last that the Arab nation represented by the UAR has succeeded for the first time, *via-à-vis* Israel, in changing by force a fait accompli imposed on it by force . . . To Israel this is the most dangerous aspect of the current situation – who can impose the accomplished fact and who possesses the power to safeguard it. Therefore it is not a matter of the Gulf of Aqaba but of something bigger. It is the whole philosophy of Israeli security. Hence I say that Israel must attack.'[57] He went on to say that the international situation was such that Egypt would have to allow Israel to strike the first blow and concluded, 'Let Israel begin. Let our second blow then be ready. Let it be a knockout.'[58]

Jordan had watched these developments with exreme anxiety. Its army intelligence had revealed no evidence of a build-up of Israeli troops on the Syrian borders.[59] Consequently they concluded that Russia was trying to inflame the already tense situation. They knew that Russia was anxious to preserve the Syrian regime because it offered them an important foothold in the Middle East. They also believed that both Russia and Syria had an interest in drawing Nasser into a war with Israel which would result in his defeat. For the Syrians, this would remove their main rival from the political scene. For the Russians, it would force Nasser to become more dependent on the Soviet Union. This interpretation of Russian activity was also expressed in the Western press.[60]

As the situation became progressively more alarming King Hussein became increasingly apprehensive. Although he hoped that together the Arabs might prevent Israel from capturing their land, he knew that any confrontation would be fraught with danger. Nasser's inflammatory statements were also a cause of anxiety since they suggested that he was being carried away on the wave of enthusiasm he had created. The King felt that Nasser was blind to the realities of the situation and believed that it would not be long before the struggle for power between Egypt and Syria would reap its reward in the form of a full-scale attack by Israel on its Arab neighbours. At a press conference held on 28 May King Hussein stated that he was 'worried, really concerned, that Nasser and his command were extremely confident, happy with their preparations and that if war did occur there was nothing to worry about'.[61]

Nasser's over-confidence seems to have been based on an inaccurate assessment of Arab–Israeli military capabilities and a failure to observe the massive support Israel was receiving from the West. Nasser's commanders appeared to have supreme faith in their ability to defeat an Israeli attack. Riad writes that on 29 May he asked Nasser about the efficacy of the Egyptian air force. Nasser answered that Field-Marshal Amer (the Vice President of Egypt) 'had assured him of our preparedness'. At the beginning of June, Amer told Riad that 'if Israel actually carried out any military action against us I could, with only one third of our forces, reach Bersheeba'. According to Riad, the Minister of War, Shams Badran, made the extraordinary claim that Egypt's air forces were capable of handling the intervention of the US Sixth Fleet.[62] In an interview in *Al-Musawar* General Sudki Mahmoud, Commander of the Egyptian air force, claimed that the Egyptian 'warning system and air defences are capable of discovering and destroying any air attack by the enemy, no matter how many aircraft were involved, or from what direction they come'.[63]

The Secretary General of the Egyptian President's Office, Abdul Majid Farid, makes a similar claim. He writes that Nasser's decision to close the Straits was based on military reports provided by Amer who told him that Egyptian 'armed forces are not only capable of repulsing Israel but are also capable of moving east to secure a defence line on the Egyptian border, stretching from Bersheeba to Gaza, so that Egypt can establish a position from which to impose its own political conditions and to force Israel to respect Arab and Palestinian rights within the framework of the UN resolution'.[64]

On the morning that Nasser announced the closure of the Straits he visited the Bir Gifgafa air base. Without any reservation, Nasser's officers expressed certainty that they could completely destroy the Israeli air force in a matter of hours. They assured Nasser that Tel Aviv and other Israeli cities would then be at their mercy.[65]

Nasser's intelligence service also played an important part in misleading him. Juma'a comments that 'Egyptian intelligence deceived the Egyptian President during those dark moments . . . It failed to provide him with accurate information about the enemy's striking power'.[66] This is confirmed by Sudki Mahmoud.[67] Nutting also claims that when he told Nasser about Israel's military capability Nasser replied that his intelligence service had assured him that his Russian MiGs and Sokhois were more than a match for anything possessed by Israel.[68]

Egyptian intelligence also misinformed Nasser about the intentions of the superpowers. Nasser acted in the belief that he had the full support of the Russians. A week before the war began he told members of the Egyptian National Assembly that he had 'met with the War Minister, Shams Badran, and was told what had occurred in Moscow. I wish to tell you today that the Soviet Union is a friendly Power and stands by us as a friend . . . When I met Shams Badran yesterday he handed me a message from the Soviet Premier Kosygin saying that the USSR supported us in this battle and would not allow any Power to intervene until matters were restored to what they were in 1956'.[69] In fact, the Soviet Union had made repeated pleas for restraint which Badran failed to convey to Nasser.[70]

The same misperception occurred in relation to the intentions of the West. Nasser felt sure that a full-scale war on all fronts was not in the offing because he was certain that Israel would not act without support from the West and this did not appear to be forthcoming. Like the Jordanians Nasser seems to have held the memory of 1956 in his mind when Israel had been held in check by America. He noted that neither the French nor the British seemed to be prepared to go to war on behalf of Israel. Although he was known to be pro-Israel, President Johnson's public statements advised both Egypt and Israel to act with restraint and not to undertake aggressive action. According to senior Jordanians Nasser was misled by his intelligence service 'into believing that he had won the political round against the USA, Britain and Israel and that the USA's haste to invite [Vice President] Zakaria Mohiedin to Washington to meet with the American President to seek a peaceful solution to the crisis amounted to a back down, if not defeat, of American policy in the area and that any Israeli military adventure was highly unlikely, if not impossible'.[71] Nasser's senior politicians also shared his belief. Amer's Battle Order No. 2 which was issued to the Egyptian troops on 2 June stated that: 'It is now clear that the American Government will not on any account enter into any military adventure on the side of Israel.'[72]

Nasser's intelligence service also confirmed his belief that Israel did not intend to go to war. Nasser told Nutting that according to 'the most reliable and recent information in his possession, Israel was not planning to attack Egypt and would not be able to do so for at least another eight months'.[73] Statements made by Israel's leaders did little to alter his views. As late as 29 May Eshkol stated that 'the USA and Britain as well as other maritime states are committed to secure free passage in international waterways and Israel will wait to see if these states fulfil their commitments'.[74] Nasser felt increasingly confident that Israel was afraid of Egypt and that either it would not enter into battle at all or if it did, it would do so with limited aims which the Egyptian army could defeat. According to Nutting Nasser seemed 'convinced that he could ride out the storm provided he offered Israel no further provocation'.[75]

Nutting also observed that Nasser was convinced that the

> Israelis would not be prepared to fight a war on two fronts, if only for fear of the striking power of Egypt's Russian-equipped air force. Therefore he believed that unless they could count on the West joining in the fighting, at least to the extent of providing air cover . . . he would be able to thwart their plans by showing that Egypt would fight if they went for Syria. If, on the other hand, the West should decide to play an active military

role alongside their Israeli clients then he reckoned that Russia could not fail to respond.[76]

The Jordanian perception of the situation was quite different from Nasser's. They believed that the situation had reached a point of no return and were convinced that Nasser had walked into the trap set for him by Syria and that Israel would not let him go unscathed. The Jordanian intelligence department had reported that Syria's moves were aimed 'at implicating Nasser in a war with Israel with the intention of harming him. The Department reported to the authorities on these matters'.[77] This interpretation was shared by Khammash: 'Nasser had walked into the trap laid for him of his own accord. The Syrians had pushed him into a conflict for which he was not ready.'[78]

The press of the time is full of reports describing King Hussein's anxiety that war was about to erupt. On 28 May King Hussein stated at a press conference that the situation looked serious and he feared that 'Israel and Zionism might succeed in setting off an explosion'.[79] When Nasser announced the evacuation of UNEF from the Straits, Jordan's leaders concluded that it would only be a matter of days before war broke out. This is evident from King Hussein's description of his reaction to the news:

> I was in Aqaba when I heard of Egypt's decision to call for the withdrawal of the international police force from Sinai and to place the Egyptian Army in its place and to close the Straits of Tiran. At that particular moment I knew that we had fallen into a trap; that war was imminent there was no doubt and that a tragic miscalculation had occurred. I thought at the time that the Egyptian leadership had several options but this was the worst of them.[80]

This quotation reveals that the Jordanian leadership had hoped that Nasser would use other tactics which would demonstrate his commitment to Syria and the Arabs in general, but which would fall short of embroiling them in the war.

The King continues: 'on the morning of 22 May I was stunned by the news. For such a measure, lacking in thought and consideration, would only lead to disaster because the Arabs were not ready for war. There was no co-ordination, no co-operation, no common plan amongst them'.[81] This certainty that war was imminent is echoed by Khammash: 'Once Nasser announced his intention on 16 May to mass his troops in Sinai in order to deter Israel from invading Syria we became absolutely convinced that war was imminent'.[82]

Jordan's leaders had no doubt that Nasser's activities had given Israel the pretext it needed and that its leaders would not let their advantage slip away. King Hussein remarked that 'the Israelis had planned their manoeuvres and we acted exactly as they hoped we would'.[83] He believed that Israel's passive response was a front designed to lead Nasser on to a point where his actions would result in a wave of sympathy for Israel which would allow it to act as it desired. Even though Eshkol declared: 'I tell the Arab countries once more, especially Egypt and Syria, that we have no aggressive plans against them and that we have no interest in threatening their security or territory',[84] the Jordanians did not believe him. They regarded Israel's declaration that it would wait to see if the USA and Britain would try to open the Straits on Israel's behalf as part of a deliberate deception.[85]

The Jordanians knew that in November 1966 Eshkol had raised the period of military service from twenty-six to thirty months, since when Israel had been close to a permanent state of alert.[86] The fact that after the removal of UNEF from Sinai and Gaza Israel had refused the UN's invitation to accept UNEF forces on its side of the border was also regarded with suspicion, because to have done so would have hampered confrontation with Egypt. When Israeli radio commented that if UNEF were to withdraw from Gaza Egypt would then be in a position to threaten Israeli shipping the Jordanians felt that this was an invitation to Nasser to do precisely that.[87]

Of particular importance to Jordanian perception was that in the past the Israelis had made it plain that they would regard any attempt to close the Straits as tantamount to a declaration of war. According to this interpretation a *casus belli* had already been provided by Nasser and this was the argument that the Israelis presented to the West.[88]

Jordan's leaders had no doubt that Israel must regard the present situation as ideal for launching war.[89] Nasser's closure of the Straits and Shukairy's bellicose statements – that the time had come to annihilate the state of Israel and that the Arabs would throw the Jews into the sea – had alienated world opinion to such an extent that military activity by Israel would be regarded with positive favour. America had also expressed its support of Israel, although this appeared to fall short of offering military aid. The Jordanians were aware that President Johnson was known to be sympathetic to Israel. He was strongly influenced by the American Jewish vote, which had been an important factor in bringing him to power. The Rostow brothers were also firmly pro-Israel. Both were in positions of considerable influence at the White House. Eugene Rostow was Under Secretary of State in June 1967 and his brother, Walt, was National Security Adviser.

In May 1966 the Arabs were also far from meeting the requirements that had been laid down by the UAC in 1964. The Arab front-line states were eighteen months short of the earliest possible date that the UAC had considered they would be ready to deal with an Israeli attack. Both Egypt and Iraq had a significant part of their armies tied up elsewhere. Of equal significance was the fact that the Arab world was profoundly divided. Both Egypt and Syria were still railing against the 'reactionary' Arab states, including Jordan, which appeared to be completely isolated and without external military support. Although the Arabs were closing ranks rapidly, even if they succeeded in coming together, the preceding period of friction and disunity would ensure minimal levels of co-ordination on the Arab front. The UAC had been proved to be virtually non-existent, so there was no longer any unified plan for Arab confrontation with Israel. The Egyptian–Syrian defence pact had only been in existence for six months and was unlikely to be able to co-ordinate Egyptian–Syrian military activity effectively. As a result of these factors, the Israelis had little to fear from a concerted Arab effort against Israel.

At the end of May this was confirmed to Israel's politicians by the Americans. At their meeting Johnson told Eban that the Israelis had nothing to fear from the Arabs even if the latter fought in unison. Thus, at the beginning of June Eban was able to assert what the Israeli military had always known: 'Nasser would have the beating of his life'.[90] At a press conference held at the end of May Eban declared that Israel would make any sacrifices necessary to open the Gulf of Aqaba. When asked how long it would be before Israel responded he replied: 'You can say it will not be years or months . . .' He added that Israel was also receiving strong support from the West.[91] These statements confirmed the view of senior Jordanians that they were on the brink of war.

Jordan's conviction that war was imminent was confirmed by Israel's activity. On 20 May Israel called up its reserve troops and completed a partial mobilization.[92] Five days later Eban flew to Washington for talks with high-ranking American officials. There was also mounting pressure in Israel for Eshkol's replacement as Minister of Defence (a position normally held by the Prime Minister) by Moshe Dayan. Dayan was a more militant man than Eshkol and many Israelis believed that he would lead Israel to victory in the impending war.

Although King Hussein was deeply unhappy at the prospect of war, the pressure on him to participate was overwhelming. He believed that the kingdom was in grave danger whether or not Jordan played an active role. Israel's raid on Samu had convinced him, and many of his political and military advisers, that Israel made no distinction between Jordan and more aggressive Arab nations. He was sure that if hostilities opened between Israel and either Syria or Egypt, Israel would invade the West Bank no matter what Jordan did. This belief is reflected in a statement he made during an interview with the *New York Times* which was published on 29 May. He said that he was certain that if war resulted in the defeat of the UAR 'our position here is finished'. Jordan would inevitably be attacked 'because Israel views the Arab world as one'.[93] The same view is expressed by Khammash: 'What was of particular interest to us in the army was Israel's intentions towards the West Bank. We did not need to ask many questions to understand that if Israel waged war against Egypt, Syria or both, the West Bank was a primary target and would not be spared because Israel had succeeded in manipulating international opinion in its favour.'[94] Zaid Rifai makes a similar remark: 'Even if Jordan did not participate directly in a war that was started by Israel it would not only be destroyed by the Arab world and even blamed for the loss of the war but our turn would be next. If we were isolated from the mainstream of Arab politics, we would be an easy target.'[95]

King Hussein knew that Israel would have no difficulty in finding an excuse to attack Jordan. Even if the Jordanian army stood aside and did not fire a single shot Israel could use previous guerrilla raids against Israel from Jordan to justify its invasion of the West Bank. If, as was more likely, the Jordanians demonstrated their support of Egypt and Syria by limited shelling of Israeli targets and artillery fire, Israel could use this as its excuse to attack Jordan once it had defeated Syria and Egypt. If the Jordanian army was confronted with the full weight of the Israeli army it would stand little chance of defending the West Bank.

For this reason, King Hussein concluded that Jordan's only hope of preventing such a tragedy was to form an alliance with Egypt and Syria. He later wrote: 'since no Arab country was capable of meeting the Israeli threat alone it seemed essential that we co-ordinate everyone's capabilities before the battle was joined'.[96] He reasoned that if Jordan was likely to be attacked no matter what it did it might as well make the best of an impossible situation, fight as part of an overall Arab effort and thereby 'minimise the danger'.[97] If confrontation with Israel occurred after the defeat of Egypt and Syria Jordan would not stand a chance. If, however, Jordan joined forces with Egypt and Syria, thereby forcing Israel to fight a war on three fronts, Israel would only commit a maximum of one-third of its forces against Jordan. As part of a united Arab effort Jordan would also enjoy an enhanced military capability. Jordan's embryonic air force was a major weakness in its defence system. Without adequate air cover the troops would be exposed to debilitating air attacks, which would weaken their manoeuvrability and cause devastating losses. The provision of air cover by Egypt, Syria and Iraq would even the balance and give Jordan's ground forces a chance to show their worth. Jordan also had insufficient troops to provide second lines of defence. The acceptance of troops from other Arab nations would remedy this and make Israel's penetration of the West Bank that much more difficult.

King Hussein's decision to form an alliance with Egypt and Syria may also have been influenced by the memory of the accusation levelled at his grandfather. Although the Arab Legion had fought well in 1948 it had fought on its own and King Abdullah's critics had accused him of acting in self-interest. Consequently King Hussein may have felt that if, like his grandfather, he acted on his own he could still be accused of betraying the Arab nation. If Jordan fought alongside Egypt and Syria and allowed troops from other Arab nations onto Jordanian territory it would be difficult for such criticism to be made.

Thus, although King Hussein did not want to go to war, and believed that it was the worst possible option open to the Arabs, by the end of May he was certain that the Arabs had gone beyond the point of no return and that war was inevitable. He concluded that the Jordanians' most logical and wise course was to act in unison with their fellow-Arabs. Unlike many less well-informed people, the King was aware that the Arabs were embarking on an extremely dangerous path and he had no illusions that they could defeat Israel. However, he failed to foresee the crushing defeat that would occur. Although he commented that he 'doubted that [Egypt and Syria] could defeat Israel . . . In the most optimistic light I could see a slight advantage but I never believed in total victory',[98] he later admitted that neither did he think 'that Israel would win so easily'.[99] He and other members of the Jordanian elite believed that if the Arabs forced Israel to fight a war on three fronts and bolstered up each others' weak points in the way described above, they would be capable of fending off the Israelis for long enough to allow international pressure to bring an end to the war. According to Abu Odeh, the King believed that 'even if developments turned against him his destiny was with the West and he therefore depended on the Western powers to interfere before it was too late'.[100]

This situation at home also made it imperative for King Hussein to bring Jordan into line with the Arab confrontation states. Syrian, Egyptian and Arab propaganda blared over the radio their message of war, vengeance and victory and were listened to by millions of Arabs throughout the Middle East. They claimed that the hour of reckoning was at hand and that the Israelis would receive the retribution they richly deserved. This produced a massive response in favour of war amongst the Arabs of Jordan. They were filled with excitement at the prospect of imposing their will on Israel after the humiliation of previous defeats and had little understanding of the risks that were involved. Nasser was hailed as the hero of the hour who would lead the Arabs to victory. Demonstrators took to the streets calling Nasser's name and shouting for victory to the Arabs and death to the Israelis. They were filled with a lust for battle which could not be denied. King Hussein's commanders warned him that they could not hold their men in check for much longer and that there would be a serious crisis if Jordan failed to act.[101]

The pressure of public opinion in favour of war was so strong that King Hussein knew that if he failed to participate he ran the risk of civil war. Recognition of this is reflected in Sharif Zaid Ben Shaker's[102] statement at a press conference held at the end of May: 'If Jordan does not join the war a civil war will erupt in Jordan'.[103]

King Hussein also realised that if Jordan did not participate he would become the scapegoat for any failing on the part of the Arabs to achieve their aspirations. The charge of being an imperialist agent would be reiterated with renewed venom and he would be accused of protecting Israel through his inactivity. Nussaibah commented that 'Jordan might have been exposed to extinction or collapse if it had not joined the war . . . because it would have been maligned by all the neighbouring Arab countries even if the outcome of the war had been a stalemate. Jordan would have been a scapegoat. The regime would definitely have been threatened had it failed. They would have said that if Jordan had joined then it would not have ended that way and we could have achieved victory'.[104]

The King describes his dilemma:

> The atmosphere that I found in Jordan, particularly in the West Bank, was one where, frankly, we had the following choice: either to act at the right time with no illusion of what the results might be but with a chance to do better than we would otherwise, or not to act and to have an eruption occur within which would cause us to collapse and which would obviously immediately result in an Israeli occupation of probably the West Bank or even more than the West Bank, and we never separated the West Bank from the rest of Jordan or the Arab world in anticipating such action. That was really the reason why I went to Egypt to meet Nasser to his surprise.[105]

This quotation reveals King Hussein's belief that he had nothing to lose by participating in the war because the civil turmoil that would inevitably erupt if Jordan stood aside would provide Israel with yet another excuse to occupy the West Bank 'or even more than the West Bank'.

In addition, King Hussein felt that Jordan was committed to joint Arab action because this had been formalized in the formation of the UAC, which had never been officially disbanded. He later wrote: 'In my heart of hearts I felt that I was deeply committed to the Arab Joint Defence Treaty signed in Cairo in 1964. It was totally incomprehensible for my country not to adhere to its commitments or to respect its signature when she had always been at the vanguard of the Arab forces' wars of liberation throughout the last fifty years.'[106] This quotation also reveals the King's commitment to the Palestine cause and to Arabism, which made it impossible for him to stand aside. He believed that the 'potential war related to Palestine and Jordan administered a large part of it. I was extremely concerned with this conflict which was on the verge of eruption . . . I was certain that if war came – which every day was becoming increasingly evident – we should commence the offensive. If Israel attacked I would not stand aside and my armed forces would join the Arab peoples'.[107] The King believed that the Jordanian army could make an important contribution to the Arab war effort and that it was his duty to ensure that it did. As a Hashemite he had been brought up to believe in the importance of Arab unity. Now, when the Arab world was combining in a way rarely seen before, he felt that he had to be true to his values and participate in the general Arab action.

Rifai points out that King Hussein 'was committed to the Arab cause. He was anxious to have as much unity in Arab decision-making as possible and therefore he was not always free to choose what he thought was best . . . I think he knew that we were going to lose the war. He knew that the time for war was not right and yet if the war took place he knew he had no choice but to be part of it'.[108] King Hussein had often declared that Jordan was the natural springboard for the liberation of Palestine and that he attached more importance to finding a solution to the Palestinian problem than any other Arab ruler. How could he stand aside when the Arab world was on the verge of a war which it believed would result in the long-awaited liberation of Palestine?

Arab propaganda had succeeded in placing the Jordanian elite in the same position the Syrians had placed Nasser. When the Syrians had called into question Nasser's sincerity in relation to the Palestinians he had been forced to provide a clear demonstration of his commitment. The same principle now applied to the Jordanians. Egypt and Syria had created a situation in which Jordan's declarations of support for the Palestinians were suspect and it was accused of supporting imperialism against the needs and desires of the Arabs. Abu Odeh remarked that Jordanian members of Parliament 'had always been accused by Nasser's propaganda of being false in their expressions of commitment to the Arab cause . . . and were waiting for an opportunity to show the electorate that they did support the trend. Therefore they supported Nasser's efforts enthusiastically and wholeheartedly, apart from a few individuals. Most were in favour of war because they believed that this was the only way in which they could clear their reputation'.[109]

By the third week of May, the question King Hussein was asking was not whether he should fight Israel with his Arab brethren, but how he could achieve this. Syria had shown itself to be the implacable enemy of Jordan so Egypt represented the only route whereby Jordan might become integrated into the total Arab framework. Soon after Nasser announced that UNEF had been asked to leave Sinai and Gaza King Hussein called a meeting with Juma'a, the Cabinet and high-ranking officers of the Jordanian army, which was placed on a full alert. At this meeting he explained his belief that war was inevitable and that the Jordanians would fight. The same day he received the Ambassadors of Turkey and Britain as well as the Chargé d'Affaires of Iran. He conveyed Jordan's determination to stand with its Arab brethren against any aggression.[110] The day after Nasser's announcement of the closure of the Straits of Tiran to Israeli traffic Jordan made a request for Iraqi and Saudi Arabian troops to be stationed in Jordan 'in order to discourage the inevitable Zionist offensive or at least to limit the damage'.[111] Now that the threat of an Israeli invasion was real the fear that Israel would use the troops as an excuse to invade Jordan became irrelevant.

The day that Nasser announced the closure of the Straits of Tiran to Israeli traffic, Radio Jordan, which up to that moment had continued to criticize Nasser, changed its tune. It praised Nasser and expressed support for his actions. This was followed on 24 May by an official proclamation of support for

Nasser from the Jordanian government.[112] On 23 May units of the 40th armoured brigade and a battalion of heavy artillery were sent through the main streets of Amman on their way to the West Bank in order to provide a visible demonstration that Jordan had thrown in its lot with the other front-line states. The next day the American Ambassador was summoned to meet King Hussein and Juma'a and warned that Jordan would react strongly if the USA continued to support Israel against the Arabs. King Hussein told the Ambassador that Jordan would not stand passively aside but would participate with the Arabs. Jordan was committed to the Arab side and its ability to defend the West Bank depended on this. He then 'implored them as well as the rest of the world to see if anything could be done to avert an eruption or collision and to try to find a political solution'. However, the Americans did not give King Hussein any advice, nor did they offer him any assurances.[113]

This negative reaction led to a statement issued by Juma'a on 27 May deploring American policy and warning that it was adopting a position which, if maintained, would result in a severe deterioration in Arab–American relations.[114] Despite this, the Americans still made no response. Jordan received no assurances that America would stand by the Tripartite Agreement and ensure that Israel would not seize the territory of any Arab nation. Nor did America promise that it would use diplomatic means to prevent war from erupting.

This lack of support or advice from America increased Jordan's determination to join sides with its fellow-Arabs. The Jordanians shared with Eban the realization that 'public opinion was on [Israel's] side . . . and so were many of the people high up in [the American] Government'.[115] This meant that Jordan would be unable to rely on America and would therefore be wise to enlist the support of the Arabs. Consequently, Radio Jordan began to co-ordinate its pronouncements with those of Radio Cairo and attacked America for its support of Israel.

In order to try and effect a reconciliation with Nasser, on 21 May King Hussein sent Khammash to Cairo. However, although Khammash was politely received by Egypt's military commanders he failed to meet Egypt's leaders and his efforts to discover Egypt's preparations for war, or to co-ordinate Jordan's plans with them, were in vain. What he found did little to allay his fears that Egypt had embarked on a course of action without being fully alive to its consequences. He later said:

> In Cairo I was received by the UAC's Commander-in-Chief, General Ali Ali Amer, and his deputy, General Abdul Munim Riad, and a liaison officer from the Egyptian High Command. He [the liaison officer] knew nothing and could answer no questions. The Commander-in-Chief and his deputy knew nothing about war plans and I felt that they were deliberately kept in the dark. I tried to meet with the Egyptian leaders but they were all too busy to receive me. I soon concluded that the Egyptian leaders had no war

plans and did not expect that there would be a need to fight a war. As a soldier I knew that if you were facing a potential war you would want to co-ordinate with your allies even if you hated their guts. The British and the Americans fought the Second World War alongside the Russians! There was no prospect of co-ordination even though the offices of the UAC seemed to be available. Clearly the Egyptians were playing a political game rather than preparing for war. On my return I reported to His Majesty that it was apparent to all of us that nothing short of an initiative by the King would help to soothe our anxiety.[116]

The morning that Khammash flew to Cairo King Hussein held a meeting with Juma'a and his military commanders to review the situation. He then called in the Ambassadors and diplomatic representatives of Egypt, Syria and Iraq. Juma'a writes that King Hussein 'asked them to convey to their governments his sincere concern and Jordan's total readiness to co-operate and co-ordinate and to place the Jordanian armed forces under a unified command, if necessary, as long as we can face the enemy together'.[117] However, the various Arab countries proved unwilling to co-operate. King Hussein had asked Iraq to send its troops to the Jordanian front-line to help defend it, but angered by his earlier refusal, Iraq turned down the request and stated that such a decision would have to be ratified by the UAC.[118]

Three days of silence followed. King Hussein and his advisers became increasingly anxious. The news from Khammash was particularly disturbing since it suggested that Egypt did not realize that the outbreak of hostilities was likely to occur in a matter of days. King Hussein states that 'it was frightening to see that the Egyptians were probably considering the crisis as a political manoeuvre rather than a prelude to war'.[119] Although Jordan's relationship with Syria appeared to be beyond repair King Hussein had hoped that Nasser would respond to his overtures of friendship. However, this had not been the case. Instead Nasser was declaring that 'the imperialist agents, the allies of Zionism and the fifth column . . . say they want to act in concert with us. We cannot co-ordinate our plans in any way with members of the Islamic alliance because it would mean giving our plans to the Jews and to Israel.'[120]

Despite the discouraging situation Juma'a arranged a further meeting between King Hussein and his military commanders. The defence of the West Bank was the main topic of discussion. All the commanders felt that this was the primary concern and had no doubt that it would be subject to attack by Israel.

Khammash describes what took place:

A meeting was held in which we debated our position and our strategy. The main points were:

1. If we wanted to be true to our principles our commitment to the Palestinian cause would not allow us to refrain from joining a war being held in the name of Palestine.

2. Our military strategy, particularly since 1965, was based on joint Arab action.

3. Israel's strategic target is and always has been the West Bank. Any setback on the Egyptian front would automatically give Israel the incentive to launch an onslaught on the West Bank. Thus, by playing our role in a joint Arab action we would minimize the danger and perhaps halt the Israeli advance, particularly if our forces were given the air cover we badly needed.
4. Israel's fighting strategy, as we knew it, was always based on drawing Arab front-line states to fight separately and not together. By knocking down the strongest (Egypt) all our efforts on our own would be in vain. Samu taught us that Israel's intention had been to eliminate or at least minimize any possibility of joint Arab action by creating situations that would increase Arab divisions thus making the possibility of Arab co-operation impossible.
5. With the Egyptian and Syrian propaganda campaigns we knew too well the disastrous effects on our population if we refrained from fighting Israel alongside our Arab brethren. We did so in 1948 and were ready to do the same in 1956 until Nasser asked us not to involve ourselves.

We concluded that our chances of co-operation with Syria or even of Iraqi troops coming to our aid were non-existent. Our request to the Iraqis prior to my visit to Cairo [on 21 May 1967] was turned down by their defence minister three days later. Following this development His Majesty called us together for another meeting to debate the new situation. The only solution was an initiative by His Majesty who decided to fly to Cairo himself.[121]

On 28 May Juma'a called the Egyptian Ambassador to his home. There he found King Hussein, who told the Ambassador that he was certain that Israel was about to launch a full-scale attack and that he wished to travel to Cairo in order to meet Nasser, convey his feelings to him directly and discuss how they could co-ordinate their battle plans. The reply came the following day: 'Come as soon as you can.'[122] The wheel had now turned full-circle and Jordan stepped back into the Arab fold.

Chapter 6

On the brink of war

The signing of the Egyptian–Jordanian Mutual Defence Treaty

On the morning of 30 May 1967 King Hussein flew to Cairo to meet Nasser. He was accompanied by his Prime Minister, Saad Juma'a, his Foreign Minister, Ahmed Toukan, his Chief of Staff, Lt General Amer Khammash, the commander of the Royal Jordanian air force, Brigadier Saleh Al-Kurdi and an air force captain as aide de camp. At Cairo airport the Jordanians were met by Nasser and his four vice-Presidents. They went immediately to the Kubbeh Palace for talks. The Egyptian delegation included Nasser, the foreign minister, Mahmoud Riad, the Secretary-General of the Egyptian President's Office, Abdul Majid Farid, and the four vice-Presidents of the UAR, including Field Marshall Amer. Later they were joined by General Abdul Munim Riad, the Chief of Staff of the UAC, and Ahmed Shukairy, the leader of the PLO. The result of these talks was the Egyptian–Jordanian Mutual Defence Treaty. The signing ceremony of the Treaty was broadcast live over Cairo Radio[1] and was followed by a press conference attended by the two heads of state and Ahmed Shukairy.

According to the Treaty, 'the two contracting powers consider any armed attack on either state or its forces an attack on both. Consequently ... they commit themselves to hasten each to the assistance of the attacked state and immediately take all measures ... including the use of the armed forces to repulse the attack' (Article 1). In the event of military operations the Jordanian Armed Forces were to be placed under the command of the Chief of Staff of the United Arab Republic (Article 7), the Egyptian General Muhammad Fawzi. The Egyptian General Abdul Munim Riad was accordingly appointed Commander of the Eastern Front which covered the Israeli–Jordanian–Syrian frontiers. He was to operate from an advanced post in Amman in co-ordination with the Commander-in-Chief of the Egyptian Army, Field Marshall Amer.

In order to strengthen Arab defence of the Jordanian Front, King Hussein agreed to the entry into Jordan of Arab troops from Egypt, Iraq, Syria and Saudi Arabia. It was arranged that Riad would visit Syria and Iraq in order to negotiate the quick despatch of these troops. During the meeting a telephone call was made to President Aref of Iraq to ask him to rescind his earlier refusal to send troops to Jordan. Aref agreed to this and ordered the immediate despatch of troops to Jordan.

Nasser also agreed that Jordan's minuscule air force should be augmented by air support by Egypt and Iraq. He gave King Hussein his assurance that the Jordanian army could depend on the protection of the Egyptian air force.[2] It was also decided that two Iraqi Hawker Hunter squadrons should be stationed at, and operate from, H3 base near the Jordan–Iraq border. This promise was of the utmost importance to the King since the absence of air cover for the Jordanian army had been one of this greatest anxieties.

During the meeting King Hussein conveyed to Nasser his belief that war with Israel was inevitable and his concern that the Arabs were not ready for a military confrontation with Israel. He recalled the Arabs' recognition only the previous year that even in combination their armies were no match for Israel's.[3] It was agreed that Jordan's role in the event of war would be to prevent Israel from attacking each confrontation state in turn. Jordan was to tie down a substantial proportion of Israel's army which would otherwise be used against Egypt and Syria. This would increase the potential of Arab success on these two fronts. A concerted effort of all three Arab states would at least prevent an early Israeli victory and allow enough time for the superpowers to intervene and impose peace. For the Jordanians, joining the war was both an opportunity to demonstrate their commitment to the Arab cause and a calculated act designed to increase their chances of fending off what they believed would be the inevitable Israeli march into the West Bank.

King Hussein warned Nasser of the possibility that Israel would start the war by launching a surprise attack. He pointed out that Israel's first objective would be the Arab air forces and that their 'first assault would quite naturally be directed against the Egyptian air force'.[4] Nasser replied, 'That's obvious. We expect it . . .'[5] He assured King Hussein that his army's military capability had grown to such an extent that it was now ready to confront Israel and would have no difficulty in repulsing an Israeli attack. He laid particular emphasis on the strength of the Egyptian air force which he believed represented a formidable challenge to the Israelis. He led the Jordanians to a room which contained maps depicting the deployment of the air force. This displayed an impressive number of squadrons and air bases.

The Egyptian commander of the air force then told them that for the last few days squadrons of Egyptian aircraft had been flying into Israeli air space unchallenged. He believed that this indicated that Israel's fear of the Egyptian air force was sufficient to prevent them from challenging it. The Jordanians were then taken by Nasser to an air base near Cairo where the strength and preparedness of the Egyptian air force was displayed to them.

On the whole, the Jordanians appear to have been impressed by the

Egyptians' display of confidence. Juma'a recalls: 'from what Field Marshall Amer said at the time, it seemed to me that if armed conflict took place, the Egyptian Armed Forces, together with the Jordanian Armed Forces, would achieve all Arab military objectives inside Israel within a few days'. Accordingly, Juma'a felt that 'winning the battle would be of no difficulty to those huge and mighty striking forces'.[6]

This point of view was not shared by all of Jordan's leaders. As a politician who had only recently come to the peak of power, Juma'a had little knowledge of the realities of the Arab–Israeli military balance and he was carried away by Nasser's display of confidence. He was not typical of other Jordanian politicians such as Tal and Zaid Rifai, who possessed a hard-headed realism which precluded any illusion about what they might achieve in a confrontation with Israel. They knew that there was no question of achieving objectives inside Israel but believed that they were capable of fending off an Israeli attack until a ceasefire was declared. This was also the view of the Jordanian military. Although they were reassured by Nasser, they had their reservations, as Khammash explains: Although the Jordanians' 'reservations about Egypt's preparations for war were turned into enthusiasm by Nasser's comforting reassurances, my inner thoughts remained sceptical and I felt that the Egyptians were mounting a deterrent force rather than preparing for war. However, we all felt that if war came the Egyptian military capability was sufficient to meet any Israeli offensive'.[7]

Similar expectations were expressed by King Hussein. He knew that the Arabs could not hope to overrun Israel and was only concerned with ensuring the territorial integrity of the nation and demonstrating his commitment to the Arab cause. He was not seeking to attack Israel but to defend Jordan from what he believed would be an inevitable Israeli assault.[8] He was convinced that joining forces with Egypt represented the best chance for achieving this objective.

The King's awareness of the need for Arab unity made him abandon all the obstacles which had prevented this in the past. His reconciliation with Nasser involved making important concessions. As well as accepting the presence of Arab troops on Jordanian territory and Egyptian military leadership, King Hussein agreed to the withdrawal of Jordanian forces from the Syrian border and the release of political prisoners, including members of Al-Fatah and the PLO. Most spectacular of all was the King's reconciliation with the leader of the PLO, Ahmed Shukairy, who sat next to King Hussein at the press conference and returned to Jordan with him. In response to these Jordanian demonstrations of commitment to Arab unity, Nasser ordered the immediate stoppage of the Egyptian propaganda campaign against Jordan. When Nasser declared that he and King Hussein 'had agreed on everything'[9] he was not exaggerating.

King Hussein returned to Jordan later that day. He was accompanied by Shukairy who had not set foot in the country since the King had withdrawn his recognition of the PLO the previous year. King Hussein received a tumultuous welcome from the general population, which was jubilant at the prospect of the role they believed Jordan would now play in the battle against Israel. 'People danced in the streets and the hillsides were crowded with thousands as the Royal procession drove to the hilltop palace';[10] the King was left in no doubt that his people approved of his latest decision.

The Prime Minister, Saad Juma'a, spoke to the Chamber of Deputies the following day, outlining the details of the defence pact. Jubilant members voted overwhelmingly in favour of the pact and despatched cables to King Hussein and Nasser expressing their delight.[11]

Preparations for war

The signing of the Defence Treaty represented the final major development before the outbreak of Arab–Israeli hostilities. The period that followed was marked by many signs that war was not far off. Although Israel appeared to be waiting for the outcome of America's diplomatic efforts, it was obvious to the Jordanians that they were preparing for war. On 25 May Israel declared the total mobilization of its forces. This meant that four out of every five citizens were now on active service and the Israeli economy ground to a standstill. The Jordanians interpreted this as an indication that soon Israel would open hostilities because they knew that 'Israel could not tolerate such a total stoppage for very long'.[12]

The differences that had been weakening the Israeli government dissolved as it closed ranks. A government of National Unity was formed on 2 June in which General Moshe Dayan was appointed Minster of Defence. Narkiss describes how Dayan's appointment sent the morale of the Israeli army 'sky-high',[13] presumably because its members felt that this move could only mean that war was at hand. The Jordanians interpreted Dayan's appointment in exactly the same way. Although the following day Dayan declared that it was too late for Israel to implement a military response to Egypt's closure of the Straits,[14] the senior Jordanian leadership was not convinced.[15] Israeli troop movements had been carried out with great secrecy but intelligence reports received by the Jordanian GHQs on 3 June informed it of an imminent Israeli offensive. They described a build-up of Israeli armoured, mechanized and infantry formations in forward concentrations west of Latrun and in the Afullah region opposite Jenin.[16]

On 4 June King Hussein held a press conference at which he told reporters that he believed war was only a few days away. He expressed his disappointment at the pro-Israeli line Britain and America appeared to be taking, and warned them that if this continued they might lose the friendship of the Arab world forever.[17]

The same day, the Jordanians re-established diplomatic relations with Syria, even though Syria had expressed unhappiness at the Egyptian–Jordanian Treaty and maintained its attacks on the Jordanian regime.

The Jordanians made it plain that when hostilities broke out they would be active participants on the side of the Arabs. On 31 May they announced the call-up of their reserves. Arrangements were also made for the deployment of the troops which had been promised by other Arab nations. Khammash and Al-Kurdi visited Baghdad for this purpose, while Riad, who had visited Baghdad as a member of an official Egyptian delegation, went on to Damascus to discuss the despatch of Syrian troops to Jordan. By 2 June Jordan had been promised the support of at least one armoured division from Iraq, one Saudi Arabian brigade, two Egyptian commando battalions and one Syrian brigade.[18]

On 1 June Riad arrived in Jordan, bringing with him a staff composed of Major General Hosni Eed, Air Brigadier Mustafa Al-Hinnawi, the Head of Air Operations of the UAC, Colonel Munir Shash, Lt Colonel Hosni Mekki, his head of staff, and a signal officer whose duty it was to keep in constant contact with General Muhammad Fawzi in Cairo. Senior Iraqi officers were also expected to join him.[19] On 3 June Riad visited the West Bank to survey the area and to draw up a plan for its defence.[20] That evening in Amman he met King Hussein, Khammash and other senior military personnel in order to discuss Jordan's military strategy and the preparation of a new troop deployment plan.

Jordanian defence plans

The Jordanians faced severe problems in organizing the defence of their country. It was not merely a question of inadequate resources or their long border with Israel. There were also political and topographical difficulties. The Israeli side of the border was flat and covered with high trees and dense orange groves. This provided excellent cover for any troop movement. They had at least thirty-three places from which to launch an attack on Jordan and it was impossible for the small Jordanian army to defend all these areas. They also had an excellent transport network which enabled them rapidly to mobilize their forces. These factors gave them a freedom of choice and of movement which made it impossible for the Jordanians to predict precisely from which direction they would strike.[21]

While the Israelis possessed considerable strategic flexibility, the Jordanians did not. Apart from the narrow strip of land containing the towns of Qalqilya, Tulkarem and Jenin, the West Bank consisted of mountainous terrain which made the movement of troops visible and exposed them to the threat of air attack. It also made travel slow and prevented their rapid deployment.

The defence of Jordan was further exacerbated by political factors. The loss of parts of Central Palestine and the West Bank to Israel in 1948 and 1949[22] had resulted in an outcry throughout the Arab world and left scars which never healed. The constant accusation by Egypt and Syria that the Jordanian government was failing to protect its citizens meant that the army had to be visibly present along the length of the border. Even under the most favourable circumstances the army was far too small to defend the 630 km armistice line in the West Bank with a further 400 km in the East Bank.[23] By spreading the army in this way its fighting capability was considerably reduced. Frequently a brigade was covering a point extending 50 km or even 100 km and was therefore offering no more than a psychological reassurance to the inhabitants of the area. Under these circumstances it was impossible to concentrate forces in strategically critical areas such as the Old City of Jerusalem and Nablus.

The topography of the area and military logic indicated that the most important lines of resistance were along the defiles and passes that lay astride the routes and approaches of the two main axes of probable Israeli advance from the coastal plains to the heights of Nablus and Jerusalem. However, while such a strategy was tactically sound it might have resulted in the loss of the fertile and heavily populated strip along the border. The political repercussions throughout Jordan and the Arab world would have been too great for the Jordanian government. Similarly, from a purely military point of view, an extra brigade deployed in the area of Jerusalem would have been tactically more advantageous than stretching the army's resources by deploying it in the hills around Hebron. However, public opinion would not allow Hebron to be left unprotected in this way. This contradiction between political and military requirements was something the Jordanians never resolved. As it was, the spread of the army was advantageous to Israel because it gave them the initiative to choose which part of the border to penetrate. Jordanian military strategists[24] believe that it was precisely this spread of the Jordanian army that was the underlying objective behind Israel's border raids.

In considering Jordan's defence requirements the army had to take into account two possibilities: local attacks of limited aggressive intention and an all-out Israeli offensive on one or more axes with the aim of occupying the West Bank. The first possibility required spreading the army along a series of small observation posts which could give warning of any military unit approaching the border and delay its advance. For each possible axis of Israeli advance Jordan needed to provide military units which would at least equal those likely to be deployed by Israel. The second possibility required a concentration of forces of two brigades or more along the main axes of probable Israeli advance, and the presence of a strong reserve force in the rear capable of mounting a counterattack and air cover.

At no point did the Jordanian army possess anything like the military capability required for either of these potential threats.[25] In the case of the first possibility Israel had always launched its raids with more than one brigade. Since there were thirty-three points of entry from Israel, Jordan needed a minimum of thirty-three brigades. In the case of the second possibility, the political factors discussed above prevented a concentration of forces in the way military logic dictated. The Jordanian army was also incapable of providing adequate second lines of defence and could only offer its troops a minimum of air cover.

Despite these problems, plans were made for fending off a full-scale Israeli invasion of the West Bank. Following the successful Arab summit conferences of 1964 and the formation of the UAC, a Jordanian plan for the defence of the West Bank in the event of an Israeli invasion was drawn up in September 1965 and approved by the UAC, of which Jordan was a member at the time. Under this plan[26] the Jordanians anticipated that Israel would deploy ten infantry brigades, two armoured brigades and one parachute brigade against Jordan if operations were limited to the Jordanian front, while point C of the plan envisaged a deployment of six infantry, two armoured brigades and one parachute brigade under Israel's Central Command if action against Egypt was carried out at the same time. This assessment proved to be correct.

Jordan's inability to meet its own defence requirements had made it eager to allow the entrance of additional Arab troops into Jordan in the event of an imminent full-scale Israeli attack. Accordingly, although the Jordanians expected to fend off the initial attack, the arrangement made under the UAC allowed for the entry of the following reinforcements from other Arab nations: one Iraqi infantry brigade, one Saudi infantry brigade, one Iraqi armoured brigade, an Iraqi squadron of twelve Hawker Hunters and six Iraqi Illusion fighter bombers. Jordan therefore depended on other Arab nations to provide air cover and second lines of defence.

The plan was essentially defensive because of Jordan's limited military capability.[27] Israeli raids, together with the other psychological and political factors discussed above, prompted the Jordanians to adopt the strategic concept of 'Offensive-Defence' with a forward defence posture to ensure that not one inch of the West Bank was abandoned without a fierce battle.[28] Hence, according to the plan, nine of the eleven active brigades (seven infantry and two armoured) were deployed for the defence of the West Bank. The front-line units were instructed to attack the enemy and to obstruct its advance while the remainder of the units occupied the vitally important areas and major axes behind them. Should the front-line units be forced to retreat, they were to withdraw to the second line of defence and join the other forces in fending off Israel.

Five of the seven infantry brigades on the West Bank were stretched along 650 km of the border from Jenin in the north-west to Samu in the extreme south via Tulkarem, Qalqilya, Latrun, Jerusalem and Hebron. The task of counterattack – an essential ingredient of the concept of dynamic defence – was entrusted to two brigades, one infantry and one armoured, in the Jerusalem sector west of Jericho. Two other brigades, one infantry and one armoured, were positioned for the same purpose in the vicinity of the Damia bridge in the Jordan Valley. The plan was that once Israel's main thrust was identified in either sector, the opposing Jordanian force would engage it in battle to resist its advance and prevent it from making territorial gains.

According to the concept of active defence the Jordanians would seek to hit the Israelis whenever they could in limited engagements. One of the most important of these limited offensives was called Operation Tariq. This plan had been developed at the time of the Arab Legion; it was concerned with the encirclement of the Jewish Jerusalem enclave and was credible in so far as the configuration of the border made defence of the Israeli side of Jerusalem difficult. The communication lines of Jewish Jerusalem with the rest of Israel pass so close to the armistice line that the Jordanians were in a position to cut them in several places, surround Jerusalem and seal it off from the rest of Israel. According to Operation Tariq, the Jordanian army would tie a noose around Jerusalem by striking from the north and cutting Jerusalem off from Nabi Samuel to Houssan in the south, thereby isolating it from the coastal plain of Israel.

Operation Tariq was important because the Jordanians believed that if they could seize Jewish Jerusalem it could be used as a vital pawn to recover all the Jordanian territory the Israelis might have occupied when a ceasefire was imposed. For this reason, from 1949 onwards, Operation Tariq was a crucial part of Jordan's military strategy. Tal describes how it was central to Jordanian military calculations and formed 'part and parcel of all [Jordanian] Staff Officers' calculations. It was part of our training, of our preparations and we were fully alert to its importance all the time and thus were capable of carrying it out with a high potential of success'.[29]

The key to Operation Tariq was the swift occupation of Mount Scopus – an Israeli enclave within Jordanian Jerusalem which was the site of two Israeli establishments, the Hadassah Hospital and the Hebrew University. Under an agreement signed in 1948 the Israelis were allowed to keep a police force of eighty-five and thirty-three civilians on the Mount, but were not allowed more than a minimal amount of weaponry or other military personnel.[30] However, although the number of personnel was not increased, over the years the Israelis smuggled in large quantities of arms and by 1967 had turned it into a veritable fortress.[31]

Just as Mount Scopus was of vital strategic importance to the Jordanians, so the Jordanians knew that it was a primary objective of the Israelis. If the Israelis succeeded in taking the territory between the Mount and Jewish Jerusalem they would be able to encircle and occupy the whole of Arab Jerusalem and the area stretching to Bethlehem, thus cutting it off from Ramallah.[32] The validity of the Jordanians' assessment is confirmed by Narkiss 'through the years the destiny of Mount Scopus was basic to the deliberations and considerations of Central Command'.[33] The Jordanians realized that gaining control of the Mount was essential so they had built strong fortifications around the Mount and in the areas of Sheikh Jarrach, Ammunition Hill and the Police School.

The Jordanians were also aware of the tactical importance to the defence of Jerusalem and Ramallah of the heights of Biddu, Nabi Samuel, Beit Iksa, Beit 'Inan, Beit Hanina and Tal Al-Ful. They lie between Latrun in the west and Ramallah in the east, with Jerusalem a short distance to their south-east. From these heights the Jordanian forces were able to dominate the main Jerusalem–Tel Aviv highway and the city of Jerusalem itself. They were also close to Latrun, which is a mere 25 km from Jerusalem on the mountain road which runs through Nabi Samuel and Biddu to Lydda and the Israeli coastal plain. The heights were of immense importance to the successful implementation of Operation Tariq because they were 7 to 8 km away from Mount Scopus. For this reason, the Jordanians knew that another Israeli objective would be their occupation of these heights because this would frustrate any attempt by Jordan to encircle Israeli Jerusalem and cut it off from Israel. It would also help Israel advance north along the Nablus–Tulkarem–Qalqilya triangle and to strike the rear of any Jordanian forces that might drive there towards the area of Natanya.

In addition to specifying the occupation of Mount Scopus, the 1965 plan designated other areas as of vital strategic importance. These included the Jordan Valley–northern Dead Sea axis, Jerusalem–southern Dead Sea axis and the area around Aqaba. The areas of Nablus, Jerusalem, Ramallah and the road which leads from Jenin to Qabatiya were so important that the army was instructed to defend them at all costs. Nablus is at the centre of a nexus of communications through which pass almost all the roads from the Western coastal plain to the Jordan Valley and the East Bank. Jerusalem and Ramallah are the key centres of communication in the centre of the West Bank. All major routes from the coastal roads of Israel lead to these two towns.

The September 1965 plan envisaged that Israel would invade along two main axes in a pincer movement to encircle the West Bank. These axes were Jenin–Nablus–the Jordan Valley and Jerusalem–Jericho–the Jordan Valley.[34] According to Jordanian expectations, an alternative axis would have been along the Bissan–northern Jordan Valley, where an Israeli thrust might push down from the north along the Jordan Valley to encircle the West Bank when it reached the Jerusalem–Jericho road.[35] The Jordanians also knew that the area of Tulkarem and Qalqilya would be a primary Israeli objective because of their fear that Jordan would try to cut Israel in two by driving through its narrow waist to Natanya. Although the Jordanians knew that such an attempt was impossible in view of Jordan's limited military capability,[36] the Israelis were very sensitive to this threat. At this point Israel is no more than 16 km wide and the successful occupation of the area would cut communications between north and south Israel, isolate Haifa from Tel Aviv and threaten its most important strategic region.

Thus, the Jordanians anticipated that Israel's operations in the West Bank would take the form of a pincer movement. In the northern part of the West Bank it would consist of a thrust from the north and the occupation of Jenin and Nablus, followed by a drive towards the Damia Bridge. In the southern part of the West Bank it would begin with an attempt to occupy Ramallah and Jerusalem and then advance towards Jericho. The two arms of the pincer would then link up in the region between Damia and Jericho. This would result in the isolation of Hebron and the complete encirclement of the West Bank. Later events proved that this assessment of Israel's concept of operations in the West Bank was entirely accurate. In anticipation of this pincer movement the two armoured brigades, the 40th and 60th, were placed in strategic positions ready to counter an Israeli attack along these routes. The 60th brigade was located near Jericho, east of Jerusalem, and the 40th brigade was located west of the Damia bridge. Each brigade was composed of two armoured regiments equipped with American M-48 and M-47 Patton tanks and one mechanized infantry battalion equipped with American M-113 armoured personnel carriers. Their role was to act as a mobile striking force and as such they were the elite of the Jordanian army.

The command structure of the Jordanian army consisted of a GHQ at Amman composed of a Commander-in-Chief, Field Marshall Habes Majali, a Deputy Commander-in-Chief, Major General Sharif Nasser Ben Jamil, and an executive Chief of Staff, Lt General Amer Khammash. The defence of the East and West Banks was divided into two operational Headquarters, the Western and Eastern Commands headed respectively by Major General Muhammad Ahmed Salim and Brigadier (later General) Mashour Haditha Al-Jazzi. The Headquarters of Western Command was at Ramallah and that of Eastern Command was at Zarqa. The Western Front was divided into the following sectors: the Jordan Valley, Jenin, Nablus, Ramallah, Jerusalem and Al-Khalil (Hebron). The Eastern Front was divided into northern and southern sectors. Seven of Jordan's nine infantry brigades were placed under the direct control of Western Command. In addition, both the 40th and 60th independent armoured brigades, which were composed of General Headquarters troops as part of Army Reserve, were placed in support of Western Command. The two remaining infantry brigades were located in the East Bank, one of which was permanently deployed at Aqaba while the other was charged with the task of defending the heights of the East Bank which overlooked the northern Jordan Valley sector from Shunah in the south to Irbid in the north. The main logistic base and installations for the Jordanian army were located in the East Bank, with supply dumps on the West Bank. Administrative groups attached to the infantry and armoured brigades were responsible for ensuring their supplies.

Although the UAC had ceased to be effectual by the summer of 1966, Jordan's strategy for the defence of the West Bank remained largely unchanged, apart from the fact that Jordan was once again left with the problem of insufficient forces to provide secondary lines of defence and virtually no air cover for its troops. Two of the most significant changes that did take place were the result of the Israeli attack on the village of Samu. The wave of Arab criticism against the Jordanian regime resulted in an even greater spread of the Jordanian army along the length of the armistice line. Consequently, the Jordanian army was incapable of dealing with a full-scale Israeli offensive unless radical alterations were made. The second effect of Samu was the cessation of training programmes for new recruits which further depleted the strength of the Jordanian army. The criticism of the Jordanian Government that followed the Israeli raid was also a major factor behind the Arab League Defence Council's decision in early 1967 to end financial aid to Jordan, thus stopping the strengthening of the Jordanian army. Jordanian strategists[37] believed that this was one of Israel's objectives behind the raid. By making military co-operation between Jordan and the other Arab confrontation states difficult it made it even harder for Jordan to provide adequate defence of the West Bank.

As the situation in the Middle East became increasingly volatile throughout April and May 1967, King Hussein realized that he was no longer dealing with the threat of local attacks by Israel but with the threat of a full-scale invasion. He knew that he had to find additional support for the defence of the West Bank because to change from static to active defence in order to deal with the latter threat the Jordanian army needed additional land forces as well as adequate air cover for its troops. This realization was one of the factors which eventually led to the formation of the defence pact with Egypt at the end of May 1967. However, although the situation had changed entirely, the deployment of the Jordanian army remained essentially the same. Even though Jordan had been promised additional troops and was fighting as part of an overall Arab effort, the alterations made by Riad at the meeting on 3 June were limited and did not alter the broad lines of Jordan's original strategy.[38] They were concerned with the deployment of the Arab troops promised to Jordan, particularly the Iraqi division. They also took into account the provision of air cover by the Egyptian and Iraqi air forces. This was regarded as of the utmost importance for the protection of the limited engagements which the Cairo meeting had agreed that Jordan would carry out.[39] The most significant point about these new directions was that the dates at which the Arab troops were expected to arrive at their new positions were all *after* 5 June – which, as it turned out, was too late to be of use to the Jordanians.[40] The only significant changes made by Riad were plans for heavy artillery to shell Israeli airports and air bases and for Jordan's long-range guns to be brought to the front.

As arranged in Cairo, it was agreed that in the initial stages of war on the Egyptian front Jordan's role would be to maintain a defence posture and to open hostilities on a limited front with the aim of neutralizing a portion of Israel's forces which otherwise would be deployed on the Egyptian and Syrian fronts. This limited engagement was only to be expanded after the fulfilment of two conditions: the arrival of Iraqi and other Arab forces at the front[41] and positive information that events on the Egyptian front were proceeding as planned.[42] Only when these two conditions had been fulfilled were the Jordanians to extend operations along the front and enter into the offensive phase of the operation. However, even this was to be limited. Both King Hussein and Khammash point out that the term 'offensive' is an exaggeration since all it meant was a joint artillery and air operation to put Israeli airfields out of action, as well as limited operations behind the enemy lines at specific targets.[43]

Riad also suggested that since the Jordanian army was stretched far beyond its resources Syria should be asked to commit some of its army to the defence of Jordan. According to King Hussein, Riad was of the opinion that Syria could protect its own front with only one-third of its forces and that consequently it could afford to send ten of its fifteen brigades to defend the Jordanian–Israeli frontier.[44] However, although Riad made this request to the Syrians and through Amer, they remained silent.[45]

As in the original plan, the 40th and 60th armoured brigades were briefed to support and sustain the front infantry brigades. The 40th armoured brigade was assigned the task of supporting the two brigades stationed in Jenin and Nablus and of protecting the northern Jordan Valley and Damia Bridge areas. This provided additional defence for the Jenin–Nablus axis. The 60th armoured brigade was assigned the task of covering the southern section of the Jordan Valley with particular attention being paid to supporting the brigades defending Jerusalem and Hebron. This provided additional defence for the Jerusalem–Jericho axis.[46]

Riad was also working on a new strategy for Jordan which would have used the additional support promised Jordan by Egypt, Iraq, Syria and Saudi Arabia more effectively.[47] It proposed a limited offensive against Israel once hostilities opened.[48] However, the war began before this plan was fully developed.

Distribution of Jordanian forces

On the morning of 5 June the Jordanian Forces were deployed in the following manner:

The 6th (Qadisiya) brigade was situated in the Jordan Valley near the Damia

Bridge. It was reinforced by a tank squadron of 12 M-47s, one platoon of field engineers and a 25-pounder field regiment.

The 25th (Khalid Ibn Walid) infantry brigade was situated in the region of Jenin. Two of its battalions were on the border and a third was behind them in the region of Qabatiya. It was reinforced with an M-47 Patton tank squadron, one battery of 25-pounder guns, one battery of 155mm heavy guns and one platoon of field engineers.

The 1st (Princess Alia) infantry brigade was situated in the Nablus–Tulkarem–Qalqilya region. One battalion was in Qalqilya and Tulkarem, and two were in the rear, south of Nablus. It was supported by two batteries of 25-pounder guns and two batteries of 155mm guns.

The 2nd (Hashimi) infantry brigade was situated in the Ramallah region. One of its battalions was in the Latrun enclave, facing the Jerusalem Corridor, with a second acting as a reinforcement in the rear.[49] A third battalion was deployed along the Ramallah-Beit Hanina-Biddu triangle. The brigade was supported by a field regiment minus one battery of 25-pounder guns, one battery of 155mm heavy guns and one platoon of field engineers.

The 3rd (Talal) infantry brigade was situated in the Jerusalem region. It was reinforced by a battalion of the Imam Ali brigade, one field engineer platoon, one field artillery regiment of 25-pounder guns and one platoon of anti-tank guns (3.5 launchers).

The 29th (Hittin) infantry brigade was situated in the Hebron region. One of its battalions was deployed between the Mar Elias Monastery and Houssan Village, south of the Jerusalem Corridor. A second was at Mount Zion and the third was south of Mt Hebron. It was reinforced by a field artillery regiment of 25-pounder guns and one armoured regiment minus one squadron of Centurion tanks.

The 27th (Imam Ali) infantry brigade, minus one battalion, was situated between Jericho and Jerusalem. It was a reserve force to be used to protect Jerusalem and as a second line of defence for that sector.

The 60th armoured brigade was situated in the Khan Al-Ahmar region west of Jericho supported by one artillery regiment equipped with 105mm SP guns, one regiment minus one battery of 40mm twin anti-aircraft guns and one squadron of field engineers.

The 40th armoured brigade was situated in the Damia Bridge region. This brigade was reinforced by an artillery regiment of 105mm SP guns, one battery of 40mm anti-aircraft twin guns and one squadron of field engineers.

The Hussein Ben Ali infantry brigade of Eastern Command was situated between Amman and Aqaba.

The Yarmouk brigade was deployed between Amman and the area stretching from the heights controlling Israel's approaches to Irbid and the northern Jordan Valley.

The Royal Guard brigade was deployed in the area of Amman. The 40th and 60th armoured brigades constituted the main strike force of the Jordanian army and, with the addition of one heavy artillery regiment minus two batteries of 155mm guns, formed the GHQs main reserve force.

This deployment reflects the Jordanians' belief that the Israelis were most likely to invade in the form of the pincer movement described above. Accordingly, four of the infantry brigades were deployed in the Jerusalem, Ramallah, Hebron, Khan Al-Ahmar and southern Jericho areas and were supported by the 60th armoured brigade in the Jericho area for the purposes of counterattack on the Jerusalem–Hebron–southern Jordan Valley axis. Three infantry brigades were deployed in the Jenin, Nablus, northern Jordan Valley areas, supported by the 40th armoured brigade west of Damia for the purposes of counterattack on the Jenin–Nablus–northern Jordan Valley axes. However, the Israeli offensive took place while the army was still spread more thinly along the length of the armistice line than military logic required.

The Jordanians were also expecting the arrival of an Iraqi division which was to include 150 tanks, two Egyptian commando regiments, one Saudi Arabian brigade, a Syrian brigade and two squadrons of Iraqi planes.[50]

On the eve of the war the general feeling amongst the Jordanian military and political elite was optimistic. Although they realized that Israel's military capability was far more powerful, they had been impressed by the Egyptians' display of confidence. They did not believe that they would regain the land Israel had seized in 1948, other than the territories assigned in the partition plan, but they did believe that with their capabilities enhanced by support from their Arab allies they could engage their enemy in combat, prevent it from seizing their land and perhaps gain a political victory, as had happened in 1956. Khammash expresses the view of many leading Jordanians at the time:

> a concerted and well-planned Arab effort on land and in the air was bound to thwart Israel's aggressive objectives. That is why the army officers thought that with the new defence pact signed in Cairo and with Arab forces joining together, particularly with the Arab forces coming to our support – Iraqi, Syrian and Saudi Arabian – we were bound to put up a good show against Israel. We were not expecting such a quick conclusion to the war as did, in fact, take place.[51]

Chapter 7

The war

The war record

On 3 June King Hussein received the Turkish Ambassador who informed him that Israel would start its offensive on 5 or 6 June with an air strike on Egypt's air bases.[1] According to Juma'a this information was confirmed by the Iraqi Ambassador who visited him on 4 June and told him that according to their information Israel would open hostilities the following morning, that is, on 5 June. Juma'a and the Iraqi Ambassador then visited King Hussein to inform him of this development. King Hussein immediately told Khammash who informed Riad of the news. At King Hussein's request it was conveyed at once to the Egyptian High Command in Cairo.[2] The Egyptians replied that they were expecting such an attack and were prepared for it.[3]

This was the third time that Jordan had warned Egypt that Israel was likely to commence hostilities in this way. The previous occasions had been at the meeting with Nasser on 30 May and 3 June when King Hussein had told Nasser that all the information coming into Jordan pointed to a surprise attack by Israel on Egyptian airfields on 5 or 6 June.[4]

At 7 a.m. the next day the Jordanian radar station at Ajloun showed intense aerial activity over Israel. This information was conveyed to Riad who immediately passed it on to the Egyptian High Command. However, the Egyptian High Command did not receive this message and consequently no alert was issued to its air force.[5]

The radar at Ajloun was recording the flight of virtually the entire Israeli air force to Egypt. The leader of the IAF, General Mordechai Hod, had taken the enormous risk of putting the IAF's full strength attack on Egyptian air fields with the hope of knocking the EAF out of action while it was unprepared and unable to counterattack. After their initial attack the Israeli aircraft flew back to Israel, refuelled, and set off once more for another attack. The rapid turn-around time of the Israeli air force meant that they were able to conduct far more sorties than the Egyptians had anticipated.[6] In nearly three hours of continuous attacks the IAF virtually annihilated the Egyptian air force.

The destruction of the Egyptian air force determined the course of the war in general.[7] The Egyptians and the Jordanians had depended on Egyptian air cover for their troops. Without this, their forces were prey to the attentions of the IAF which could pick them off with ease.[8] The speed with which the IAF destroyed the EAF enabled them to catch the Syrian, Iraqi (the two squadrons at H3 base) and Jordanian air forces by surprise that afternoon and eliminate them from the battle. From the afternoon of the first day of the war the Arabs fought with virtually no air cover at all. As a result the war was lost almost as soon as it had begun.

Instead of informing their ally of this dire development the Egyptians passed the Jordanians completely false information. At 9.00 a.m. (10 a.m. Egyptian time) the Egyptian Commander-in-Chief, Amer, passed Riad the following coded message:

Israeli planes have started to bomb air bases of the UAR and approximately 75 per cent of the enemy's aircraft have been destroyed or put out of action. The counterattack by the Egyptian air force is under way against Israel. In Sinai UAR troops have engaged the enemy and taken the offensive on the ground. As a result, Field Marshall Amer has ordered the Commander-in-Chief of the Jordanian Front to open a new front and to launch offensive operations according to the plan outlined the day before.[9]

Amer's entirely false claim that the Egyptian air force was engaged in a counterattack on Israel and had destroyed 75 per cent of the Israeli air force coincided with the information provided by the radar at Ajloun. After recording the initial wave of aerial activity over Israel the radar showed hectic air activity in the air space of both Israel and Egypt. Aeroplanes in large numbers appeared, travelling in both directions and in both zones.[10] The conclusion drawn by the Jordanian observers was that the EAF was launching its counterattack on Israeli planes and air bases following the Israeli raids on Egyptian bases. King Hussein explains that 'when . . . our radar screen showed planes flying from Egypt towards Israel, we didn't give it a thought. We simply assumed they were from the UAR air force on their way to a mission over Israel. They weren't. They were Israeli bombers on the way home, their first mission against Egypt accomplished!'[11]

Later that morning a second message arrived from Amer. In it he stated that Israel's air offensive was continuing but that 75 per cent of their air force had been put out of action. He claimed that UAR bombers had put many Israeli air fields out of action and that the ground forces of the Egyptian army had penetrated into Israel through the Negev.[12] At about 12.30 Nasser phoned King Hussein and repeated to him what Amer had claimed. He then asked King Hussein 'quickly to take possession of the largest possible amount of land in order to get ahead of the UN's ceasefire. "For", he said, "I've been informed that the Security Council is intervening tonight to stop the war."'[13]

The same morning another instruction came from Amer to move the 60th armoured brigade to Hebron to provide support to an Egyptian division advancing towards Bersheeba in the Negev. The 40th brigade, near the Damia Bridge, was to replace its positions in the hills west of Jericho. According to this message the northern sector of Jericho which the 40th was vacating would be protected by a Syrian brigade as previously instructed by Cairo.

On learning of these orders, the Jordanian officers were horrified because they signified a complete departure from the planned strategy[14] and put Jordan on a dangerous course of action which stood little chance of success. They could not understand the orders' military logic and they had no plans to open hostilities along the entire Jordanian front and no strategy for the capture of Israeli territory apart from Mt Scopus and the encirclement of Jerusalem.[15] Moreover, they had previously agreed that they should not enter the phase of active defence without waiting for definite news of events on the Egyptian front. They pointed out that if the Israelis defeated the Egyptians they would deploy more of their forces against Jordan which would easily be overrun. If this happened their only achievement would have been to provide the Israelis with an excuse to launch a full-scale assault on their territory.

The officers also pointed out that it had been agreed that they would not enter the active phase of operations until the arrival of all the reinforcements from other Arab nations which had been promised to Jordan. They believed that it would be foolhardy not to wait because if those reinforcements were late or failed to arrive the Jordanian army would find itself outnumbered.

Although the Jordanians were strongly against seizing Israeli territory, they argued that if this was necessary the best strategy in the Jerusalem area would be to implement Operation Tariq. Major General Salim and Brigadier Atef Majali were particularly keen to implement it because the Jordanian army was fully prepared and it stood a good chance of success. If they could take Mount Scopus and encircle Jewish Jerusalem it would place them in an excellent position to bargain for the return of any land Israel might have seized.

However, Riad did not agree with this advice. He argued that the first Jordanian objective should not be Mount Scopus but Al-Mukkaber Hill in the south. The reason for this was that Mount Scopus lay in northern Jerusalem and Riad believed that it was the southern sector that would be the most strategically vital area. The reason for this belief was the information passed to him by Cairo GHQs that Egyptian troops were advancing north into the Negev. Consequently he concluded that the main axis of operations would be Bersheeba–Hebron–Bethlehem–southern Jerusalem. If this was the case the Egyptians would need the Jordanians to conduct an offensive operation along the frontier in southern Jerusalem and Hebron rather than in north Jerusalem where Mount Scopus was situated. Accordingly, Riad must have felt that if the Jordanians occupied Al-Mukkaber they would offset any attempt by Israel to advance into the area. The Jordanians could not help disagreeing with this point of view. They had always believed that the main focus of Israel's attentions would not be in the south but in the north of Jerusalem – in the area of Mount Scopus, the hills lying to the north west and in Latrun. However, Riad was not convinced.

The Jordanian officers also pointed out that in addition to the strategic objection, the Jordanian force Riad proposed using to take the hill was far too small. The Israelis had large armoured units south of Jerusalem which would be used to launch a counterattack and which the Jordanian infantry battalion could not hope to fend off since it was not being provided with any artillery or armoured support. Consequently the Jordanians believed that it would not be long before their troops would be forced to retreat and Israel would take the hill. Such a development would seriously affect Jordan's ability to defend the Jerusalem sector.

Tal describes how the question of the occupation of Al-Mukkaber hill 'was debated at length in the operations room whilst Staff Officers [Egyptians and Jordanians] quarrelled and insulted one another'. 'After a long and heated debate the late Atef Majali [Riad's Director of Military Operations] became furiously angry and putting on his Arabic head-dress made as if to leave the operations room. Abdul Munim Riad and the Commander of the Western front [Major General Salim] exchanged insults and a great deal of confusion ensued'.[16] However, in the end Riad's view prevailed since as Commanding Officer he could not be overruled by his staff.

The Jordanians were equally horrified at Cairo's request for the 40th and 60th armoured brigades to be moved south. The location of these brigades had been carefully planned and were essential to protect the strategically vital areas of Jerusalem and Nablus and the expected axes of Israeli advance. If these axes were left without armoured support Israel would be free to enter them without fear of strong resistance. The Jordanian infantry brigades left in the area would be faced with a superior Israeli force which would almost certainly overwhelm them.

The movement of the 60th brigade to Hebron also made it impossible for the Jordanians to conduct Operation Tariq which required maximum strength in the area around Jerusalem. By the time the 40th brigade had replaced the 60th the Jordanians would have lost the tactical advantage of surprise since by that time hostilities between the Jordanians and the Israelis would have been opened. However, Riad's belief in the advance of the Egyptians from Sinai to the Negev led him to underestimate the importance of Operation Tariq. The information he had received from Cairo convinced him that Israel's main offensive against Jordan would come from the south – between Jerusalem and Hebron – and therefore it was essential that this area should be strengthened by the addition of an armoured force.

Although the Jordanians were convinced that Riad was mistaken and did not hestitate to tell him this, their words were of no avail. Tal describes how Atef Majali 'objected strongly to some of his decisions, but Riad was a stubborn man. The same applied to the Commander of the Western front and the brigades on the West Bank where most of Riad's orders were opposed by the officers involved. They called on Atef Majali to persuade Riad that the various orders were unwise and to plead their case before the Egyptian general'.[17] However, despite their protestations, the Jordanians were forced to accept the new instructions. As the Jordanian army was now acting as part of a joint Arab defence force the Jordanian GHQ officers were under the command of the Egyptians and were virtually mere observers of the war. Tragically these orders proved disastrous for the Jordanians and sealed the fate of the West Bank. From this point on, the war in Jordan was no longer conducted on the basis of the strategies the Jordanians had so carefully worked out. Instead it was conducted on the basis of the information and directions supplied by Cairo and faithfully implemented by Riad who had little understanding of the realities of the Jordanian theatre.

Between 9.00 a.m. and 12.00 p.m. on the morning of 5 June Riad issued the following instructions:

The Egyptian commando battalions attached to the Jordanian brigades around Jenin and Ramallah were ordered to infiltrate Israeli territory at dusk and attempt to destroy Israeli installations at the air bases of Hertzlia, Ein Shamer, Kfar Sirkin, Lydda, Ramle, Aker and their radar stations. Artillery units were instructed to take forward positions and to bombard enemy air bases.

The air forces of Jordan, Syria and Iraq (the two squadrons at H3) were put on combat alert and ordered to commence air strikes immediately.

All Jordanian artillery units along the whole of the front with Israel were instructed to take advance positions from which they could shell Israeli air fields. Light artillery and mortar fire began at 11.30 a.m. and heavy artillery was instructed to begin at 3.00 p.m.

Forces on the Western Front were ordered to despatch combat patrols along the frontier and to act in co-ordination with the Saiqa (Egyptian commando) and artillery units.

At 12.00 p.m. the battalion of the 27th (Imam Ali) brigade attached to the Talal brigade in Jerusalem was ordered to occupy Al-Mukkaber Hill in the southern section of Jerusalem. The brigade's two remaining battalions were instructed to take second-line defence positions in the area of Khan Al-Ahmar on the Jerusalem–Jericho road.

At 12.40 p.m. the 60th armoured brigade was ordered to advance to Hebron. At 1.00 p.m the 40th armoured brigade was ordered to move at 2.00 p.m. to the area between King Hussein Bridge and Jericho.[18]

The destruction of the Jordanian air force

Although Riad had issued orders for a joint Syrian–Iraqi–Jordanian air strike at 9.00 a.m. it was 11.50 before the attack was carried out. The reason for this delay was the procrastination of the Iraqis and the Syrians. Tal writes that when the Iraqis were asked to launch an air attack on Israel in co-ordination with the Jordanians and the Syrians, they replied that 'for technical reasons' they could not come immediately.[19] The Iraqi base at H3 on the Jordanian–Iraqi border is more than 800 km from Israel's coast and when the Iraqi aircraft took off from H3 at 11.00 a.m. to join the Jordanian Hawker Hunters they managed only one raid on the Israeli airport at Lydda before the Israelis mounted a counter-attack.[20]

The response of the Syrians to the Jordanians' request for an air strike against Israel was even more disturbing. Their modern MiGs and proximity to Israel made them of vital importance to any Arab air attack. King Hussein comments that 'without the help of [the Syrian MiGs] the bombing of Israeli bases would have had a negligible effect'.[21] However, when the Jordanian command contacted them at 9.00 a.m. they replied that 'they had been caught off guard: their aircraft were not ready for the strike and their fighter pilots were on a training flight'. They asked for time to get ready. At first they asked for a half hour and then an hour and so on until 10.45 when they asked for yet another delay which, King Hussein confirms, was also granted. The King goes on to say that 'at 11.00 we couldn't wait any longer. The Iraqis had already taken off and were on their way to join us. The result of these repeated Syrian postponements was that our air operations did not really get off the ground until well after 11.00 a.m.'[22] This two-hour delay meant that the possibility of raiding Israeli air bases while their aircraft lay vulnerable on the ground resupplying was completely aborted.

At about 11.50 a.m. Jordan launched sixteen of its Hawker Hunters, which bombed Israeli air fields at Natanya, Kfar Sirkin, Kfar Saba and other targets. However, they did not find many Israeli aircraft on the ground and were too few in number and limited in capability to inflict much damage on the Israeli air fields. They returned to Jordan half an hour later claiming the destruction of four Israeli aircraft.

By the time the Jordanian planes returned to their bases after three sorties over empty Israeli air fields, the IAF had finished with the EAF and was able to launch an attack on the Jordanian, Syrian and Iraqi air forces. Israeli Mirages caught the Jordanian Hunters refuelling and re-arming on the ground and destroyed them beyond repair.[23] On their return home the Israeli planes bombed and strafed other targets, including King Hussein's Palace.[24] The Jordanian radar station at Ajloun was singled out for attack by four Super

Mysteres and was destroyed. By 2.30 p.m. on the afternoon of the first day of the war the JAF had been wiped out. The Syrian air force and Iraqi squadrons at H3 base experienced similar destruction.

Most Arab and Western commentators believe that Israeli air supremacy was the most important military factor which led to the defeat of the Arabs.[25] With the destruction of the Arab air forces the Israelis had no difficulty in defeating their land forces. Throughout the war the Jordanian army was constantly bombarded with rockets and napalm bombs. The Israelis were able to raid Jordanian positions and provide support for their own forces without fear of opposition. They could delay the arrival of essential support services and supplies to Jordanian troops by hitting Jordanian transport lines. They could block the movement of advancing Jordanian forces from the air and prevent the arrival of reinforcements. Had the Israelis not knocked out the Arab air forces so swiftly there is little doubt that the war would have been more prolonged and its course in the West Bank might have been different.

The fate of the Arab troops promised to Jordan

Most of the forces Jordan had been promised from other Arab nations failed to reach their battle-positions in time. Those that made the attempt were subjected to such intense air attack that they were rendered useless.

The bulk of Iraq's 8th mechanized brigade reached H3 on the Jordanian–Iraqi border on 2 June. It did not reach Mafraq until the morning of 5 June and was instructed to proceed to the Al-Masri junction in the Jordan Valley. The advance party of the brigade managed to reach that position at 10.45 p.m. It was then instructed to deploy in the Jericho area and prepare to push forward two of its regiments to the town of Albeereh in the region of Ramallah at dusk on 6 June. However, the brigade was subjected to constant air attack by Israeli Mirages throughout its journey across the East Bank. It sustained heavy losses of equipment and supplies and by the time it reached its assigned position in the Jericho area it was no longer fit to enter battle.[26]

The GHQs in Amman had been informed by the Saudi Arabian government on 1 June that they were sending one infantry brigade to Jordan that day. In fact, it was not until 6.30 p.m. on 6 June that a Saudi Arabian brigade, minus one battalion, arrived at the town of Al-Mudawwarah on the Saudi Arabian–Jordanian border. At 5.55 p.m. on 7 June Riad instructed it to move to Al-Quwera, which its commander refused to do until he had received confirmation from his command in Tabouk. Consequently, it was not until 8 June that an advance battalion of the Saudi brigade arrived at the south Jordanian town of Ma'an. This was too late for it to participate in the fighting because by this time the war was almost over.

The 33rd Egyptian commando battalion had been appointed to the Khalid

Ibn Walid brigade in the Jenin sector. The 53rd Egyptian commando battalion had been appointed to the Hashimi brigade in the Ramallah sector. Although they did not reach their assigned position until 5 June these units were ordered to cross onto Israeli territory at dusk that day with the objective of destroying Israeli airports and radar stations.[27] The 33rd battalion managed to infiltrate Israeli territory but of the units of the 53rd battalion, only the one assigned the task of attacking Ein Shamer airfield succeeded in crossing the border. However, because of their late arrival, even those units that did cross the border failed to accomplish their missions and on 6 June they were ordered to withdraw. Some of the commandos were caught by the Israeli mechanized brigade that entered Ramallah on 6 June and were either captured, or forced to retreat to the east.[28]

A PLO battalion, which to the complete surprise of the Jordanians had crossed into Jordan with the Iraqi force, was wiped out by the IAF as it attempted to travel across Jordan to its assigned position in the West Bank.

It was not until 10.00 p.m. on 6 June that the former Syrian military attaché in Amman, Lt Colonel Adnan Tayyara, arrived at the Jordanian border. He reported that the Syrian force promised to Jordan (the 17th mechanized brigade) was en route and would soon reach the border. However, it did not arrive, and at 2.15 p.m. on 7 June, when the situation in the West Bank was rapidly deteriorating, Riad contacted the operations room in Damascus to beg for the despatch of another armoured brigade as well as the speedy arrival of the 17th brigade. It was not until about 9.50 a.m. the following day that Major General Hafiz Assad, who was then Minister of Defence, telephoned Riad to promise the immediate despatch of the 17th brigade. Despite this promise, the advance party of this brigade did not cross the border until 8.20 p.m. by which time the Israelis had gained control of the West Bank. At 10.00 p.m. Riad instructed the brigade to go to its defensive positions but the commander of the brigade refused to obey. Consequently Riad ordered it to return to Syria which it had no hesitation in doing.

The Jordanians had entered the war believing that reinforcements and air cover would be provided by other Arab nations. In fact neither of these essential requirements was fulfilled and the Jordanian army was left to fight the war almost entirely on its own.

Battles for the West Bank[29]

On 3 June Jordan's GHQs had received intelligence reports which confirmed earlier observations of a build-up of Israeli armoured, mechanized and infantry formations in two key areas of concentration. The first area was west of Latrun opposite the Ramallah–Jerusalem axis and the second was in the Affula area across the armistice line from Jenin. According to Khammash, 'Jordanian intelligence sources inside Israel conveyed to us the impression of an imminent Israeli pre-emptive strike. This information was quickly passed on to our Egyptian allies'.[30] Consequently, when at 11.00 a.m. on 5 June General Odd Bull, the Norwegian UNTSO Commander, conveyed a message from Israel to King Hussein that Jordan would not be attacked unless Jordan took the first aggressive action, the Jordanians regarded this as a cover-up for Israel's real intentions.[31] They believed that Israel was seeking to delay action on the Jordanian front until Egypt had been dealt with.[32] Although Israel did not necessarily anticipate that Jordan would enter the war quite so quickly as it did,[33] neutral military observers point out that the speed with which Israel organized itself when hostilities began shortly after 11.00 a.m. indicate that Israel had carefully planned its activities.[34]

According to the Commander of the Western Front, Salim, the only offensive action undertaken by Jordan before 1.00 p.m. on 5 June was the shelling of Israel's military installations at Tel Aviv and Ramat David air field by long range artillery. Dupuy argues that 'the initiation of large-scale ground operations seems to have been an Israeli decision prompted apparently by the threat which artillery fire from Jordanian guns posed to their ability to maintain effective air operations on the Syrian front'.[35] However, Salim believes that the Jordanian long-range artillery fire was the *casus belli* for the Israelis. The other factors which prompted Israel to rethink its plans for Jordan were Jordan's capture of Government House at about 1.00 p.m. and fear of an attack on Mount Scopus. These resulted in Israel's full implementation of its plan to seize the whole of the West Bank and its forces were reorganized for this purpose.[36]

The Jordanians had correctly anticipated the strategic importance of the Jerusalem–Ramallah axis to Israel's Central Command (General Uzi Narkiss GOC) in which the occupation of Arab Jerusalem was a key factor.[37] By encircling Jerusalem the Israelis knew that they would isolate Hebron and that Jordanian reserve forces in the Jordan Valley and Jericho could be prevented from coming to the aid of the Talal brigade in Jerusalem. Road communications would be severed on the West Bank, leaving no room for contact between Jordanian forces in the north and the south. Just as the Jordanians had anticipated, Narkiss' plan for the occupation of Jerusalem depended on securing the high ground in the north-west, which covered the area of Biddu and Nabi Samuel, and, in the north, the area between Beit Hanina and Ramallah. The operation was based on an inner and an outer pincer movement.

The inner pincer movement was very much as the Jordanians had anticipated. It began with the occupation of Mount Scopus, followed by the capture of the Mount of Olives and the high ground between Jerusalem and Ramallah. Simultaneously, the other arm of the pincer would thrust to the south and occupy Al-Tur (Dir Abu Tur), Government House and the village of Sur Baher which overlooks the Jerusalem–Bethlehem highway. This would cut communications between the two cities and help complete the encirclement of Arab Jerusalem.

The outer pincer movement sought to isolate the Jerusalem–Ramallah area. One arm of the pincer would be directed at Latrun, the Beit Ur (Beth Horon) Pass, Beituniya and Ramallah. The other arm would seek to consolidate Israel's hold on Arab Jerusalem by occupying the vital Jerusalem–Nabi Samuel–Ramallah ridge. Seizing this territory would prevent the Jordanians from encircling Jewish Jerusalem and cutting it off from Israel. It would also help the Israelis advance north in order to threaten the area of Nablus, Tulkarem and Qalqilya and to strike the rear of any Jordanian forces that might go from there to Natanya. To complete the encirclement of the area, the Israelis planned to attack from the west with the aim of occupying Tulkarem and Qalqilya and to drive from there to Nablus. Simultaneously, they planned to attack the area of Jenin and then advance south to threaten Nablus. Having captured Jerusalem and Nablus the Israelis would be able to occupy the entire southern area by taking Hebron and, by descending down the hills to the Jordan Valley along the two axes, they would seal the fate of the West Bank by gaining control of the bridges of the River Jordan. This was the strategy precisely anticipated by the Jordanians and which their original deployment had been intended to repel.

The southern West Bank

On the morning of 5 June the forces under Narkiss were composed of the following brigades:[38] one infantry brigade, the Etzioni (almost a division strong and consisting of seven infantry battalions, one tank battalion as well as artillery and support elements), located in and around Jerusalem; one infantry brigade, situated between Tulkarem and Lod; one motorized infantry brigade, situated around Latrun; one armoured brigade, the Harel, concentrated north-east of Tel Aviv; and one paratroop brigade. This had originally been earmarked for a drop on Al-Arish in Sinai, but the rapid collapse of the Egyptian front meant that by the afternoon of 5 June the whole brigade was made available to Narkiss for use in Jerusalem.

Narkiss attached particular importance to the paratroop brigade because it was composed of highly professional troops. It was to be used to storm the all-important Jordanian strongholds in northern Jerusalem, including Mount Scopus, the Police School, Ammunition Hill and Sheikh Jarrach.[39]

On the Jordanian side, in conformity with the concept of 'Offensive-Defence', Salim's Western Command deployed four infantry and one armoured brigade for the defence of the Jerusalem–Hebron–Ramallah sector. Two of these, the 27th (Imam Ali) infantry brigade and the 60th armoured brigade, were held in the Jordan Valley between Jericho and Khan Al-Ahmar as a reserve counterattack force. Thus, the main line of defence was held by three infantry brigades. The Hittin brigade, supported by a tank regiment, was given the unenviable task of defending the Hebron sector, which included 320 km of the armistice line. One of its battalions was stationed south-east of Jerusalem between Bethlehem and Sur Baher. The Hashimi brigade was assigned the task of defending the Ramallah sector and, like the Hittin brigade, it was badly over-stretched. It was deployed in linear defensive positions in the Budrus–Latrun–Nabi Samuel–Deir Nidham–Beit Hanina sector. The 3rd (Talal) brigade was given responsibility for Jerusalem and its three battalions were deployed as follows: one battalion covered the area between Bab Al-Amud (the Damascus Gate) to Shufat Hill; one battalion was located in the Old City itself; one battalion was at Abu Tur with two of its platoons stationed at Karam Al-Alami as reserves. The Talal brigade was supported by only one field artillery regiment equipped with 25-pound guns.

Jordanian military analysts[40] point out that, when it came to war, the main line of resistance in the southern West Bank was, in fact, held by only three infantry brigades because the reserve armoured and infantry brigades were prevented from reaching Jerusalem by the IAF. In Jerusalem the Talal brigade was left to deal with the eight battalions of the Etzioni brigade as well as the Harel mechanized brigade and the paratroop brigade. According to Major General Kawash the relative strength of Jordanian–Israeli forces within Jerusalem itself were: 4 to 1 in personnel; 3 to 0 in tanks; 4 to 1 in artillery; absolute Israeli air superiority.[41]

Until 12.00 p.m. on 5 June hostilities between the Jordanians and the Israelis had been confined to artillery and small arms fire and the limited action of the Jordanian air force. However, in spite of the Jordanian objections, at 12.00 p.m. Riad had ordered the reserve battalion of the 27th infantry brigade (attached to the Talal brigade) to occupy Government House.[42] By 1.00 p.m. the Jordanians had occupied the tiny wood which separated Government House from the adjacent farm. Half an hour later the Jordanians stormed Government House and occupied it. Just as the Jordanian staff officers had anticipated, it was not long before a unit of the Etzioni brigade, backed up by about twelve tanks, launched a counterattack. Approximately four battalions were deployed against the understrength and unsupported Jordanian battalion. By 4.30 p.m. hopelessly outnumbered and with many men already killed, the battalion commander ordered his troops to evacuate the area and the Israelis took the hill. One hundred Jordanians were killed, wounded or missing in this battle out of a total battalion of approximately 500.[43] Thus, Israel took possession of an area which threatened the Jerusalem–Jericho road – the only approach between Jerusalem and the East Bank.

Jordan's offensive at Government House was one of the factors that led Israel to bring forward its plans for a full scale offensive in the Jerusalem area, particularly as by this time the Israelis knew that developments in the southern front (Egypt) were in their favour.

According to Narkiss, on the morning of 5 June the Israelis had intended to respond to the Jordanians' limited activity by taking Abdul Aziz Hill, Latrun and Government House.[44] However, at 12.45 p.m. the 'Voice of the Arabs' broadcasting from Cairo announced that a Jordanian spokesman in Amman had declared the Jordanian army's seizure of Al-Mukkaber Hill. In the English translation it said that Mount Scopus had been captured by the Jordanians.[45] Although this report was premature (the Jordanians did not take Government House until after 1.00 p.m.) it had a deep impact on Narkiss. He was already anxious that the Jordanians would seize Mount Scopus and was determined to prevent them.[46] He recalled that in 1956 the Egyptians had announced operations they intended to carry out as if they had already been completed. He therefore concluded that the Jordanians 'might indeed try to seize Mount Scopus'.[47] From this point onwards Narkiss acted on the assumption that this is what the Jordanians were intending to do. Consequently he set into motion a modified version of the full-scale offensive that had been planned many years before. The paratroop brigade was told to get ready to attack Mount Scopus and the surrounding land. Expecting Jordan's 60th armoured brigade to advance towards Mount Scopus from the Jordan Valley Narkiss ordered his armoured brigade (the Harel) to be ready to intercept it at Tal Al-Ful north of the Mount.[48]

At 2.20 a.m. on the night of 5/6 June[49] the Israeli paratroopers launched their attack on Sheikh Jarrach, Ammunition Hill, the American Colony, Wadi Joz, the Police School and Mount Scopus. They met fierce resistance from the second Al-Hussein battalion of the Talal brigade which was defending the area.[50] Although at first the Jordanians succeeded in defending the position the Israelis brought in additional artillery and mortar fire. Searchlights were also used to illuminate the areas so that air strikes could be made. At 4.00 a.m. the Israelis brought in reinforcements of tanks and a third paratroop regiment.

Unlike the Israelis, the Jordanians were unable to provide their troops with reinforcements so swiftly. The original plan to use the 60th brigade as a reserve force for the Jerusalem sector had been frustrated because of the order issued by Riad at 12.40 p.m. on 5 June to move it to Hebron.[51] One battalion had already been bombed by the IAF as it travelled south to Dahriya. Between 5.00 and 5.30 p.m. on the same day a confusing series of orders and counter-orders were issued to the brigade; it was not until 6.30 p.m. that it was decided that a tank battalion (minus one company) of the 60th brigade and the Imam Ali brigade (minus one battalion) should go to north Jerusalem to counter the Israeli advance. One tank squadron of the 60th brigade was also ordered to move to Abu Dis and Ezzariyeh in south-east Jerusalem in order to relieve the hard-pressed Talal brigade.[52] However, by this time the IAF had full control of the air and their journey west was accompanied by constant air attacks with the IAF using flares to light the darkness. Both brigades were easily identifiable. The tanks of the 60th brigade were restricted to the narrow confines of the highway whilst the Imam Ali brigade was travelling along a narrow mountain track. By mid-morning the Jordanian relief force had been rendered useless. Meanwhile, in Jerusalem, the beleaguered Talal brigade was forced to retreat into the Old City. By the morning of 6 June the Israelis had reached the bottom of the valley below the Augusta Victoria heights.

It was not until dawn that elements of the 60th brigade finally reached the area of Tal Al-Ful. However, Israel's Harel brigade had already prepared an ambush. Although the Jordanians fought hard they were forced to retreat, having lost a number of their tanks, and the Israelis continued their advance on Jerusalem.

By the morning of 6 June the Israelis had seized almost all the area outside the Old City. The only areas that remained in Jordanian hands were Shufat Hill, Augusta Victoria, Al-Tur, Ezzariyah and Ras Al-Amoud (on the southern slopes of the Mount of Olives). By this time Latrun had also fallen and the only path still open to the Arabs was the road to Jericho, and even this was threatened by the Harel brigade.

By the evening of 6 June the position of the Jordanian army in Jerusalem was desperate. The whole of Jerusalem outside of the Old City had been captured with the exception of Augusta Victoria and the eastern hills directly overlooking the Jerusalem–Jericho highway. Brigadier Ata Ali's forces in the Old City were completely isolated with no hope of receiving reinforcements of equipment, fuel or men. The only road open to unoccupied Jordan was the road to Jericho and the Israelis were bombing any traffic that moved along it. When Ata Ali explained his position to his HQs he was assured that reinforcements would reach him that night. However, constant air attacks against the relief column delayed its arrival and at dawn it was still more than 6 km from Jerusalem. Realizing that his task was hopeless and that by this time most of the Jordanian army in the north and the south had withdrawn, Ata Ali concluded that he had no choice but to withdraw the remaining Jordanian forces from Jerusalem. By the early morning this had been done. At 7.00 a.m. on 7 June the Israelis attacked once more only to find that the Jordanians had disappeared. By 10.00 a.m. they entered the Old City which fell without resistance.

The same day, the remaining towns in this section of the West Bank fell to Israel. South of Jerusalem, the Etzioni brigade moved towards Bethlehem and Hebron. By this time the order for a general withdrawal had gone out and the Hittin brigade had left the area. Bethlehem and Hebron fell without resistance. Events in the area north of Jerusalem also proved that the Jordanian assessment of where Israel would direct its main effort was correct. It did not come from the south but from the north in a three-pronged attack against Latrun and the hills north-west of Jerusalem which the Jordanians had been so concerned to protect. The failure of the 60th and 27th brigades to come to the area in time meant that, by the night of 5/6 June, despite bitter resistance, the Israelis had succeeded in breaking through Jordan's inadequate defences. Simultaneously, after a savage fight, an Israeli reinforced infantry brigade succeeded in penetrating the area of Latrun, which was being held by only one battalion of the Hashimi brigade. In the evening of 6 June these two Israeli forces then converged on Ramallah, which fell with little resistance. The following day the Israelis moved on to Jericho. They arrived in the late afternoon to find that the Jordanian army had already withdrawn to the East Bank.

Total Jordanian casualties in the Jerusalem, Ramallah and Hebron areas were estimated at 1,000 killed and wounded. However, the extent of resistance put up by the Jordanians in Jerusalem is reflected in the 600 wounded and 200 dead Israeli soldiers.[53]

The northern West Bank

Jordanian forces in the area of Nablus and Jenin were composed of: the 25th (Khalid Ibn Walid) infantry brigade, which had two of its battalions stationed in Jenin and a third in Tubas. Attached to it was an M-47 tank regiment minus one squadron, one engineer company, one artillery regiment minus one battery of 25-pound guns and one battery of 155mm guns. The Princes Alia brigade was stationed at Nablus with two of its battalions deployed on the coastal plain in the Tulkarem–Azzon–Qalqilya region. Attached to it were two 25-pound artillery batteries and two 155mm gun batteries. The Qadisiyeh brigade was located in the hills west of the Damia Bridge and northern Valley sector. It was supported by one tank squadron (12-M47s), one engineers company and one 25-pound gun regiment. The 40th armoured brigade was located at the Damia Bridge. It consisted of one mechanized infantry battalion, one M-47 tank regiment and one M-48 tank regiment. Attached to it was one artillery regiment (105mm SP), one battery of anti-aircraft guns (40mm twin) and one engineers squadron.

The concept for the defence of this area was influenced by the major and direct threat that Israel presented to the Jenin–Nablus sector and by the secondary threat of an Israeli advance along the approaches from Qalqilya and Tulkarem which led to Nablus from the west. There was also the possibility of an advance along the Bissan–Damiya axis along the west bank of the Jordan River. Each of these sectors was therefore given the support of a brigade (the Khalid ibn Walid, Aliya and Qadisiyeh). The Qadisiyeh brigade was also given the task of acting as a reserve force, together with the 40th armoured brigade. Its function was to launch a counterattack in the event of a major Israeli north-south drive on the Bissan–Damiya axis. Responsibility for the southern flank of this area was given to the Hashimi brigade, which was located between Kafr Qasem and Latrun. El Edroos points out that, in effect, four infantry battalions were holding approaches along a 80 km sector, two infantry battalions and an armoured regiment were deployed in depth and the sector counterattack force was stationed in the Jordan Valley, 80 km to the east of the western border and 32 km from the focal point of Nablus. Thus an Israeli 'Main Effort' would experience little difficulty in breaking through the spreadeagled and wafer-thin Jordanian defences on any particular segment of the sector they chose.

The forces Israel deployed against Jordan in the northern area of the West Bank were Brigadier Elad Peled's Ugdah, which comprised one armoured, one mechanized and one infantry brigade; and two infantry brigades which had initially been attached to Central Command, one located in the area of Bissan and the eastern Jezreel Valley and the other deployed in the lowlands near Tulkarem.

When the Israeli GHQs realized that Syria was not participating in the war and would be unlikely to come to the aid of Jordan they seized the opportunity of breaking into the northern West Bank. The Israelis quickly transferred Peled's Ugdah from the Syrian front to the Jordanian front in order to secure the Jenin–Nablus axis and destroy Jordan's three infantry and armoured brigades deployed in the area. This force was augmented by a further two infantry brigades from Central Command which were assigned the task of protecting the southern flank of the Ugdah's advance towards Nablus. This was to be accomplished by a pincer thrust in the directions of Qalqilya–Al-Funduq–Nablus and Tulkarem–Deir Sharaf–Nablus.

Thus, Israel deployed five brigades (including one armoured) against four Jordanian brigades (including one armoured).

Israel's concept of operations in the Jenin–Nablus–Jordan Valley (Damia Bridge) axis was precisely as the Jordanians had predicted. Their main effort was directed towards securing Nablus and consisted of a frontal assault on the Jenin–Qabatiya–Arraba sector by two mechanized and infantry brigades along the Jenin–Silat Addaher–Sabastiya–Nablus and the Jalbun–Jalqamus–Zababida–Tubas–Nablus approaches. This was to be followed by a rapid thrust down the Dotan Valley to Nablus and the Damia Bridge. The armoured brigade was to be unleashed in the early hours of 6 June in an unexpected march across country from Mount Gilboa to the key road junction of Zababida 6 km east of Qabatiya on the Jenin–Tubas–Nablus axis. According to El Edroos, its effect would be 'to jar the Jordanian defences in the vital Jenin sector and to force the 40th armoured brigade to counterattack in the Qabatiya–Jenin area'[54] where the Israelis would be ready and waiting. Having destroyed the 25th (Khalid Ibn Walid) and 40th brigades the way would then be open to deal with the thinly stretched Aliya brigade which was protecting the Tulkarem–Qalqilya–Nablus sector. The brigade would be forced to abandon its defensive positions because of the threat posed to its line of communications, which was centred on Nablus. The Israelis hoped that they would then be able to pursue the retreating Jordanians to the Jordan Valley. In order to reduce the threat represented by the reserve forces of the 40th armoured brigade and the Qadisiyeh brigade the Israelis decided to create a diversion in the form of an offensive from Tirat Zevi in the Jordan Valley towards the area of Damiya.[55]

On the morning of 5 June the IAF began the Israeli offensive in the northern West Bank by attacking Jordanian positions in the upper Dotan Valley. The Israelis had little difficulty in breaking through the defences of the battalion of the Khalid Ibn Walid brigade, which was holding a frontage of over 25 km. The first battle occurred in the evening between an Israeli armoured force and a battalion of the Khalid Ibn Walid brigade west of Jenin. The battle went on throughout the night, with the Jordanians receiving reinforcements from the 12th Independent armoured regiment, which had been deployed near Qabatiya, and an armoured regimental group of the 40th armoured brigade. However, once again the Israelis brought in the IAF. This decimated the Jordanians and forced them to retreat.

On learning of the situation in the Jenin sector Riad asked the Syrians to come to the aid of the Jordanians and replace the 40th armoured brigade with their troops, as they had promised they would. However, despite his pleas and those of the Commanders in Cairo the Syrians refused to come to the aid of Jordan. They claimed that they could not allow their troops to act without air cover, which they themselves could not provide. At 7.15 p.m. on 5 June Riad sent a message to General Fawzi in Cairo telling him that Israel had penetrated the northern sector and that Jenin and Nablus might fall. He explained that the Jordanians desperately needed air cover from Syria and Iraq, and it was decided that Iraqi air sorties would begin over the area at dawn the next day.[56]

When Riad saw that the Syrians were going to stand by while the Israelis seized the West Bank, he realized that the only possibility of reinforcing the area lay with the 40th armoured brigade which was now in Jericho. Although it was exhausted, having sustained air attacks throughout its journey south, at 8.45 p.m. Riad countermanded his earlier order and instructed the brigade to return to Jenin; it set off three-quarters of an hour later.[57] The Jordanian infantry brigade defending the Jenin sector was left to fight on its own throughout the night of 5/6 June while the Israelis received reinforcements. By the early morning of 6 June the Jordanians were forced to retreat and Jenin and the surrounding area fell into their hands.

It was not until 4.45 a.m. that a tank regiment of the 40th armoured brigade reached the Qabatiya junction south of Jenin. It had taken the 40th armoured brigade seven hours to travel by night from Jericho to Qabatiya. Despite the trials they had gone through the Jordanians initially gained the upper hand in combat with an Israeli reconnaissance battalion and forced it to retreat. However, yet again, the Israelis brought in their air force which rained bombs on the defenceless Jordanian troops throughout the day and late into the night.[58] In the ensuing conflagration Jordanian tanks and supply vehicles were destroyed by the IAF and had to be abandoned by their crews. Despite the devastation caused by the IAF the Jordanians continued to resist the advance of the Israelis until the early hours of 7 June. However, the Israelis received more reinforcements and eventually the Jordanians were forced to retreat to the Damia Bridge.

Although the Jordanian army put up strong resistance the Israelis reached Nablus on 7 June and soon had the Jordanians on the retreat. By this time it had become apparent to the Jordanians that they were outnumbered and that their defence of the West Bank had collapsed. By dusk they were well on their way to the Damia Bridge and by the evening of 7 June the Israelis had more or less gained control of the West Bank.

The withdrawal of Jordanian forces from the West Bank

By the morning of 6 June signs of despair had begun to show in Jordanian GHQs after the occupation of Jenin and Sheikh Jarrach. The Jordanian army was without air cover, the radar at Ajloun had been knocked out and a large number of tanks had been destroyed. Under these conditions it seemed impossible to maintain resistance.[59]

Another element that helped create this sense of defeat were the exaggerated reports sent to the GHQs by Jordanian commanders at the front.[60] These reports emphasized the tremendous losses the Jordanians were sustaining and the odds against which they fought. This resulted in an inflated assessment of Jordanian losses and was one of the factors which led the GHQs command to conclude that they stood no chance of maintaining control of the area and that they faced the stark choice of putting up a hopeless defence or a retreat in which no more lives would be lost than necessary.

In his telephone call to King Hussein on the morning of 6 June[61] Nasser suggested that Riad should send Amer a cable describing the situation on the West Bank. Although Nasser appeared to be worried he continued to claim that the EAF was raiding Israeli air fields. At midday on 6 June Riad sent the following message to Egypt's GHQ in Cairo:

> The situation on the West Bank is rapidly deteriorating. A concentrated attack has been launched on all axes, together with heavy fire, day and night. Jordanian, Syrian and Iraqi air forces in position H3 have been virtually destroyed. Upon consultation with King Hussein I have been asked to convey to you the following choices:

1. A political decision to cease fighting to be imposed by a third party (the USA, the Soviet Union or the Security Council).

2. To vacate the West Bank tonight.

3. To go on fighting for one more day, resulting in the isolation and destruction of the entire Jordanian Army.

King Hussein has asked me to refer this matter to you for an immediate reply.[62]

Half an hour later King Hussein sent a personal telegram to Nasser supporting Riad's earlier cable, stressing the dire situation on the Jordanian front and asking for his advice.[63]

At about the same time (12.30 p.m.) Amer replied to Riad's message. He advised the Jordanians to withdraw and suggested that the general population be issued with arms. However, the Jordanians decided to try to hold on in the hope that a ceasefire would be imposed while they were still in the West Bank. By the afternoon of 6 June news had begun to filter through to the Jordanian GHQs of the true situation on the Egyptian Front. This had a devastating effect on the Jordanian command. With the discovery that the Egyptians were on the retreat in Sinai and that Egypt's air capability had been destroyed came the realization that Israel was free to deploy a substantial proportion of its forces against Jordan. This spelt certain defeat for the Jordanians since they were already on the retreat. The Jordanian forces were prey to constant air attack and neither supplies nor reinforcements could reach the front lines. They felt that it was impossible for them to maintain resistance in such conditions. With these factors in mind Riad drew the conclusion that any regrouping operation was doomed to failure. Consequently, at about 10.00 a.m. an order for a general withdrawal of all Jordanian forces to the East Bank went out.[64]

Late in the evening of 6 June Nasser replied to King Hussein's cable. As well as praising King Hussein and the Jordanian army he advised him that the best solution was to vacate the West Bank that night while pressing for a ceasefire. In this telegram Nasser also provided the Jordanian GHQs with official confirmation of the destruction of the Egyptian air force.[65]

Shortly after the order for the withdrawal had been issued, the Jordanians were informed that the UN Security Council was meeting to consider a resolution for an unconditional ceasefire. On learning of this the Jordanian command decided that the order for withdrawal had been premature, since if a ceasefire went into effect that day they would still be in possession of the West Bank. Consequently, the order was countermanded and those forces which had already withdrawn were asked to return to their original positions.[66]

This counter-order led to considerable confusion amongst the forces in the West Bank and in many cases the troops found it impossible to return to their original positions. Khammash explains that some of the Jordanian 'units had already abandoned vitally important positions and they could not return. This naturally influenced the fighting from the third day onwards and was detrimental to the total war effort'.[67] In other cases the counter-order was not received because the front-line units had either cut or lost communication with their Commands. Throughout the war the Jordanians had experienced communication problems between army units and their commands. This was later attributed to interference by Israel.[68]

The Security Council ceasefire resolution was passed unanimously at 11.00 p.m. on 6 June. However, Jordan's hope that this would enable it to hold the West Bank was destroyed when Israel continued its offensive. On learning of this Riad once again ordered a complete withdrawal from the West Bank as he feared that failure to do so would result in the annihilation of the remains of the Jordanian Army. By nightfall on 7 June most elements of the army had withdrawn to the East Bank and by mid-day on 8 June Jordan was once again the Transjordan of King Abdullah, while Israel completed total occupation of historical Palestine.

Chapter 8

The war in perspective

Analysis of military operations in Jordan

The universal feeling amongst the Jordanian and military leaders who were either observers or actively involved in the 1967 war was that their major mistake was to rely on the help and leadership of other Arab nations. Although they do not believe that Israel could have been prevented from seizing the West Bank they do feel that they would have put up a harder fight on their own.[1] King Hussein later commented:

> In my view our first error was the fact that we did not organize our military operations on the basis of our own plans and according to our own capabilities. For so many years they talked to us about the Arab Command, the Commander-in-Chief of all the Arab armies and the assistance we could expect from our brethren . . . We relied on that which was natural. We should not have done so. For if we had not depended on the potential of outside support . . . war with Israel would undoubtedly have taken a totally different course. When one expects the air cover that I expected it was imperative that one acted the way I did. If our men had known from the beginning that they could not expect support from either Egypt, Syria or Iraq our strategy would have been different and Jerusalem would have been ours today. For during the first few days of this rapid war we placed Arab interest above our own. This is how I understood solidarity. Unfortunately no one else adhered to the same principle.[2]

The same feeling was expressed by Kawash:

> If we had stuck to a strategy of fighting our own battle with no expectations of Arab air cover, Arab troop reinforcements or a massive Egyptian and Syrian build-up in the southern and northern fronts which the previous propaganda campaign had led everyone to expect, the situation might have been different. We would have fought according to our own plans and strategy and would have put up a more determined stand, knowing in advance that we were alone, that there would be no air cover apart from our small, modest air force of 21 Hawker Hunters and that, accordingly, we should expect and plan how to handle a vastly superior air force and armour . . . If Jordan had been attacked by Israel in an all-out war without prior Arab defence pacts or agreements we would have been able to deal Israel a bloodier blow than it received from us in June.[3]

The Jordanians entered the war in the belief that two of their most urgent military requirements would be fulfilled by their Arab allies: air cover and troop reinforcements. The fact that neither of these requirements was fulfilled proved catastrophic.

The supremacy enjoyed by the IAF hindered every movement of the Jordanian troops and their support services. All the officers involved in the war speak with amazement of the way in which the IAF 'shot at anything that moved'[4] with an accuracy that they found incomprehensible unless the Israelis were receiving assistance from a superior power. Whenever the Jordanians succeeded in beating off an Israeli offensive the IAF was brought in and ensured an Israeli victory.

Kawash describes how Israeli troops

> received immediate air support whenever they requested it. They would not engage in a ground battle with Jordanian forces until those forces had been subject to heavy bombardment by Israeli aircraft over several sorties. The enemy air activity went on during the hours of darkness using flares. That was how the enemy could penetrate the Jenin sector and confront the infantry brigade there, and how it could penetrate the front lines of the Jordanian brigade north of Jerusalem while another Jordanian infantry brigade was engaged in bitter fighting inside Jerusalem itself, where the enemy was unable to achieve any success along the front line of the brigade.[5]

Khammash also describes the effect of Israeli air supremacy on the Jordanian army:

> In the three days of fighting our forces showed tremendous spirit and fighting capability but every move was subjected to fierce air attacks which hindered their capability tremendously. We were not merely fighting infantry and armoured forces. With our limited capability we were also fighting air strikes that were continuous night and day.[6]

The failure of Arab troops to arrive at their assigned positions in time was another important reason for Jordan's defeat. Khammash points out:

> We fought in co-ordination with our allies. Our operations were supposed to be part of a total, concerted effort and therefore the occupation of any particular position should have been part of that total effort. According to the defence pact, once the promised Arab forces arrived and were deployed in their positions, the JAF was meant to deploy in vital strategic positions so that this would enhance the operations from there on. In the event we were not able to do this, first, because the Arab forces did not arrive in time, and secondly, those forces that did arrive had been subjected to tremendous air attacks which rendered them ineffective by the time they reached the positions they were supposed to occupy.[7]

Israel launched its attack on Egypt before the troops which had been promised to Jordan had arrived at their assigned posts.[8] Cairo instructed Jordan immediately to implement its strategy of active defence on the basis that the promised troops would soon arrive.

The failure of Syria to enter the offensive against Israel was a major factor behind the loss of the northern West Bank. Jordan had joined forces with Egypt on the basis that Egypt and Syria would be the main fronts because of their large armies which if they acted in concert, should have been capable of defending their territory. Jordan's role was seen as a relatively minor one because of its limited military capability. Its function was to tie down a portion of Israel's forces and so minimize the strength of the Israeli offensive against its allies. Thus, when Jordan went on the offensive it was on the assumption that a large proportion of Israel's forces in the north would be occupied on the Syrian front. If the Syrians had attacked Israel they would have prevented it from transferring two armoured and two infantry brigades from the Syrian front to the Jordanian front. Instead, Israel was able to place additional troops in the Jenin–Nablus sector and, despite the valiant and prolonged resistance of the Jordanian army, eventually overrun it.

Syria's culpability in this regard was all the more damaging because it failed to provide Jordan with the aid it had promised. The Syrians had told Riad that they would send at least one brigade to Jordan. Consequently, when Riad received a message from Amer telling him that the Syrians would cover the northern West Bank he did not question it. It was on the basis of this information that he insisted that the 40th armoured brigade move to Jericho, despite the protests of the Jordanian officers. The fact that the Syrians failed to replace the 40th brigade opened the way for Israel's occupation of this area. Their complete refusal to respond to the pleas of Riad and Fawzi to come to the aid of Jordan when Israel was seizing the West Bank was one of the most bitter betrayals ever experienced by the Jordanians. Although the Syrians sent the 17th armoured brigade it arrived too late to participate in the war and it was quite apparent that it had no intention of fighting.

Syria's behaviour during the war confirmed every suspicion the Jordanians had ever had about their role in bringing about the war. Having embroiled Jordan in the war by inflaming Arab–Israeli tension and accusing Jordan of failing to support the Arabs, Syria sat back while Israel seized the West Bank. It was no wonder that after the war King Hussein felt that his Arab allies had let him down.[9]

Placing themselves under the leadership of Egypt was disastrous for the Jordanians. During the war the Egyptians were entirely caught up in the events taking place on their own territory and paid little attention to what was happening in Jordan. This is reflected in the fact that Nasser took twelve hours to reply to King Hussein's desperate telegram of 6 June asking for advice on how to deal with the rapidly deteriorating situation in the West Bank.

This point is made by Kawash:

> After the Egyptian air force had been crippled by the Israelis, the Egyptian command was trying to salvage its forces from Sinai and paid very little attention to the operations

on the West Bank after they had misled our command into believing that it was the Israeli air force that was crippled following its initial raids on Egyptian bases and after having requested Riad to launch operations on the Jordanian front.[10]

This was damaging to the Jordanians who had placed themselves in the hands of the Egyptians without any reservations and were dependent on their guidance.

The Egyptians also misled the Jordanians about events in the south. Their instructions had presented an illusory picture which had no foundation in fact. The Jordanians disregarded their carefully laid plans, which led to disaster. Most damaging of all were Egypt's instructions that Jordan should commence offensive operations at a time when Amer had already issued orders for a general withdrawal from Sinai. Riad was also misled and drew the conclusion that since the Egyptians were advancing into the Negev, Israel's main offensive would come from the area between Hebron and Jerusalem. In fact, it came along the Ramallah–Jerusalem axis in precisely the way the Jordanians had predicted. Thus, while Syrian inactivity cost the Jordanians the northern West Bank, Egyptian misinformation and misdirection cost them the southern West Bank. Tragically, although the Jordanians realized that the orders coming from Cairo did not make sound military sense, and in some cases were incomprehensible, they still carried them out because they believed that the need to co-operate with their allies and participate in a concerted Arab effort overrode all other considerations.

One of the points made by many Jordanians is that they should not have allowed a non-Jordanian to command their troops. Lt General Haditha remarked that

a Jordanian Commander would not only have known the topography of the region but also the men he commanded and what every step meant to them, regardless of his experience or his ability to command in times of war. For example, a decision to withdraw from any part of the West Bank would have been calculated by a Jordanian Commander on the basis of the knowledge of the importance of one position or another, no matter how small or unimportant that position might seem on the map. The knowledge that a decision to withdraw from any position in the West Bank might mean abandoning that position forever was bound to be viewed from a different perspective by the men in the field and a Jordanian Commander.[11]

The same view was expressed by Field Marshall Habes Majali:

The outcome would have differed drastically if the Jordanians had been left to conduct their own operations. We knew every inch of our land, we knew the exact locations that were to our advantage or disadvantage and the logic behind this, we knew which of our field commanders possessed sufficient initiative to take advantage of situations and which did not. In times of war you cannot and should not be expected to have to explain all these matters to an outsider in an operations room, even if that outsider was as competent and capable a commander as Abdul Munim Riad.[12]

Despite their belief that Riad was a capable commander, many Jordanians are critical of the decisions he made during the June war. They argue that his strategy for defence in the West Bank was ill-conceived and point out that the original deployment of the Jordanian forces had been based on preventing limited Israeli raids on Jordanian border towns, not on repulsing a full-scale Israeli invasion. When the Arabs realized that the situation was escalating into full-scale war, that it was almost certain that Israel would invade the West Bank and that Jordan had the support of other Arab troops and the promise of air cover, there should have been a complete redeployment of the Jordanian forces to concentrate them along the two main axes of probable Israeli advance.

Of particular concern to the Jordanians is Riad's failure to implement Operation Tariq. They argue that he did not appreciate the importance of Jerusalem and that his strategy in this area was at fault. Salim explains that

> left to myself on the morning of 5 June I would have moved the 27th (Imam Ali) infantry brigade from the Jericho area to the eastern and northern hills of Jerusalem immediately upon receiving the order to initiate operations in the West Bank. This would have enabled us swiftly to storm Mount Scopus. This was essential because we knew that any Israeli thrust towards Arab Jerusalem would aim to break through our defences in Sheikh Jarrach and establish contact with the Israeli garrison on the Mount and from there threaten to encircle Arab Jerusalem. If we had been allowed to do this we might have thwarted the Israeli advance and engaged them in a long and protracted battle. It would have given our defence of Jerusalem the right depth in the right area, in the north-west, which was more important to the Israelis than the value of Al-Mukkaber to us – even though this was a vital strategic point. As it happened, two-thirds of the brigade remained in the Jericho area and despite belated orders never managed to put its weight into fighting for the city. Only one battalion of this brigade was given the task of occupying Al-Mukkaber and this was forced to retreat less than three hours later, sustaining heavy losses in the process.
>
> Moreover, I would have requested and insisted on deploying another artillery battalion to augment the defence of Jerusalem as well as moving some tank companies to strengthen and support the two infantry brigades.
>
> In the event, the occupation of Al-Mukkaber was given priority over Mount Scopus and Riad insisted on this ill-fated and unrealistic operation.
>
> Operation Tariq would have enabled our forces in the Jerusalem, Ramallah and Hebron sectors, as well as the 60th armoured brigade, to encircle Jerusalem and totally upset Israel's plans for that axis. However, this operation should have been initiated as soon as hostilities began in order to avoid the anticipated Israeli air raids.[13]

If one examines the course of events in Jerusalem one can see that Salim's strategic concept would have been correct. Acting on the basis of the information provided by Cairo, Riad anticipated an Israeli attack from the south. In fact, it came from the north – between Jerusalem and Ramallah. Had Riad given more credence to the Jordanian point of view which correctly foresaw this action, he would have provided additional forces for the defence of

Jerusalem and Ramallah. This would have given that axis the extra depth it badly needed to resist the Israeli thrust towards Sheikh Jarrach and Mount Scopus and to prevent the encirclement of Jerusalem by Israel. Keeping the 27th infantry brigade as a reserve force in the Jericho area did not help Jericho when Jerusalem fell, nor did it help defend the northern approaches to Jerusalem.

Two further observations can be made. First, Jericho is separated from Jerusalem by a distance of about 50 km of difficult and arid mountainous terrain. Troops moving along this road were an easy target for air raids and their efforts to participate in the fighting were frustrated. For this reason, keeping the 27th infantry brigade as a reserve force in the area of Jericho was a grave tactical error. A commander who was knowledgeable about the topography of the area would have hastened to move at least two battalions of the brigade to the eastern hills of Jerusalem in Abu Dis, Ezzariyah, Mount of Olives and Al-Tur, which overlook the Old City. This would have made any attempt by Israel to encircle Arab Jerusalem via Mount Scopus difficult and costly.

Secondly, a military commander with experience of the area would have anticipated that given the importance of Jerusalem, the Israelis would attack it in great strength, using infantry and armoured units. In fact, Jordanian intelligence indicated the possibility that Israel would use some of its paratroops in order to make a quick and effective breakthrough of the extremely well-prepared Jordanian positions north-west of Jerusalem in the areas of Sheikh Jarrach and French Hill. Counterattacking the Israeli paratroops with elements of the 27th brigade without armoured support was doomed to failure. Riad should have sent units of the 60th armoured brigade to Jerusalem much earlier than he did, leaving other units as reserves in the Jericho area.

If a battalion of the 60th armoured brigade had been sent to Jerusalem as soon as hostilities opened, together with the 27th infantry brigade and a second artillery battalion, events in this sector would have been markedly different. One infantry brigade, supported by only one artillery battalion, put up tremendous resistance for two days and two nights against Israel's superior force. Therefore it is not difficult to imagine the strength of Jordanian resistance if those forces had been doubled and given the support of an armoured battalion. Jordan's military experts conclude that such a deployment of Jordanian troops might have preserved the whole of Arab Jerusalem or at least parts of it, such as Al-Tur, the Mount of Olives and the eastern hills, from falling into Israel's hands. Had Jerusalem not fallen before the UN ceasefire was imposed it is possible that the West Bank as a whole might have been saved.[14]

It is clear from Israel's operations in the area west of Jerusalem that the Jordanians' assessment of Israel's strategy was correct. Israel's GHQs appreciated the great strategic importance of the area west/north-west of Jerusalem (this is the narrow western path known as the Jerusalem Corridor which connects Jerusalem with Tel Aviv) in determining the destiny of the city and influencing its final battle, as well as the battle for the whole of the West Bank. In Latrun the Israelis dedicated one armoured brigade and one mechanized infantry brigade. However, because Riad was expecting the Israeli offensive to come from the south the Jordanians failed to match the strength of these forces. The Jordanians' insistence that they should initiate Operation Tariq was correct. It would have cut off the strategically vital path connecting Jewish Jerusalem with Tel Aviv, prevented the passage of Israeli forces to and from Jerusalem from the west and isolated the city from Israel.

By defending the hills of north-west Jerusalem the Jordanians would have increased their chances of successfully defending Latrun and confusing Israel's plans and preparations for the occupation of Arab Jerusalem. However, since the Jordanians were fighting under the command of the Joint Arab Command and were subject to Egyptian leadership, they were unable to implement their plans.

Another Jordanian criticism of Riad is that he should not have taken Amer's report about the destruction of 75 per cent of Israel's planes at face value.[15] Field Marshall Majali argues that the failure of Egypt to reply to Jordan's report about intense air activity over Israel on the morning of 5 June, and to the cable Riad sent to Cairo at 12.45 p.m. requesting information about the situation on the southern front, should have been taken much more seriously. Riad should have found out why Cairo had twice failed to respond to his messages and been alert to the possibility that communications were being interfered with. He should also have been suspicious when Egypt reported the destruction of 75 per cent of the Israeli air force and tried to verify it either through Jordanian intelligence or aerial reconnaissance. Such a response did not require extraordinary perception.[16] Dr Nussaibah claims that a number of Jordanian politicians who listened to Radio Cairo spontaneously concluded that its claims about Egyptian successes could not be true and that, in fact, it must signify that something had gone badly wrong on the Egyptian front.[17] This perception was lacking in Riad and it cost the Jordanians dear.

Field Marshall Majali is also critical of Riad's failure to listen to the Jordanians' point of view. He remembers that Riad 'refused to listen to or take into account views of Jordanian field commanders and actually quarrelled with Brigadier Atef Majali. He insisted on carrying out his orders to the letter despite the fact that he was made aware of the dire consequences which would result'.[18] This reluctance to take notice of the advice of the Jordanian commanders is extraordinary considering that they had been planning and training to deal with an Israeli offensive for years. Had Riad paid more attention to their views the events of 5–7 June might have been different.

Despite these criticisms of Riad most Jordanians also admit that in view of the rapid collapse of the Egyptian front and Syrian inaction the ultimate outcome of the war would probably have been the same, no matter who had been commanding the Jordanian forces. For example, Haditha said that 'the final outcome would not have differed very much in view of the superior power we faced both on the ground and from the air and also in view of the collapse of the front on which we depended so heavily'.[19] King Hussein also commented that 'considering the peculiar character of the three days battle in Jordan which Riad directed, knowing neither the terrain nor the capacities of the men under his command, while at the mercy of the fantastic misinformation regarding the situation on the various allied fronts, he could not have done better'.[20]

Kawash expressed the same view:

> Given the realities of the Jordanian Front, the enemy's overwhelming superiority and the quick collapse of the Southern front [Egypt], any commander of the Jordanian Front would have found himself with little or no room for manoeuvre. In fact the military alternatives available to him would have been very few . . . If a Jordanian commander had been in charge he might have conducted operations on the Jordanian Front differently, but the outcome would have been exactly the same.[21]

Khammash argues somewhat differently. He points out that Riad 'was quick to grasp the realities of the situation in the few days he spent in Amman before the war started', and that the real problem was Egypt's misdirection: 'The main fault was in Cairo's conception of our requirements and strategy rather than Riad's command.'[22]

Salim makes the same point: 'The outcome would have been no different if a Jordanian rather than an Egyptian had been in command. Besides his total adherence to his superiors' instructions, Riad's problem was the lack of air support and the rapid collapse of the Egyptian front which enabled Israel to concentrate its forces against Jordan and later Syria.'[23]

Riad's real problem was that he was caught between two conflicting demands and lacked the knowledge or the will to choose between them wisely. He found that he had been placed in command of an area of which he had limited knowledge. He received information from Cairo which painted a false picture and was given a series of orders which represented a complete departure from the strategy which had been previously agreed. These orders were bitterly opposed by his Jordanian officers, who, although of lower rank, were more knowledgeable of the strategic realities of the area than he was. Thus, he found himself in a most unenviable position. His solution to this dilemma was to obey the orders of his superiors to the letter. However, that he was not always sure about the wisdom of the orders is evident from his handling of Operations Directive No. 7. This order concerned the controversial and ultimately catastrophic decision to move the 40th and 60th brigades to Jericho, and

Hebron respectively. Whilst Riad signed every other order 'General Abdul Munim Riad, Commander of the Advanced Post in Amman', this one is signed 'General Muhammad Fawzi, Commander-in-Chief of the Joint Arab Command, under delegation by General Abdul Munim Riad'. This indicates that, on this particular occasion, Riad was dissociating himself from the disastrous consequences which he realized might result from the order.

Jordan's acceptance of the Egyptian's claim that they had destroyed 75 per cent of Israel's air force and were on the offensive in Sinai played a crucial part in the events that followed. King Hussein described the effect of Egyptian misinformation:

> We were misinformed about what had happened in Egypt when the Israelis attacked the UAR air bases. A new message from Amer informed us that the Israeli air offensive was continuing. But at the same time, he insisted that the Egyptians had put 75 per cent of the Israel air force out of action! The same message said that UAR bombers had destroyed the Israeli bases in a counterattack and that the ground forces of the Egyptian army had penetrated into Israel by way of the Negev!
>
> These reports – fantastic to say the least – had much to do with our confusion and false interpretation of the situation.[24]

Egypt's false claims of success had four significant effects on the war in Jordan.

The belief that Egypt had successfully beaten off the Israeli attack and had entered the offensive led the Jordanians to concur with Amer's directive that Jordan should not wait for the arrival of the troops promised by Iraq, Saudi Arabia and Syria but should immediately mount its plan for active defence and open fire along the entire front. This was a major tactical error. First, the Jordanians opened fire without any clear strategy or set of objectives. Instead of launching attacks according to carefully devised plans against vital targets inside enemy territory, the Jordanian General Command issued orders to its forces to open fire with their artillery and machine guns at enemy positions facing them, reaping very little strategic or tactical benefit. Mustafa points out that although 'this fire cost the enemy more than a few casualties and inflicted on its establishments and deployments some substantial destruction, it did not affect the enemy's efficiency or operations or stop its forces from setting into motion their plan to attack Jordan'.[25]

Secondly, the Jordanians opened hostilities against a numerically superior force which they had little chance of defeating. The belief that the Israelis were still engaged in combat in Sinai meant that the Commander of the Advanced Post misjudged the strength of the forces which Israel was able to pitch against Jordan. The rapid collapse of Egypt enabled Israel to deploy forces intended for Egypt against Jordan. The parachute brigade which played such an important part in the battle for Jerusalem and which had originally been detailed for

El-Arish is an example of this. The result of this uneven balance of forces was the decimation of the Jordanian army.

In spite of Israel's protestations to the contrary, any military analyst should have recognized that the arrival of large numbers of Arab troops and Iraqi planes in Jordan would inevitably make Israel anxious swiftly to act against Jordan before these new forces were fully deployed. Therefore, Jordan should have realized that it was absolutely essential to avoid giving Israel any excuse to launch an offensive against it before those troops had reached their battle stations. Instead, the Jordanians opened the offensive along the length of the border, thus obviating any need for Israel to hold back. The decision to go on the offensive was also influenced by Egypt's message that a ceasefire would be imposed that night and that the Arabs should therefore try to press home their 'advantage'.

Field Marshall Majali is critical of Riad for acting so hastily. He feels that he should not have taken Amer's message on trust but should have assessed the nature of the Israeli thrust on all fronts and found out what forces were available to Israel for deployment against Jordan. The army should have been instructed to do no more than engage Israel in limited activity in order to test its strength.[26]

Salim argues that the Jordanians should have waited twenty-four hours in order to see how events were progressing on the Egyptian front before embarking on the offensive.[27] In fact, this was one of the major points agreed at the talks in Cairo on 30 May. Tal also writes that Jordanian commanders felt that as the weaker power of the Arab alliance Jordan should have waited for definite news of the outcome of the battle between Egypt and Israel.[28] By going on the offensive the Jordanians were acting against all their previous plans. They had never believed they would be able to occupy Israeli territory as instructed by Nasser and Amer on the morning of 5 June, and to try to do so without troop reinforcements, and without knowing the extent of the opposition, was unrealistic.

Amer's false information also influenced Jordan's decision to wait for Syria and Iraq to join them in conducting air strikes against Israel on the morning of 5 June. The Jordanians believed that since the Israeli air force was already under attack by the Egyptians, and apparently badly hit, a delay on their part would not alter the effect of their own air attack. In fact, the three-hour delay proved disastrous. Many Jordanians[29] and other military observers[30] believe that if the Arabs had succeeded in launching a well-planned and well co-ordinated attack on Israel's air fields while the IAF was engaged in attacking Egypt, they would have been able to destroy Israeli planes refuelling and rearming after their first raids on Egypt or while returning to their base with empty tanks and no ammunition. They would also have been able to cause extensive damage to Israel air fields, making it difficult for the returning Israeli planes to land. By causing the destruction of a large number of Israeli planes in this way the Arabs might have been able to jeopardize Israel's air supremacy. As it was, by midday the Israelis had finished their attack on Egypt and were able to turn their attention to the other Arab air forces.[31]

The information passed by Egypt to Jordan was one of the reasons for the sense of panic and confusion that characterized operations on the Jordanian front. Because they were acting on false premises the Jordanians were completely unprepared for the strength of the Israeli offensive both on land and in the air. They were also implementing activities for which they had no pre-arranged plans. Consequently, considerable chaos and confusion resulted at GHQs in Amman and in the field. Order was followed by counter-order, which did little to increase the morale of the soldiers. For example, at 12.40 on 5 June the 60th armoured brigade was instructed to prepare to advance to Hebron that afternoon. At 5.00 p.m. this order was countermanded: one of the 60th armoured brigade's tank squadrons was instructed to join the Hashemite brigade in Ramallah and another was instructed to join the Imam Ali battalion in Jerusalem. At 5.15 p.m the brigade was placed under the direction of Western Command and two of its regiments were given further instructions to reinforce other areas. Quarter of an hour later all these instructions were countermanded and new orders issued.[32] This pattern of order and counter-order was repeated many times throughout the war and depleted the Jordanian soldiers' fighting ability.

This sense of confusion was increased by the air bombardment the Jordanian troops received from the IAF, which was all the more stunning since the Jordanians believed that Egypt had knocked out a large number of Israeli planes. The troops found that every move they made was subjected to fierce air attack, which made it almost impossible to implement their orders. The communication difficulties experienced by the various army units added to the sense of chaos and lack of direction. Under these circumstances it is hardly surprising if the Jordanian army did not do justice to its fighting capability.

Egypt's false information about its destruction of the Israeli air force made Israel's air supremacy incomprehensible to the Jordanians. It was hardly surprising that this was one of the factors which led King Hussein to concur with Nasser when the latter accused America of providing Israel with air support. The conversation held between Nasser and King Hussein was intercepted by Israel and broadcast by them to the world.[33] This false accusation alienated public opinion and helped quell Western criticism of Israel's aggressive action in Jordan.

The evidence of the radar at Ajloun also appeared to indicate that Israel was receiving help from a foreign aircraft carrier. Juma'a describes how the 'radar screen showed successive waves of aircraft in great numbers land in Israel from the direction of the Mediterranean sea. The viewers watching this became confused so they conveyed what was recorded on the screen to the [Advanced Post of] the JAC [in Amman] which, in turn, believed that these waves were foreign aircraft taking part in the battle ... anyone seeing the radar screen would have concluded that these fighters were coming in from the sea, presumably from an aircraft carrier near by'.[34] The radar appeared to show the presence of aeroplanes at two points over the Mediterranean. One was 40 km north of Bardaweel and the other was north-east of Port Said. These planes flew towards Israel and disappeared from the screen in the area of Lod airport. The screen also showed the presence of stationary objects in the Meditteranean.[35] The only explanation available to the Jordanians was that American aircraft carriers were being used to bolster Israel's activities.

King Hussein explains that another reason for his acceptance of Nasser's claim was the fact that Jordanian pilots and ground forces mistook Israeli Mysteres for Hawker Hunters to the extent of not firing on them when they attacked Jordanian troops. Since they knew that Israel did not have any Hawker Hunters they concluded that they must be foreign planes fighting on the side of Israel.[36]

Jordan's acceptance of Egypt's claim that on 5 June one of their divisions was marching into the Negev resulted in one of the most disastrous episodes of the war. This was the movement south of the 40th and 60th armoured brigades. This claim was made when, in reality, the Egyptian air force had been annihilated and the Egyptian army was actually retreating from Sinai. The destruction that resulted from this instruction was exacerbated by the failure of the Syrians to provide support for Jordan's right flank as instructed by the Joint Arab Command in Cairo.

Many Jordanians are particularly critical of this decision of Riad's.[37] Majali argues that instead of moving the 60th armoured brigade south, Riad should have sent it to Jerusalem as soon as hostilities opened in order to strengthen the Jordanian forces there because the 'defence of Jerusalem was a million times more important to Jordan than the possibility of meeting up with an alleged advance of an Egyptian division. Riad should have waited at least twelve hours to find out the situation of that division before embarking on such a risky move'.[38]

Riad defended his decision by arguing that he acted reasonably in view of the information passed to him by his superiors in Egypt. He had been told that the Israelis were concentrated in the region of Bersheeba and to the west and were expected to attack along two axes: Jerusalem (Nabi Musa) and Al-Khalil (Hebron) north of the Dead Sea. Although it was possible that the Israelis might also seek to enter at Jenin, he felt that according to the intelligence reports available at the time it was more likely that they would seek to enter from the south. He pointed out that 'change of positions during a battle because of a new surprise element is a sound procedure that needs to be understood'.[39]

However, if intelligence reported that Israel had concentrated its forces around Bersheeba and to the west, this indicated that Israel was intending to deploy these forces against the Egyptian front and not the Jordanian front. Mustafa points out that it is therefore

> inconceivable that the enemy should aim to attack the Hebron sector from Bersheeba because the ultimate objective of this attack was to reach the vital area of Jerusalem. But the enemy could have attacked Jerusalem directly without advancing towards it from Bersheeba, which is a distance of about 130 km. Hebron was always of second or third importance to the defence of the West Bank. We therefore disagree with the late commander that the situation dictated strengthening with the 60th armoured brigade since there were other Jordanian sectors of greater importance which had a more desperate need of armour – for example, the Jerusalem sector and the Jerusalem Corridor running through Latrun, as well as Jenin and Nablus.[40]

In fact, the primary importance of the Jerusalem sector should have dictated moving part of the Hittin (infantry) brigade from the Hebron sector and deploying it in Bethlehem and Sur Baher to be ready for use in the battle for Jerusalem.

Mustafa also argues[41] that if the 40th armoured brigade had remained where it was the Jordanians might have been able to hold Jenin for longer. Moving the brigade to Jericho made it extremely difficult for it to return in time to be of use. The distance between Jericho and Jenin is approximately 80 km and takes four hours for armoured vehicles to cover. In fact, it took the brigade over eight hours because it had to travel by night in order to avoid the IAF. It had already sustained significant losses from the IAF on its journey south and so had been weakened even before it engaged the Israelis in combat in Jenin.

A close examination of the terrain of the northern West Bank leads to the conclusion that if the Jordanian GHQs had assessed the situation correctly it would have recognized that Israel's air superiority (regardless of what had happened on the Egyptian front) dictated that it should have moved the armoured reserve for the Jenin axis to an area closer to that axis where it could launch a counterattack as soon as the enemy broke through Jordanian positions. As the duty of the brigade was to cover the northern sector of the West Bank and to be prepared to counterattack in several directions, Tubas would have been an appropriate location.[42] From there it would have been close to all the important approaches which Israel was likely to attack in the northern part of the West Bank, including Jenin, Nablus and the northern sector of the Jordan Valley. It would have been in a position to help all these approaches and to initiate a rapid counterattack on Israeli forces breaking through any of them.

Mustafa further argues that if 'the Jordanian forces in the area of Jenin had attacked the enemy in the first few hours of the war when Israel was still engaged in its air raids on Egypt and attempted to co-ordinate this with further attacks in Tulkarem and Qalqilya, supported by Jordanian and Iraqi air forces and perhaps the Syrian air force', Jenin might have been saved. However, he admits that in the circumstances, although such tactics would have delayed Israel's occupation of Jenin they would have not prevented its ultimate fall. The only thing that would have prevented this would have been, if, in addition to the measures described above, Syria had launched its offensive from the north, thereby occupying the forces which, in fact, were used against Jordan in the Jenin–Nablus axis.[43]

Ebeidat points out that 'in a defensive battle a commander can control the situation and repulse the enemy offensive by a balanced distribution of forces. If he alters this balance prior to the battle by making unnecessary movements he loses the initiative and throws himself to the will of the enemy and consequently loses the battle'.[44] In fact Jordanian armour was well distributed when the war began. There was no need to alter this balance until the situation on the Egyptian front was clear. If the information contained in Amer's cable had been correct, the situation did not warrant the despatch of the 60th brigade to the Hebron area. If Egyptian defences had managed to destroy or damage 75 per cent of enemy aircraft and were mounting a counterattack in Israel, and Egyptian land forces were attacking the enemy in the Negev, this could only mean that Egypt's position on the southern front was strong and did not need the assistance of one Jordanian armoured brigade in its advance in the Negev. This armoured brigade and all the other Jordanian armour was needed to attack vital areas on the Jordanian front which were considered to be the heart of Israel, such as the area of Jerusalem, the road connecting it with Tel Aviv and the strategically important hills lying north-west of Jerusalem. This would have been more helpful to the Egyptian war effort than despatching the 60th brigade to Hebron. According to Mustafa, attacking these sensitive areas 'would have confused the enemy's military leadership, upset its plans and forced it to redirect a large part of its efforts and forces to the Jordanian front which, as such, would ultimately have facilitated the task of the Egyptians in the south'.[45] All the military observers referred to above also ask if it was right to deploy Jordanian armour to ease the pressure on the Egyptian forces in the south, thereby depriving the Jordanian forces of half their armour at a time when the front was open to Israel's onslaught.

Jordanian military strategists[46] also point out that Riad's instructions to the armoured brigades were a serious tactical error, which also led to their fragmentation. The armoured brigades were supposed to be used as a counter-penetration striking force of great weight which would prevent the enemy from penetrating any particular sector. By breaking the brigades up into small units this capability was destroyed and they were no longer able to present a serious threat to Israel's superior force of armoured and mechanized units. This is illustrated by the experience of a battalion of the 60th armoured brigade which was overrun by the Harel brigade at Tal Al-Ful near Jerusalem on the second day of the war.

The Jordanian leadership is critical of some of its front-line commanders who sent back exaggerated reports of the losses their units had suffered during the battle. King Hussein notes that these reports gave rise to greater pessimism than the situation warranted.[47] This is evident from King Hussein's telegram to Nasser which refers to the loss of one Jordanian tank every ten minutes. This assessment was undoubtedly a major factor behind the first order to withdraw late on 6 June. Majali feels that these reports were

> a reflection of the personal cowardice of those commanders and their urgent desire to escape from a battle which they never realized would be so destructive and intense – particularly when they found themselves under constant, ruthless air attacks.[48]

However, in spite of this, he goes on to say that

> all the heroic stories we later heard about men fighting gallantly to the bitter end and never contemplating withdrawing, but preferring to stay and face certain death, is the true fighting spirit of the Jordanian armed forces. Even Israeli commanders had to admit in their memoirs the determined and brave stand put up by the Jordanians during the June war.[49]

The early issue of the order to withdraw from the West Bank on the evening of 6 June and the confusion that surrounded it is one of the most crucial mistakes made during the war. It can be argued that the first of the three choices Riad put to Nasser, to ask for a ceasefire, was in contradiction with the second, to withdraw from the West Bank immediately, since there was no point in getting a ceasefire unless the Jordanian forces held on to their existing positions. For this reason it was wrong to think of withdrawing from the West Bank at all. Most Jordanian military experts[50] share the view that the only salvage of the situation would have been to remain in the West Bank until the end – particularly if a ceasefire resolution had been pressed for more urgently.

Khammash is one of those Jordanians who argue that the order to withdraw came too soon. He believes that they 'should have regrouped in certain positions and pressed for a Security Council Resolution before really contemplating total withdrawal. In fact, the Security Council Resolution did come at the end of the second day – after Riad had issued the order for withdrawal'.[51] King Hussein also admits that the decision to withdraw was wrong. He argues that the ceasefire resolution came when the Jordanian army still held many areas of the West Bank, but unfortunately Riad had just issued an order for its withdrawal.[52] The order also had a detrimental effect on the Jordanian units at the front lines. According to Ejailan, Haditha was furious about the withdrawal order because he felt it was premature, and expressed great relief when it was cancelled one hour later.[53]

The same point is illustrated by the telegram sent by Brigadier Turki Baara, the Commander of Princess Alia brigade, to Khammash on the evening of 6 June. He expressed the unit's displeasure at having to withdraw from their secure positions and then attempting to return to them. Only his Command and forty soldiers succeeded in returning because of the intense air attacks of the IAF.[54]

Majali and Haditha argue that a Jordanian commander would never have given in to the Israelis so easily but would have fought longer and harder.[55] As Commander of the Eastern Front, Haditha was in charge of all the reserve troops situated on the East Bank. He says that in his view 'this withdrawal was not necessary. I was not defeated. I did not even take part in the fight'.[56] His complaint is not that the war could have been won, but that the Jordanian 'defeat was so cheap to the Israelis'.[57] Like many other Jordanian military leaders, he believes that the Jordanians should have attempted to regroup the army around Jerusalem in order to put up the fiercest resistance possible before contemplating a complete withdrawal. When the order for withdrawal was issued, many Jordanian army units in Jerusalem were still in their positions, including some in the Old City and eastern hills. He stresses that the reserve infantry brigade situated behind Jerusalem and the brigade at Hebron were ordered to withdraw before they had participated in any serious fighting. When the Jordanian army units in the West Bank received the order to withdraw, many of them were furious because they were fully prepared to continue the battle to defend their land.[58]

Haditha feels that

> despite Israeli air superiority we were capable of regrouping and perhaps changing our fighting strategy to a protracted fight, particularly in certain positions like Jerusalem. I know the logistics may have been extremely difficult in view of the continuing air attacks on our forces day and night, but this should not have been sufficient to force us to abandon our positions before putting up a determined and strong fight. Jerusalem was worth every bit of a fight to the finish. Had we regrouped and decided on such a fight we would have given Israel a hard time and, I believe, a bloody nose as well.[59]

This view is repeated by Majali. He argues that the order for the withdrawal should only have been given after the Jordanians had tried to regroup by withdrawing units and reorganizing them in new defence lines. No place should have been abandoned without the prior establishment of a new defence line behind it. In particular he argues that the Jordanians should have attempted to form new defence lines on the Jenin–Tubas axis and between Jerusalem and Jericho. This would have forced the Israelis to enter a protracted battle and been to the Jordanians' advantage, because of the chance that a ceasefire would be imposed before the Israelis had succeeded in causing a further retreat. Like Haditha he points out that some brigades had not seen any active combat, yet Riad made no attempt to redeploy them around Jerusalem to provide protection for the units which were retreating and to make a final stand against the Israeli advance.[60]

It is important to stress that these feelings are not merely the result of hindsight. At the time, Jordanian military officers drew up plans for continued resistance in the West Bank. Kawash describes how,

> on 6 June in the afternoon, I proposed, through Brigadier Atef Majali, a plan for a counterattack by the last light of 6 June, to be launched by an infantry battalion of a brigade that remained intact in the region behind Nablus, together with a tank battalion as part of it . . . This force was to mount a counterattack against the right flank of the Israeli forces which were approaching Aqqaba Dam, the objective of the Jordanian force being to recapture the Qabatiya Triangle. This strike would have been launched, together with an assault by a battalion of the Valley Sector brigade reinforced with elements of armour, in the area of Bissan with the aim of capturing specific targets south of Bissan, thereby disrupting the Israeli plan and enemy forces within the sector.[61]

This proposal was discussed but was not adopted in view of the early withdrawal of the Jordanian army. In the evening of 6 June, when it had become clear that Israel controlled the north-western and southern sectors of the city of Jerusalem and the fate of the remaining force in the old city was uncertain, Brigadier Atef Majali suggested despatching an infantry brigade and a tank battalion (which were stationed in the region of Bethlehem and Hebron) to mount a counterattack aimed at penetrating the city of Jerusalem from the south when Israeli forces least expected it. According to Brigadier Majali: 'These forces which had captured Jerusalem were exhausted and elements of our forces were showing resistance in various pockets.' Although the proposal was discussed it was ultimately dismissed by Riad.[62]

The command structure of the Jordanian forces proved to be inefficient. The number of brigades under the control of Western Command (seven infantry and, during most of the war period, two armoured) was far more than it could efficiently co-ordinate and control. Communication between brigades and Western Command HQs at Ramallah was often difficult and occasionally impossible. While this may have been the result of interference by Israel, the heavy demands made on Western Front HQs did not help matters. There were a number of incidents in which this HQs wanted to pass new instructions to front-line or retreating units but was unable to get in touch with them.[63] The reverse situation also happened in which front-line or retreating units found that they could not get through to their HQs and some then made direct contact with GHQs in Amman.[64]

Western Front Command also had difficulty in co-ordinating the large number of forces under its control. Events moved so rapidly in the three days of war and were further complicated by the arrival (or non-arrival) of additional Arab troops. This led to confusion at both HQs and in the field, vividly illustrated by an incident that occurred on 5 June. One of the reasons for the slow return of the 40th armoured brigade from Jericho to Jenin that day was that along the narrow road connecting Jericho with Damia it encountered elements of the 8th Iraqi brigade en route and could not pass it easily. Thus, the desperately needed armour was subjected to unnecessary delay.

After the war it was recognized that the Command structure was too unwieldy and it was changed to become more streamlined and efficient.[65]

The role of politics on the course of the war

By the evening of 5 June the Jordanian GHQs realized that unless Israel could be stopped by political means they would lose the West Bank. The Jordanians hoped that a ceasefire would be imposed while they were still in control of the West Bank. By noon the following day the situation in Jordan had rapidly deteriorated. Most of Jerusalem's northern and north-western areas had been occupied and the Jordanian command realized that this, and the growing likelihood that Israel would soon have Arab Jerusalem completely surrounded, meant that they might be forced to order a full-scale retreat from the West Bank. The Jordanian Foreign Minister, Ahmed Toukan, telephoned the Jordanian ambassador, Dr Muhammad Al-Farra, at the UN HQs in New York. He told him that the war was going against Jordan and that they needed to get a ceasefire as soon as possible since Israel was seizing more Jordanian territory with every passing second. Farra adamantly refused to obey Toukan's instructions, even though Toukan explained the dire situation in the West Bank and pleaded with him to listen.[66] This was also the attitude taken by the Egyptian ambassador at the UN.[67]

The reason for Farra's extraordinary behaviour was that the Arab delegates at the UN were following the war on 'Saut Al-Arab' broadcasting from Cairo. The Egyptian radio station misled its audience about the true state of affairs because it was conveying propaganda designed to maintain the morale of the Arab masses. It claimed that the Arabs were not merely fending off the Israelis but actually had them on the retreat. Consequently, the Jordanian delegate could not understand his Foreign Minister's request to obtain a ceasefire. According to Nussaibah, the Israelis also encouraged Arab UN Ambassadors in their false belief by keeping silent about the true situation.[68]

As a result of this debacle the Israelis were given more time in which to consolidate their hold on the West Bank. It was not until 11.00 p.m. on 6 June that the UN passed a resolution demanding a ceasefire, and it was Thursday 8 June when the Jordanian government informed the Secretary General, U Thant, that they accepted it.[69]

Most Arab commentators observe that the short time allotted to the Arab allies to co-ordinate their plans was a major political cause of their defeat.[70] The underlying reason for all this was the fragmented state of Arab politics.

According to King Hussein, 'lack of co-ordination and lack of co-operation long before the war were the major reasons for the defeat of the Arab world'.[71] Khammash comments: 'We should not have entered war without a mutual and co-ordinated plan, but unfortunately Arab politics deprived us of this'.[72]

Riad also lays the blame for the Arab defeat squarely at the feet of Arab politics. He points out that

> engaging in a battle with the enemy requires previous co-ordination and co-operation. The UAC which was involved in this work had been paralysed one year before the battle. Consequently, there was no co-ordination in the true sense of the word. Preparations for the Operations stage was not done in an acceptable way. The Advanced Command set up a few days before the battle could not have done more than it did. This was a clear error of Arab politics which harmed the Arab soldier even before Israel.[73]

Whilst Jordan had a strong ideological and political interest in a unified Arab world and genuinely tried to achieve this, it was at fault for failing to recognize at an earlier stage that the need to patch up its differences with Egypt should have overridden all other considerations. Israel's raid on Samu had made the Jordanians fully aware of how vulnerable the West Bank was and aroused their suspicions that Israel was intent on war. Despite this Jordan failed to compromise on certain issues in order to establish a much-needed co-operation. The Arab world was still deeply divided one week before the outbreak of hostilities. This meant that the degree of co-ordination between the Arab allies was minimal. In Jordan Riad had no time to draw up a carefully thought-out plan of action. King Hussein points out that 'it wasn't until Riad arrived in Amman and we learned the exact potential of the Iraqi forces joining ours that we were able to consider any kind of strategy'.[74] Had there been more time to establish a coherent plan of action the damaging disagreement and chaos that prevailed at the army GHQs in Amman might not have existed.

Kawash points out that it was lack of co-ordination between the Arab allies which destroyed the effectiveness of their air strike against Israel. He believes that although Syria's tardy response did not help matters, the 'ultimate outcome would not have been different unless there had been complete co-ordination and prior planning, as well as one operations room. If that had been the case the air forces of Jordan, Syria and Iraq would have been co-ordinated. Instead, what happened was a total fiasco in which each country made haphazard raids which achieved very little ... [Effective co-ordination] required several years' co-operation and preparation but the Arab political scene did not allow us to achieve this'.[75]

There was also no time to establish proper channels of communication between the allies. King Hussein points out that his communications with Nasser were conducted over the public telephone because although the UAC had an up-to-date transmission system, this was still in Cairo.[76] Under these

Egyptian–Jordanian communications and this undoubtedly influenced the war in its favour. The poor communications between the two countries also made it easier for Egypt to mislead Jordan, with dire consequences.

The Jordanian government's failure to accept troops from other Arab nations is closely related to its failure to patch up its differences with the Arab world in general. The Jordanian argument that the presence of Arab troops would have provided Israel with an excuse to invade the West Bank became less relevant after their raid on Samu. They could have used Israel's aggressive action to justify the acceptance of Arab troops onto Jordanian soil for defence purposes – particularly since Wasfi Tal, the Prime Minister of Jordan at the time, argued that it was a 'dress rehearsal' for the June war whose purpose was to increase inter–Arab strife and so prevent the Jordanians from receiving Arab military assistance.

Mustafa points out that in view of the Jordanians' inability to defend the West Bank on their own, the only solution was the acceptance of Arab forces. Jordan's policy that it would allow Arab troops onto its territory once hostilities became inevitable did not allow for the ever-present possibility of a surprise attack.[77] As it turned out events moved so quickly that there was no time for Arab troops to reach their positions and, in effect, Jordan fought alone.

The Jordanians should have been more suspicious of Egypt's claims of success on the first day of the war. Jordanian political and military leaders noted how over-confident Nasser was and believed that until one week before the war he was playing a game of brinkmanship with no real intention of fighting. They were also aware of how, in the past, the Egyptians had played down their defeats and embroidered their victories. For these reasons the Jordanians had every reason to be suspicious when the Egyptians claimed fantastic successes. They should not have taken these claims on trust but should have made an independent assessment of the true state of play, particularly since Amer's directives entailed such radical alterations to their original plans.

Tal was one of the few politicians who realized that the reports coming from Egypt could not be true. When he heard them he concluded that the Egyptians were indulging in wishful thinking, but he was forced to keep his thoughts to himself because few people shared this belief.[78]

The Jordanian leadership admits that if it had discovered the true state of affairs on the morning of 5 June they would not have embarked on the suicidal course they did. They would have engaged in limited action on the basis of their pre-arranged strategy, which would demonstrate their adherence to the Arab cause but would fall short of providing Israel with sufficient excuse to invade the West Bank.[79]

Instead the Jordanians followed all the commands coming from Cairo and as a result grave tactical errors were made, including the occupation of Government House, moving the armoured brigades south and failing to implement Operation Tariq.

Tal points out that throughout the war the Jordanians did not have a single Jordanian liaison officer in Egypt.[80] In view of the fragile nature of Jordanian–Egyptian relations, and Nasser's over-confidence, they should have realized that this was essential. An observer at the nerve centre of the Joint Arab Command would have been able to confirm or deny reports emanating from the Egyptian leadership. He would have been able to advise on the wisdom of their directions and to inform the Jordanians of any details which the Egyptians failed to pass on. Instead the Jordanians 'were at the mercy of whatever information Egypt decided to give out'.[81]

Jordan's propaganda campaign against Egypt was partly responsible for the war. Although the politicians concerned argue that the campaign was necessary in order to defend the Jordanian government against the accusations being levelled against it by Egypt and Syria, this should be weighed against its effect. Jordan's taunts that Egypt was in a position to deal Israel a heavy blow by closing the Straits of Tiran was a major factor in Egypt's decision to do precisely that. This then provided Israel with the excuse to launch a full-scale attack on the Arabs and to seize their land without losing the sympathy of the West.

The Jordanians laid themselves open to disaster by failing to understand the extent of Syria's determination to engineer the downfall of their government. Syria had remained the implacable enemy of Jordan despite the Jordanian government's attempts to achieve a reconciliation from mid-April onwards. The Syrians had provided the Jordanians with unmistakeable evidence that they would not be moved throughout the period immediately preceding the war. The bomb at Ramtha shortly after the Prime Minister had announced various measures in support of Jordan's 'sister' Syria, should have been warning enough. Syria's profoundly unenthusiastic response to the Egyptian–Jordanian Mutual Defence Treaty provided further evidence that nothing would divert Syria from its deep antagonism to the Jordanian regime. King Hussein also confirms that he was aware of this. He says that he had 'few illusions about the possibility of aid from Damascus. The truth is that up to then the Syrians had systematically refused to co-operate with us'.[82]

In view of this the Jordanians should have been suspicious when, on 5 June, they were told that Syria would provide cover for Jordan's right flank in the northern sector when the 40th brigade was ordered to move south. A regime that was determined to destroy the Hashemite monarchy was hardly likely to defend it. The failure to perceive this opened the way for Israel's occupation of the West Bank. As Khammash says, 'our trust in the Syrians was misplaced and cost us very dear'.[83]

The Jordanians failed to perceive the full extent of America's support of Israel. The failure of America and the other signatories of the Tripartite

Israel. The failure of America and the other signatories of the Tripartite Agreement to support Jordan was the cause of much bitterness. The Jordanian politicians failed to realize that when it came to open combat Jordan's alliance with America would have no weight in comparison with America's alliance with Israel. Jordan entered the war under the illusion that America would not allow Israel to seize the West Bank. Events proved how tragically misplaced this trust was.

'Saut Al-Arab's' destructive role on the war in Jordan was not limited to the effect of its misleading information on the Jordanian and Arab UN Ambassadors. First, by broadcasting news of Jordan's capture of Government House, before any offensive had been implemented, it alerted the Israelis to this threat. Moreover, because this report was confused with an offensive on Mount Scopus, the Israelis brought forward their plans for the encirclement of Jerusalem and their capture of the territory between Mount Scopus and Jewish Jerusalem.

Secondly, 'Saut Al-Arab' broadcast news of the passage of Iraqi forces across Jordanian territory and specified their exact locations. This information was used by Israel to locate the position of the Iraqis and the IAF launched savage air attacks on the Iraqi troops, destroyed their equipment and supplies and rendered them useless.

By these means, 'Saut Al-Arab's' efforts to bolster the Arab cause in fact caused considerable damage.

The desire of the Jordanians to demonstrate their commitment to the Arab cause overrode all other considerations. The strength of their feeling is illustrated by an incident which occurred in Amman the day before King Hussein left for Cairo at the end of May. King Hussein was told that Syria was still accusing the Jordanian government of betraying the Arab cause to the benefit of Israel. He became extremely angry and turned to one of his advisers, saying, 'The Syrians will soon find out just who is loyal to the Arab cause and who is a traitor to it'.[84] Tragically his words proved prophetic. This desire to prove their loyalty to Arab unity was one of the most important factors that led the Jordanians to enter the war and which prevented them from dealing more cautiously with the instructions and information coming from Egypt.

Chapter 9

The aftermath

Defence of the East Bank

By 8 June 1967 most elements of the Jordanian army stationed on the West Bank had retreated across the bridges of the River Jordan. Shattered and having suffered a stunning defeat at the hands of their enemy, their war was over. For their commanders at GHQs, including Riad, the next urgent task was to deal with the threat that the Israeli army would continue its offensive to Amman. The remaining forces under Riad's command were redeployed on the East Bank. On 7 June the only forces left to defend Jordan were the Eastern Command troops (the Al-Hussein and Yarmouk brigades), the Royal Guard brigade, the Iraqi forces (the 8th mechanized brigade and the 1st infantry brigade) and a Syrian mechanized infantry brigade which had arrived at 2.00 p.m. that day. These forces were concentrated in the areas of Naur and As-Salt, west of Amman, with the purpose of preventing an advance of Israeli troops to the capital.

By 12 June the situation had improved. All the Iraqi forces promised to Jordan had arrived. These Iraqi troops (the Salahudin Forces) were composed of Iraq's 1st infantry, 8th mechanized, 6th armoured and 27th infantry brigades. Three Jordanian brigades which had been stationed on the West Bank had also regrouped on the East Bank. Two of these brigades, the Qadisiyeh (stationed in the Jordan Valley) and Hittin (stationed in the areas of Hebron), had escaped heavy fighting and suffered limited losses. They had withdrawn to the East Bank ready to occupy new defensive positions. What was left of the 60th armoured brigade had also succeeded in crossing the River Jordan and elements of it were still functional. By this time the Syrian mechanized infantry brigade had been ordered to return to Syria, because it had proved so reluctant to enter its appointed defensive positions. Its positions were replaced by Iraq's 27th infantry brigade.

These forces were deployed with the purpose of defending the main approaches to Amman. These were:

Irbid–Mafraq–Amman

Damia Bridge–Northern Jordan Valley–Arda–Amman

Southern Jordan Valley–Jericho–King Hussein (Allenby) Bridge–As-Salt–Amman
Southern Jordan Valley–King Abdullah Bridge–Naur–Amman
Aqaba–Ghor Al-Safi–Karak–Amman

Israel's control of the Golan Heights also led to concern that the Israelis might seek to enter Northern Jordan from the areas of Taiyba and Dira'a in southern Syria. Consequently these axes were strengthened.[1]

As well as taking these military measures, the Jordanian government also instigated political ones to prevent any further advance in Israeli forces. Shortly after the ceasefire came into effect the Foreign Minister, Ahmed Toukan, arranged an urgent meeting with all former Foreign Ministers for advice on how to deal with the threat that the Israelis would continue their offensive to Amman.[2] The main decision was that they should pursue every diplomatic channel possible to safeguard the East Bank. Toukan contacted the American Ambassador to ask him to request his government to ensure that Israel abided by the ceasefire agreement. The same request was made to the Ambassadors of the USSR, Britain and France since these nations were permanent members of the UN Security Council.

The army

Jordan's three-day confrontation with Israel resulted in the annihilation of its air force and 80 per cent of its armour.[3] According to King Hussein only six of the army's 186 tanks returned across the River Jordan. At the end of the fighting only four of the Jordanian Army's eleven brigades were still operational[4] and the 50,000 strong army had been reduced to 30,000 men. Seven hundred Jordanian soldiers were killed in the war and 6,000 were wounded and missing.[5] According to army records, loss of equipment included 179 tanks, 53 half-track personnel carriers, 2 rescue trucks, 737 3-ton trucks, 462 1-ton trucks, 429 Land Rovers, 152 90mm guns, 27 20-pound guns, 26 25-pound guns, 138 106mm recoilless guns, 201 3.5 inch rocket launchers, 348 50mm heavy Browning machine guns, 491 30mm medium Browning machine guns, 1,559 Carben machine guns, 802 Energa launchers, 1,117 30mm automatic rifles, 6,539 M-1 30mm rifles, 8,454 various types of weapons, which had been distributed to towns and villages in the West Bank. Also lost or destroyed during the three days of fighting were 7,850 precision tools, 7,000 tons of ammunition, 1,749 pieces of wireless equipment, 2,500 tons of fuel and 1,500 tons of foodstuff.

Although the leadership of the Jordanian Army was not held responsible for Jordan's defeat the command structure of the Army was altered. It was recognized that this was top-heavy and consequently the positions of Commander-in-Chief and Deputy Commander-in-Chief were abolished. Field

Marshall Habes Majali, who had been the Commander-in-Chief, was made Minister of Defence, and the Deputy Commander-in-Chief, Major General Sharif Nasser Ben Jamil, was made military adviser to King Hussein. Major General Salim, the Commander of the Western Front, was given early retirement, and Major General Khammash, the Chief of Staff, was promoted to Lt General and made Chief of the General Staff.

The organization of the field troops was altered. They were reassigned into divisions with independent divisional commands. This gave the units greater flexibility since divisional commanders had fewer troops to control and could operate more efficiently. The remnants of Western Command were reorganized into two infantry divisions – the 1st and 2nd. Each division was supported by an armoured brigade and divisional artillery troops. These divisions were given the task of defending over 95 km of the River Jordan, from the Sea of Galilee to the Dead Sea.

The 2nd infantry division was placed under the command of Brigadier Atef Majali (Riad's Director of Military Operations). The 40th armoured brigade was assigned to provide support for that division and placed under its direct command. The 1st infantry division, with the support of the 60th armoured brigade, was placed under Lt General Mashour Haditha, the Commander of the Eastern Front during the war. The Yarmouk brigade was deployed at As-Salt and the Al-Hussein brigade took up its previous position at Aqaba. In the aftermath of the war Jordan's defence strategy also reverted to its original posture of 'active defence'.

Although the Jordanian government tried to absorb the 10,000-strong Palestinian commando and militia units into the army this proved unsuccessful. Only 300 men were recruited and formed a commando force stationed at Kerama. The remaining Palestinians joined the fedayeen movement and formed their own military organizations.[6]

The Salahudin forces also remained in Jordan, stationed in the area of Ramtha–Mafraq–Zarka in support of Jordan's northern axis.

For the first two years after the war Jordan received no military aid apart from a few Western-made tanks and other essential military hardware provided as a gift by Iraq. While the armies of Egypt and Syria were re-equipped by the USSR,[7] Jordan refused to turn to the communist world for help. In mid-1968 the oil-rich Arab states came to the aid of Jordan and provided it with a $100m grant. This enabled Jordan to receive its first supply of tanks and combat aircraft since the war. In the autumn of 1969 Jordan received from the USA and the UK 300 Patton and Centurion tanks, 18 F-104 Interceptors and 24 Hawker Hunter fighter bombers.

In 1969 the Jordanian government invited an advisory mission from Pakistan to Jordan to act as consultants for the army's programme of reorganization which was already under way.[8] The task of the team of Jordanian military strategists was to organize the best deployment of forces, with particular attention being paid to topographical considerations and the threat posed by Israel. The main contribution of the Pakistani Mission was to provide a theoretical background to the redeployment of forces.

The survey of the army revealed that the army was still suffering from critical imbalances in its strength and equipment. These included manpower deficiency in all units, a need to reorganize the RJAF, to create two field regiments and one self-propelled field regiment, to provide a fourth company to the infantry battalions and to standardize the organization of armoured units. All these problems were tackled and far-reaching changes were made.

One of the most important results of the study was the recognition that, because of its small size, the Jordanian army was essentially a defensive force and that its best strategy was to organize defence in three stages.

As a result of the survey security forces were placed in observation posts in the mountain ranges overlooking the Jordan Valley. They consisted of the minimum forces necessary and were operated with a combination of reconnaissance elements including troops and/or advance positions or screens. They were assigned the task of gaining information about Israeli troop movements and of inflicting maximum casualties on any Israeli force crossing the River Jordan. This was to be achieved by aggressive patrolling and concentrating artillery on the likely avenues of an Israeli approach.

The old problem of spreading the troops thinly along the length of the border was tackled. Although the Pakistani mission recognized that it was necessary to provide cover for the local population in the border towns and the Jordan Valley, this was achieved by the use of mobile infantry platoons and a static armed police force, rather than by a large number of troops placed along the River Jordan.

The aim of the proposed defence strategy was to concentrate Jordanian forces in positions which would absorb any Israeli offensive by the application of mass fire power from unexpected places and directions. It was noted that the Jordanian army's existing defensive positions were not fulfilling many of the basic requirements of defence and that the main threat presented by Israel lay in its air superiority and employment of tank forces. Consequently, measures were taken to remedy this, including providing depth at all levels, reorientating strategy to deal with tanks, providing efficient camouflage and concealment of troops and maintaining strict fire control in order not to alert Israel to the location of Jordanian troops.

The question of reserves had always been problematic because the small size of the Jordanian army meant that no reserves were available at battalion level due to the absence of a fourth company. There were also few reserves available at brigade level due to the commitment of troops in the Jordan Valley. Armoured squadrons which could have been used as reserve forces were instead being used to man anti-tank weapons. Only at divisional level were there adequate reserves of infantry and armoured forces. Measures were taken to remedy this and to provide reserves at the levels of brigade and battalion.

When considering anti-aircraft defence it was noted that air attacks continued to be the main problem facing the Jordanian army. This problem was solved through the use of camouflage, digging in troops as much as possible and redeploying anti-aircraft guns to achieve the required concentration at vital points only.

Special concern about the vulnerability of the radar station at Ajloun was expressed. This station had been destroyed during the war and it was only rebuilt in 1969. Because of the threat represented by Israeli planes, at least one composite battery of anti-aircraft guns was stationed to guard it.

After examining the capability of joint action by land and air forces, formal air request for close air support was no longer initiated by brigades but by divisions instead. Jordan's awareness of Israel's ability to intercept wireless communications was reflected in the fact that frequencies and call signs used for air to ground wireless communications were changed daily in order to avoid any jamming or other interference by Israel. The procedure already used by the Jordanians was enhanced by stand-by frequencies in addition to the daily ones. The training programme for elements of the RJAF was also reviewed and revised.

The survey envisaged that any Israeli approach in the south would concentrate on the axis of Karak–Qantara–Amman with a subsidiary effort on Karak–Madaba–Amman. For this reason the Karak approach was strongly defended. The Pakistani mission recommended that Aqaba should be defended 'to the last man's round' as it was of such vital importance. However, the Jordanians disagreed and argued that this was more relevant in terrains such as Wadi Shuaib and Arda rather than Aqaba.

The survey advised that any Israeli offensive in the southern sector should be blunted by creating strong defensive positions in the area of Karak–Aqaba and dislocated by offensive missions into Israeli territory. These areas were therefore strengthened and contingency plans made to deal with the possibility of an Israeli breakthrough towards Amman from Karak. In general offensive plans were made for the capture of strategically vital positions in each sector.

When examining the defence of Aqaba it was anticipated that an Israeli approach was most likely to occur through Wadi Araba with a subsidiary effort to fix the force occupying the centre sector, because this avoided built-up areas and did not have the problem of heavy artillery fire from Jordanian positions. It was found that the existing Jordanian positions were not organized to meet this threat and adjustments were made accordingly.

The study revealed that existing defensive positions had been hastily occupied on withdrawal from the West Bank and had not been developed on a sound footing. Consequently important alterations in defensive positions were made, even though considerable labour and material resources had been spent to develop those positions and commanders and troops were often reluctant to change their dispositions.

Early in 1970 the Jordanian army was reorganized into four divisions. In addition to the 1st and 2nd divisions a third armoured division was created from the 99th armoured brigade (the Wasfi Tal brigade which was created after the 1967 war) and the two hitherto independent 40th and 60th armoured brigades. A fourth mechanized division was formed from one mechanized brigade and the Royal Guards brigade. The Jordanian air force was reorganized into four operational squadrons.[9] Thus, in August 1970 the overall strength of the Jordanian Armed Forces reached a total of 65,000 combatants, a semi-trained Security brigade and a police force of about 5,000.[10]

These changes involved a major redeployment of armour and reserves with one division of mobile forces of armour and mechanized units covering the main axes of probable Israeli approach in accordance with the new strategic concepts. Security forces were left to patrol main lines of defence. In certain areas, depending on the topography, the reserve forces were composed of armoured brigades, apart from one armoured regiment attached to each division.

After the war the defence of Jordan became easier because there were only six places across which Israel could enter Jordan. These were Aqaba, the bridges of King Abdullah, King Hussein, Damia, Sheikh Hussein and Dira'a-Ramtha. One of the most important of these approaches was the northern one of Dira'a because of the difficulties an Israeli approach would face along the other axes. An Israeli approach across the bridges would be difficult because the mountain range overlooking the Jordan Valley meant that Israeli troops would face a barrage of Jordanian gunfire. The south was equally difficult for the Israelis to attack. The mountains around Karak provided the Jordanians with excellent defensive positions from which to direct artillery fire. The Battle for Karama was to prove how difficult any Israeli attempt to attack Jordan from the southern Jordan Valley would be. Aqaba was also perilously close to Eilat, which would almost certainly be subjected to Jordanian attack in the event of fighting in the area. For these reasons, two Jordanian divisions were placed in the north and were instructed to attack the invading force from the north-east and the north-west in order to prepare for a frontal assault, which would be carried out by brigades held at relevant areas of concentration.

As a result of these widespread changes, by 1970 the Jordanian army was fully reorganized and ready to meet with any contingency. It had come to terms with the new defence requirements and was slowly being re-equipped to make good the ravages caused by the June war.

The economy

The economic effects of the war were as severe as the military ones. Jordan's economy prior to the war had witnessed higher rates of growth than most other developing countries. GNP had been rising at a rate of 9.4 per cent, yet was maintained with a fairly high degree of price and monetary stability. The Central Bank of Jordan points out that as

> Jordan's absorptive capacity expanded its natural resources were efficiently utilized, its human resources were upgraded and became more productive, its institutional set up modernized and developed, its stock of entrepreneurs increased under the umbrella of constitutional continuity, stability, law and order. The social overhead capital accumulated and enlarged and the capacity of the public sector in providing public services and infrastructural facilities promoted and expanded.[11]

The loss of the West Bank immediately arrested these promising developments. Although the West Bank constituted only 6.2 per cent of the total area of Jordan it was the richest and most highly populated area. According to the Jordanian Bureau of Statistics the West Bank had contributed 35–40 per cent to Jordan's gross national product. Thus, the loss of the West Bank meant the loss of one-third of Jordan's hard currency earnings, a quarter of its cultivable land and nearly half its industrial establishments. The latter sector alone had employed 37 per cent of Jordan's workers.[12] The loss of industry included the loss of commodities which had been marketed within Jordan but which now had to be imported, thus adding to Jordan's import bill. These commodities included olive oil, soap and fruit. Industry also suffered from the sharp contraction in the size of Jordan's internal market. Jordan's Seven Year Economic Development Plan (1964–70) was also arrested. Prior to the war this had envisaged a total investment of JD 275m and by 1967 most of the development projects and proposals involved in the Plan were under way.[13] However, the war either halted or put a stop to many of these proposals, including the construction of the Yarmouk Dam, the electrification of Jordan and the construction of Jerusalem Airport.

The effect of the war on Jordan's agricultural sector was devastating. The West Bank had contained the most fertile land in Jordan and was responsible for half of Jordan's agricultural exports.[14] The West Bank had supplied 65 per cent of Jordan's vegetables, 60 per cent of its fruits, 80 per cent of its olives, 30 per cent of its grain and approximately a third of its livestock and poultry farms. In 1966, forty per cent of the income generated out of the agricultural sector and almost one half of the agricultural labour force had come from the West Bank.

Jordan had depended on the tourist industry for a substantial proportion of its revenue and the West Bank had accounted for 90 per cent of this.[15] The tourist industry had been expanding before the war. Remittances from Palestinian emigrés to their relatives on the West Bank had also been substantial and it seemed doubtful that this would continue. There was also the question of whether the USA would continue to give aid to Jordan in view of the active role it had played in the war.

The influx of refugees and the general contraction of the economy led to a sharp rise in unemployment. Economic insecurity also limited investment and prevented a quick recovery. The ability of the government to meet the new demands being made on it were strained by the need to allocate a high proportion of its budget to defence instead of investment. These factors plunged Jordan into an economic recession which was all the more disheartening since Jordan had been on the way to freeing itself from the burden of external aid as a result of its economic development. Instead the high unemployment rate resulted in social and political problems, and was a major contributory factor to the growth of the fedayeen movement in Jordan.

Jordan was saved from economic ruin by aid from Arab states and the West. As a result of the Khartoum summit held at the end of August, Kuwait, Libya and Saudi Arabia agreed to provide P Stg 135m annually to the defeated countries. Jordan's share of this was to be P Stg 40m.[16] The remittances sent by Palestinians abroad to their relatives in Jordan continued unabated and this eased the situation. In addition the phosphate industry continued to prosper, even though the war delayed the implementation of a potash project which was scheduled to commence operations in 1968 with an initial production capacity of 500,000 tons. Despite this, over a million tons of potash were exported in 1967 and this increased the following year. The mineral industry was also located on the East Bank and its contribution to the GNP continued to rise steadily. The government launched an emergency programme designed to absorb the economically active labour force seeking work and also implemented those projects from the Seven Year Economic Development Plan which had been intended for the East Bank.

The farming sector did not fare so well. The growth of guerrilla activity in the years following the war resulted in a rise of Israeli raids and air and artillery bombardments on land in the Jordan Valley. This damaged irrigation schemes and farms and made it difficult for farmers to tend their produce. In the summer of 1969 the East Ghor Canal was put out of action by the IAF, which further handicapped the recovery of the agricultural sector. According to the Central Bank of Jordan the total loss in the East Bank caused by Israeli raids in the Jordan Valley amounted to the equivalent of JD 97.2m in 1975 prices.[17]

The tourist industry also failed to re-establish itself since the visitors who had once come to Jordan as the Holy Land now went to Israel.

Despite these problems foreign aid kept Jordan solvent. In 1967 this amounted to P Stg 179.5m, of which P Stg 134.3m consisted of grants which came mainly from the Arab world. At the end of 1967 Jordan's balance of payments showed a surplus of JD 33.2m as opposed to JD 8.9m the previous year. Although economic development staggered again between 1970 and 1971, since then it has continued to revive.

The Palestinians

Israel's capture of the West Bank resulted in an influx of 300,000 Palestinian refugees into the East Bank, bringing the total number of refugees in Jordan's care to 850,000.[18] Many of these people were refugees for the second time having originally fled from territory occupied by Israel in 1948. The immediate task of the government was to settle them as quickly as possible. Juma'a describes how the government's main task at the conclusion of hostilities 'was to face the catastrophe with determination. We worked day and night receiving every morning tens of thousands of refugees, providing them with food and shelter'.[19] With the help of UNWRA, by the winter of 1967 the refugees had been resettled in temporary camps in Amman and Jerash. Eleven permanent camps were later built to house the refugee population.

However, the Jordanian government's failure to find a permanent solution to their problem, and Israel's continued occupation of the West Bank, made these camps fertile grounds for recruitment to the fedayeen movement. In a short time the camps were virtually military establishments and in the winter of 1967 Palestinian fedayeen began to cross the Jordan River to the West Bank to attack Israeli settlements and military posts. The fedayeen were supported by Egypt and Syria, although neither of these countries allowed them to operate from their own territory. The Israelis responded to the guerrilla attacks with reprisal raids in the form of air attacks and artillery shelling of Jordanian army positions, border towns and villages.

The Jordanian government had initially been against fedayeen action because of the grave consequences this would have for the citizens of the West Bank. However, popular pressure led to a reversal of this decision, but Israeli reprisals and the lawless activities of some of the popular Palestinian organizations eventually made a government clampdown inevitable. On the whole the fedayeen movement became an anarchic element in Jordanian society. Two out of the three main Palestinian organizations, the Popular Front for the Liberation of Palestine (PFLP) and the Popular Democratic Front (PDF), were openly against the Jordanian government and sought to overthrow its Hashemite monarchy. The carrying of arms by the fedayeen and their dislike of Jordanian rule brought them into increasing conflict with the army as well as with many ordinary Jordanian citizens. Violent clashes between the fedayeen and the Jordanian army began to occur from 1968 onwards. The first took place in November and resulted in the death of twenty-eight Palestinian fedayeen and four Jordanian soldiers. By the end of 1969 the political and military confrontation between the fedayeen and the government had reached a critical stage. El Edroos describes how 'the Commandos had established a de facto government within a state and openly flouted Jordanian order- and law-enforcing agencies. A decisive showdown between the Hashemite Government and the commandoes was inevitable'.[20]

By 1970 the use of mobile patrols, pursuit tactics and an electronic anti-infiltration barrier had successfully put an end to fedayeen infiltration into the occupied territories from Jordan. In order to circumvent this the Palestinian guerrillas changed their tactics and shelled Israeli border towns and settlements. Since Israel's response was to shell Jordanian border towns and villages popular pressure forced the government to try and prevent the guerrilla activity. The twofold danger of Israeli reaction and fedayeen lawlessness made the general populace and the army increasingly unhappy. Army leaders began to urge King Hussein to control the fedayeen. The Minister of the Interior, Hassan Al-Khayed, issued a statement declaring that 'Jordan is determined to strike with an iron fist those who threaten the country's security by their actions ... and thus provide Israel with justification to mount further pressures on Jordan'.[21] However, at first King Hussein was reluctant to crush the Palestinians partly for ideological reasons and partly because of the inevitable Arab criticism. Another point which he had to take into account was the presence of 25,000 Iraqi troops in the area of Zarqa and Mafraq.

Consquently King Hussein agreed to some of the demands made by the Palestinian leaders and for a short time this eased the situation. However, in July the same year an assassination attempt on the life of the King and his senior ministers resulted in fighting between the fedayeen and the Jordanian army. Once again reconciliation between the government and the fedayeen was achieved but this was finally blown apart in August when King Hussein and Nasser accepted the Rogers Initiative and a ceasefire was imposed. This plan advocated an Israeli withdrawal from the Jordanian and Egyptian territory occupied by Israel in 1967 in return for a comprehensive peace settlement. All the Palestinian organizations regarded acceptance of the plan as a betrayal of their cause and accused King Hussein and Nasser of colluding with America. The two most left-wing organizations now openly called for the overthrow of the King.[22] The result was daily clashes between the fedayeen and the Jordanian army.

By mid-September the situation could no longer be contained and on 15 September King Hussein agreed that the government would have to take military action. A military government was established and on 17 September civil war broke out. The week long war resulted in victory for the Jordanian government, although it earned the condemnation of the Arab world.

Government and politics

In the immediate aftermath of the war the Minister of Information, Sharif Abdul Hamid Sharaf, a relative of King Hussein, resigned from his post. He had been closely associated with Jordan's propaganda campaign which had accused Egypt of hiding behind UNEF and allowing Israeli shipping into the Straits of Tiran. Since this campaign was regarded as an important factor behind Egypt's decision to close the Straits, thereby providing Israel with the excuse to attack Egypt, Sharaf took the unusual step in Middle East politics of resigning in spite of the fact that it was Wasfi Tal who had initiated and planned the campaign.

Shortly after this Wasfi Tal resigned from his post as Chief of the Royal Diwan and was replaced by Sharif Hussein Ben Nasir. This was followed by the resignation of the whole of the Jordanian Cabinet on 1 August. The same day King Hussein asked Saad Juma'a, the Prime Minister, to form a new Cabinet. King Hussein also appointed a Consultative Council to help him deal with internal and external affairs. Its members included prominent Jordanian politicians, including Saad Juma'a, Suleiman Nabulsi, Wasfi Tal, Bajhat Talhouni and Sharif Hussein Ben Nasir, as well as Field Marshall Habes Majali.

A few months later, on 7 October, Juma'a resigned from the Premiership and Bahjat Talhouni took his place. Juma'a was associated with pro-American policies and this change reflected a move away from the West and towards Nasser whom Talhouni had always favoured.

Nasser's support of King Hussein was perhaps the latter's only compensation for the loss of the West Bank. Mahmoud Riad, Egypt's Foreign Minister at the time, describes how 'Nasser was deeply impressed by how King Hussein of Jordan had stood shoulder to shoulder with him during the war'.[23] On 22 June Nasser wrote to King Hussein, paying tribute to his heroic struggle and 'offering to put all we have in the service of the common destiny of our two peoples'.[24] The support of Nasser was of vital importance to King Hussein who believed that in the aftermath of the war the Arabs needed a fresh approach to the issue of Israel. He believed that the bellicose way in which the Arab world had approached the Arab–Israeli conflict had been one of the main causes of the disaster that had befallen it. The aggressive statements of the Arab nations and their threatening gestures had given Israel all the excuses it had needed to seize Arab land. Their approach had also been responsible for the negative international attitude to the Arabs which had allowed Israel to achieve its objectives with little or no condemnation.

As the war had left the armies of the Arab confrontation states completely broken, King Hussein decided that his only hope of winning back the West Bank was through diplomacy. Accordingly, the remainder of the year was dedicated to seeking political means of persuading Israel to relinquish the land it had seized. King Hussein's first journey was to Europe and America, but before leaving he visited Nasser who gave the King his full support to use every diplomatic channel open to him to win back the West Bank. He told King Hussein not to worry about Sinai which was unimportant compared with the West Bank. He declared: 'For the sake of getting back the West Bank, forget about my losses and go to Lyndon Johnson and do what you can to make him give you back the West Bank.'[25] He also made it clear that he wanted King Hussein to take the lead at the UN. He urged the Jordanian monarch 'to negotiate with the Americans in any way he wanted to and for as long as he wanted to for a peaceful settlement in the West Bank which would lead to total Israeli withdrawal, as long as he refrained from signing a separate peace treaty, going so far as to end officially the state of belligerency with Israel, and even, if he wanted, concluding a joint defence agreement with the United States'.[26] Nasser realized that King Hussein's connections with the West were valuable to the Arabs because after the war Egypt and Syria had become even more deeply committed to the Soviet Union. King Hussein was also valuable to Nasser because of his close connections with the oil-rich Arab states who were in a position to provide him with the money he urgently needed to put his country back on its feet.

Between 24 June and 7 July King Hussein travelled to Europe and America. In America he visited the UN General Assembly and delivered a speech describing the Arab position and offering peace in return for territory. He then went on to Washington to explore American intentions. During his meeting with President Johnson King Hussein explained the Arab point of view. He said that he was willing to offer Israel peace if it would return the West Bank, which he was prepared to demilitarize. However, Johnson replied that Jordan would have to enter direct negotiations with Israel. This demand closed the door on any prospect of settlement since Arab public opinion against direct negotiations was so strong. According to Mahmoud Riad, Johnson offered King Hussein 'nothing beyond vague general promises'.[27] At the end of the meeting on 28 June a White House statement said that the King and Johnson had been unable to arrive 'at an identity of views' in their discussions about the Middle East.[28] When discussing this point in an interview King Hussein stated that in the immediate post-war period he was aware that any moves the American administration made would be in favour of Israel.[29] This was a source of disappointment to King Hussein who had regarded the USA as Jordan's ally. He left America for Europe where he visited many capitals, including London and Paris, to discuss ways of regaining the West Bank. King Hussein writes that in London Prime Minister Wilson and Foreign Minister George Brown showed a great deal of understanding. In Paris Charles de Gaulle also expressed his sympathy with the Arabs. However, since public opinion in the West was hostile to the Arabs as a result of Arab accusations that Israel had received help from Britain and America during the war, neither of these leaders was able to offer Jordan any practical help.[30]

Immediately after his return from the West King Hussein visited Nasser to inform him of the result of his talks with Western leaders. He told Nasser that seeking a solution at the UN was futile at that time not only because of US delaying tactics but equally because of widely differing stands by the Arab delegates who were outbidding each other. He proposed holding an Arab summit meeting. The two men agreed that since Israel was not going to withdraw from the occupied territories unconditionally they would have to offer some concessions. King Hussein also made it plain that he would not act unilaterally but only in concert with the Arab world as a whole, because the issue of Palestine was one that concerned all Arabs.

Nasser continued to urge King Hussein to pursue his diplomatic contacts with the USA[31] and gave him a mandate to act as spokesman for the Arabs on the issue of Palestine. However, Syria, Iraq and Algeria continued to oppose any form of negotiation on the issue of Palestine. This division in the Arab world made it impossible for the formulation of a uniform policy which King Hussein believed was an essential prerequisite for the return of Arab land.

Ever since the war had ended King Hussein had pressed for an Arab summit in order to surmount this problem. On 17 June he had sent a cable to all Arab heads of state calling for a summit meeting to be held within the week. He received a lukewarm response. Nasser was reluctant to attend such a conference because he believed it would be fruitless.[32] The radical Arab states including Syria, Iraq, Algeria and Sudan decided that they wanted nothing to do with the moderates. However, by the end of July a summit seemed to be in the offing and King Hussein visited various Arab capitals in order to sound out the intentions of Arab states and to try and formulate proposals on the issue of Palestine which would be acceptable to them all. According to Farid one of the reasons for Nasser's decision to attend the conference was his recognition that any delay in restoring Jerusalem and the West Bank to Jordan would increase the likelihood that Israel would retain them. For this reason he wanted to make it clear that he was willing to give King Hussein a mandate to speak on his behalf.[33]

At his meetings with political leaders in Kuwait, Iran, Saudi Arabia, Libya, Tunisia, Morocco and Lebanon, King Hussein presented proposals on the Arab–Israeli issue which he intended to put forward at the forthcoming Arab summit in Khartoum. The basis of his plan was an offer of peace to Israel in return for the West Bank. He also intended to offer to demilitarize the West Bank after its evacuation by Israel. At the same time, he made it clear that he would not recognize Israel, sign a peace treaty with it or agree to the internationalization of Jerusalem. On 29 August the heads of state of the Arab world met together at Khartoum. At the summit Nasser made it clear that there was no question of pursuing the rights of the Palestinians by military means since the armies of the confrontation states were not in a position to wage war. The situation called instead for the use of political weapons. King Hussein then urged the Arab world to recognize that it was only through diplomacy that the inhabitants of the West Bank would be freed from Israel's rule.[34]

At the end of the summit Nasser focused particular attention on the problem of the West Bank and Jerusalem. He pointed out that there had now emerged in Israel a hard bloc in the form of the Gahal Party which 'insists on retaining the whole of the West Bank, refusing to give up one inch of the land'. He went on to point out:

> This is why we must move quickly and exert our utmost efforts to regain Jerusalem and the West Bank through the means available to us at present, for if we delay neither Jerusalem nor the West Bank will return to us.
>
> Is it possible to regain the occupied lands by military means at present? I believe the answer to this question is evident. This road is not open before us at the present time. Thus we have before us only one way by which to regain the West Bank and Jerusalem: political action ... I believe King Hussein should approach the Americans and agree with them on the restoration of the West Bank. I am ready to announce this publicly because America alone can order Israel to take its hands off the West Bank.[35]

This statement at the closing session of Khartoum provided King Hussein with the support he needed for his discussions with America and marked a definite departure from the previous Arab approach of military confrontation with Israel.

At the end of the Khartoum summit the Arab heads of state issued a statement affirming their unity and declaring Arab willingness to unite their political effort at the international and diplomatic levels to eliminate the effects of the aggression and to ensure the withdrawal of Israel from the occupied Arab lands. The statement concluded that no negotiations, no recognition and no peace treaty would be concluded with Israel, that none of the rights of the Palestinian people should be relinquished and that annual aid should be provided to Egypt and Jordan.

The Khartoum summit was a victory for King Hussein because of its stress on the need to seek a political solution to the problems created by the 1967 war. This major change of policy was to reap significant results in the form of Arab acceptance of UN Resolution 242. King Hussein was also publicly supported by Nasser who allowed him to negotiate on behalf of Egypt as well as Jordan. This increased his chance of finding a peaceful solution to the problem of the West Bank because of the increased prestige it gave him. *The International Herald Tribune* pointed out that King Hussein and Nasser had now obtained 'tacit Arab sanction for prospective indirect negotiations with Israel through third nations looking towards an Israeli withdrawal'.[36]

Although the presence of the three noes in the final statement issued by the Arab leaders at Khartoum appeared to be uncompromising, their presence was a means of assuring the Palestinian people that their cause had not been forgotten in the face of Israel's aggression. Riad writes: 'We who attended the Conference had seen how the Palestinians feared that the climate of military defeat in the June war would open the door to the abandonment of their rights. Consequently many Conference members emphasized that as long as Israel remained in occupation of Arab territories, no trafficking with Israel would be feasible'.[37] The decision to seek political solutions left the way open for negotiations even if they were not direct. Riad later pointed out to the Foreign Affairs Committee of the Egyptian National Assembly that although the Arabs had never officially accepted Israel's existence they had accepted it as a fait accompli as long ago as 1949.[38] A refusal to sign a peace treaty with Israel did not rule out the possibility of offering it secure borders and the demilitarization of land adjacent to it.

Despite this major step forward the presence of the three noes in the Khartoum resolution proved to be a major stumbling block in the way of an Arab–Israeli settlement because they enabled Israel to ensure that no strong pressure would be placed on it to withdraw from Arab lands. Israeli leaders used them as an illustration of Arab intransigence, thereby deflecting attention from the genuine possibility for peace that the discussions at Khartoum represented. Zaid Rifai points out that 'the Arabs had accepted Israel's right to exist, they had accepted that the pre-1967 borders should become the recognized international boundaries which in actual fact represented all the conditions asked of the Arabs by Resulution 242. This is what we accepted and what Nasser accepted so if Israel had decided to withdraw we would have achieved a peaceful settlement – something which would have been unattainable before the 1967 war'.[39]

Another important result of the summit was the decision to offer substantial aid to Jordan and the UAR 'until the effects of the aggression are eliminated'. Riad describes how at a 'separate later meeting of the delegations who would provide the aid and representatives of Egypt and Jordan, the Jordanian Minister of Economy asked that Jordan receive P Stg 40m. I informed Nasser and proposed that we increase Jordan's share from P Stg 15m to P Stg 20–25m. Nasser disagreed and said: "Let Jordan immediately take what it wants . . . King Hussein has been brave and honest with us . . . if they want P Stg 40m, let it be so and let it be part of Egypt's share so that we don't have to ask the Arab states for more money."'[40] This money was one of the factors which enabled Jordan to recover its economic equilibrium.

Following the Khartoum summit, King Hussein visited Nasser in Cairo in order to agree on how he would approach the West. At this meeting Nasser agreed that they should be willing to recognize the rights of all states in the

Middle East, including Israel, to exist in peace and security, to terminate the state of belligerency, and to open all international waterways, including the Suez Canal, to navigation by all states. These concessions were to be offered in exchange for Israel's withdrawal to pre-war borders and for a solution of the refugee problem which would give all Palestinian refugees a choice – in accordance with all relevant UN resolutions – between returning to their former homes and accepting compensation.[41]

After this meeting King Hussein visited a number of Western capitals, including Madrid, Paris, Bonn, London, Washington and later Moscow. The aim of his tour was to achieve a better understanding of the Arab cause amongst the international community, to negotiate according to the principles formulated at Khartoum and on the basis of his discussions with Nasser, and to gain the support of the three Western members of the UN Security Council (USA, Britain and France) in his proposal to offer Israel peace in return for the West Bank and Sinai.

In the West King Hussein pointed out that the Arab world had taken a great step forward in its readiness to recognize Israel's right to exist and its willingness to use diplomacy to settle the issue of Palestine. He felt that Israel should therefore be prepared to drop its insistence on direct negotiations.[42] He made it plain that the Arabs were prepared to issue a statement recognizing the right of all nations in the Middle East to live in peace and security if Israel withdrew from the territory occupied in 1967 and offered a genuine settlement of the refugee problem.[43]

King Hussein believed that this time his meetings with Johnson and other American leaders had gone some way towards achieving his aims. According to Robert Stephens, during his meetings with King Hussein, Arthur Goldberg, the American Ambassador to the UN, promised him 'that the United States would work for the return of the West Bank to Jordan with minor boundary rectifications and the United States was prepared to use its influence to obtain a role for Jordan in Jerusalem' if Jordan accepted the US sponsored Resolution which was about to be put to the UN.[44]

This favourable impression was confirmed by Abdul Munim Rifai: 'Johnson gave written promises, written commitments to exert pressure to compel Israel to withdraw. The talks with the King in 1967 when we went to the UN, his talks with the leaders of Congress and the policy makers in Washington and with the Secretary of State were also along these lines'.[45] Although specific written promises are unavailable for observation, Royal Palace sources confirm that correspondence on the prospects for and conditions of peace in the area was exchanged at the time.

However, Mahmoud Riad, Egypt's Foreign Minister, was not so optimistic. He comments:

When I met King Hussein in New York he told me he had received assurances from Washington on Israel's complete withdrawal from all the Arab territories if we would accept the US draft resolution. I told King Hussein that . . . I was firmly convinced that Johnson would never change his policy of supporting Israel's aggression . . . Why did the US not include in its draft resolution a clear statement stipulating Israel's withdrawal from the Arab territories?

Once again King Hussein emphasized: "But I believe all the assurances of President Johnson . . . These are assurances given at the highest American level and we cannot take them lightly."'[46]

At the meeting of the UN Security Council in November 1967 a British sponsored resolution, which represented a compromise of both Arab and Israeli views, was accepted unanimously. It stated that

The Security Council, expressing its continuing concern with the grave situation in the Middle East, emphasizing the inadmissibility of the acquisition of territory by war and the need to work for a just and lasting peace in which every state in the area can live in security, emphasizing further that all member states in their acceptance of the Charter of the UN have undertaken a commitment to act in accordance with Article 2 of the Charter,

(1) affirms that the fulfilment of the Charter principles requires the establishment of a just and lasting peace in the Middle East which should include the application of the following principles:

(i) withdrawal of Israeli armed forces from territories occupied in the recent conflict;

(ii) termination of all claims or states of belligerency and respect for and acknowledgement of the sovereignty, territorial integrity and political independence of every state in the area and their right to live in peace within secure and recognized boundaries free from threats or acts of force.

(2) affirms further the necessity:

(a) for guaranteeing freedom of navigation through international waterways in the area;

(b) for achieving a just settlement of the refugee problem;

(c) for guaranteeing the territorial inviolability and political independence of every state in the area through measures including the establishment of demilitarized zones.

(3) requests the Secretary General to designate a Special Representative to proceed to the Middle East to establish and maintain contacts with the states concerned in order to promote agreement and assist efforts to achieve a peaceful and accepted settlement in accordance with the provisions and principles in this resolution.

(4) requests the Secretary General to report to the Security Council on the progress of the efforts of the Special Representative as soon as possible.[47]

The unanimous acceptance of this resolution (known as Resolution 242) was a triumph for King Hussein since it was based on the principles he had suggested. He believed that the resolution would open the way for a 'just and durable peace in the Middle East'.[48] The Special Representative of the

Secretary General elected to act as mediator between the states concerned was Gunner Jarring, the Swedish Ambassador to Moscow. He was charged with promoting a peace settlement in the Middle East under the terms of the Security Council Resolution.

Despite this optimism the Jarring mission did not meet with success. Syria did not accept Resolution 242 and Israel made demands which were not specified in the Resolution itself. According to Rabin American support for the Resolution had been based on an earlier promise to it by Israel which was later withdrawn. An Israeli cabinet meeting of 19 June 1967 had offered the withdrawal of Israeli forces from Sinai and the Golan Heights to the borders of 4 June in return for, *inter alia*, peace treaties, minor boundary alterations in Israel's favour, demilitarization of the territories concerned, and assurance of the right of navigation. On the insistence of Dayan and Begin a similar offer was not made to Jordan.[49] America was asked to communicate the offer to Egypt and Syria, neither of whom made any response because of the exclusion of Jordan. According to Farid, Nasser's response to Israel's offer was that it should be 'postponed for the time being . . . it is more important for the Jews to withdraw from the West Bank and this will only be possible by political means'.[50] By August Israel had withdrawn its offer to Egypt and Syria[51] and in November Eban announced at the UN that 'the June war ceasefire lines will not change except for secure borders and peace treaties which would terminate war with the Arab countries'.[52] On 3 September Eshkol declared that the decisions taken at Khartoum represented a grave fact which 'made the prospect of peace in our region more remote'.[53] Israel's leaders continued to stress that they were only prepared to discuss the Arab–Israeli problem in direct negotiations with the Arabs, even though they knew that this was something no Arab leader could afford to do.[54] On 17 October the Israeli Cabinet announced that in view of the decisions taken at Khartoum Israel would 'fully continue to maintain the situation established by the ceasefire agreements and to safeguard her position'.[55] This policy remained the same despite every effort of the UN mediator, Gunner Jarring, to change it.

Although the Jarring mission did not produce the desired results, Resolution 242 has remained of importance in Arab–Israeli relations as the embodiment of the international consensus on the principles that should govern the solution to the territorial dispute.[56]

Chapter 10

Conclusion

This account of Jordan's role in the 1967 Arab–Israeli war has highlighted many aspects of the difficulties imposed upon Jordan as a result of the contradictions arising from its impoverished state, its pro-Western policies and its commitment to Arabism. It has also stressed the deep divisions within the Arab world that characterized the 1950s and 1960s, as well as revealing aspects of the 1967 war which have only previously been fleetingly described.

The intimate relationship between foreign and domestic affairs in Jordan has been evident throughout this study. Two reasons for this coalescence can be discerned: Jordan's political and economic dependence on other nations and its Palestinian population. Political dependence stems from its weak military capability and fear that its powerful neighbour, Israel, had never forsaken its desire to expand its territory. Consequently, Jordan turned to other nations for financial support for the maintenance of its army and sought to belong to a regional defence system. Jordan's economic dependence stems from its meagre natural resources and its underdeveloped economy, forcing it into a position of dependence on foreign financial aid. Its limited internal market also made it essential for Jordan to seek markets abroad, particularly in neighbouring Arab states. As a result Jordan has been vulnerable to external pressures.

Jordan's Palestinian population is also responsible for the intimate relationship between Jordan's foreign and domestic affairs. Over half of Jordan's citizens are Palestinians and, prior to 1967, many were highly susceptible to the propaganda of Egypt, Syria and the PLO which accused the Jordanian government of failing to meet its commitments to the Palestinians and to the ideal of Arab co-operation. The riots which followed Israel's raid on the Jordanian border village of Samu provide a good example of the way in which the feelings of Jordan's Palestinian citizens can influence Jordan's foreign policy. Although this was not the only reason for the King's decision to enter a defence pact with Egypt, it was a major factor.

In consideration of the events leading up to the 1967 Arab–Israeli war it was emphasized that in many respects the war broke out as a result of inter-Arab rivalry and divisions. The issue of Israel was one of the principal axes around which the struggle for leadership of the Arab world revolved. Each

Arab nation sought to outdo the others in its support of the Palestinians and thus brought the possibility of war ever closer. The rhetoric of Arab unity enabled the Arabs to goad each other on to their destruction. The use of propaganda as a means of influencing the general Arab populace has been revealed as a powerful but dangerous technique that unleashed a torrent of popular feeling which no Arab leader could afford to ignore. Jordan had long been subjected to this destructive form of foreign policy implementation, but Israel's attack on Samu led to a storm of abuse by the radical Arab forces. The Jordanian government was accused of being a traitor to the Arab cause, of deserting the Palestinians in their hour of need and of being too soft on Israel. The resulting wave of civil unrest ensured that the Jordanian government would find it almost impossible to refrain from participation in any Arab–Israel confrontation. Consequently, the Jordanian elite was forced to participate in a war which it knew it could not win.

The role played by Syria in the period leading up to war, and during the war itself, provides an excellent example of the destructive effect of an ideology which had little foundation in fact. Syria's provocative policy towards Israel was directed at drawing the Arabs into a confrontation with it, even though Syria knew that Israel was far more powerful than the Arabs. The Jordanians believed that Syrian claims to support the Palestinians under the guise of Arab unity masked a desire to win the leadership of the Arab world. They believed that Syria was using the issue of Israel to defeat both King Hussein and Nasser, either by demonstrating their lack of integrity or as a result of military defeat by Israel.

Syria's role in forcing a confrontation with Israel is even more ironic when one considers its passive stance when war eventually broke out. Syria had constantly exhorted the Arabs to confront Israel by force, although the military body established at the first summit conference in January 1964 (the Unified Arab Command) had warned the Arabs that they could not hope to be victorious over Israel until 1970 at the earliest. When it came to war, Syria stood aside despite its defence pact with Egypt, while Israel overran Gaza, Sinai and the West Bank. Throughout the critical days between 5 and 8 June 1967 the Egyptian political and military leadership begged Syria to fulfil its commitments and to support Jordan's efforts, but it refused to respond even though Jordan had entered the war in the belief that it would be supported by Syria and Egypt. Syria's inactivity was especially destructive because Jordan moved one of its two armoured brigades from its position opposite northern Israel, further south, on the basis of Syrian promises that their forces would take its place. When they failed to do so Israel swiftly moved in to take the northern areas of the West Bank, including the cities of Jenin and Nablus.

The destructive role of Arab propaganda is also evident when one considers the effect of the radio station 'Saut Al-Arab'. Far from promoting Arab unity its daily outpourings deliberately sought to destabilize the conservative Arab regimes and created deep national and regional conflicts. During the 1967 war the excesses of the station hampered the Arab war-effort in at least three ways. Its description of the 'victorious' march of Arab troops to the front line made it unnecessary for the Israelis to use any of their surveillance techniques to locate their position. The Israelis only had to listen to 'Saut Al-Arab' to know precisely where to direct their aircraft to smash the hapless Arabs before they had a chance to relieve the beleaguered Jordanian troops. The misleading broadcasts of Arab victories prevented the Egyptians and Jordanians at the UN from pressing for an early ceasefire which, if it had been successfully imposed, would have limited Israel's territorial gains and prevented thousands of people from being made homeless. Their premature description of the taking of Mount Scopus alerted the Israelis to this danger and ensured that they moved swiftly to prevent this and brought forward their plan for the occupation of Arab Jerusalem.

The reasons for Jordan's participation in the 1967 war can be found in four main areas: Jordan's commitment to Arab unity and co-operation; its commitment to the cause of Palestine; domestic pressures; external pressures. Perhaps the most important of these four areas is Jordan's commitment to Arab unity and co-operation. The remaining three can be related to the pursuit of this ideal. The view of most observers is that Jordan joined the Arab war effort either as a result of a mistaken belief that the Arabs would be victorious, or because it had no choice. The evidence described in this text shows that the first of these contentions is false. It is clear that King Hussein joined forces with Egypt in the knowledge that there was no possibility of overrunning Israel. Instead he sought to preserve the status quo. He believed that he could not stand aside at a time when Arab co-operation and solidarity were vital and he was convinced that any Arab confrontation with Israel would be greatly enhanced if the Arabs fought as a unified body. The plan of action devised at his meeting with Nasser in Cairo on 30 May was established on this basis. It was envisaged that Jordan would not take an offensive role but would tie down a proportion of Israel's forces and so prevent it from using its full weight against Egypt and Syria. By forcing Israel to fight a war on three fronts simultaneously King Hussein believed that the Arabs stood a chance of preventing it from making any territorial gains while allowing the Arabs a chance of gaining a political victory, which may, eventually, lead to peace.

King Hussein was also convinced that even if Jordan did not participate in the war Israel would take the opportunity to seize the West Bank once it had dealt with Syria and Egypt. He decided that for this reason the wisest course of action was to bring Jordan into the total Arab effort. This would provide his army with two elements which were essential for its efficient operation – additional troops and air cover. When King Hussein met Nasser in Cairo it was agreed that these requirements would be met.

The second contention that Jordan joined the Arab war effort because it had no choice is misleading. There is no doubt that Jordan faced a dangerous situation in the months preceding the war. Arab propaganda had whipped up feeling within Jordan in favour of war and had cast doubt on the Jordanian Government's commitment to Arabism and to Palestine. Although the riots that followed in the wake of Israel's raid on Samu were contained, popular feeling in favour of war was still strong and King Hussein was forced to take it into account. He believed that if he failed to contain this feeling he ran the risk of civil war. However, King Hussein has faced many similar situations but has not given way to the popular mood. For this reason, his decision to enter a defence pact with Nasser must be seen in terms of his commitment to Arab unity.

This is borne out by the fact that the King was prepared to place the Jordanian army under the direction of Egyptian commanders. There is no evidence to suggest that this was imposed on him against his will. Instead the evidence suggests that he freely consented. Such an action can only be understood in terms of King Hussein's determination to operate in harmony with his Arab brethren. If he had merely wanted to still the clamouring of his Palestinian population he would not have done this. Further evidence of his primary motivation is provided by comparing Jordan's actions during the war with those of Syria. When asked to enter the offensive Jordan did not hesitate but responded wholeheartedly, even though Jordanian army officers had serious misgivings. Syria, on the other hand, took only limited action despite the plight of the Jordanian army and the pleas of Egyptian leaders.

The description of the first day of war in Jordan reveals that the decision to bring Jordan into what was meant to be an overall Arab action was disastrous. By attempting to place Arab interests above all others, the Jordanians allowed Egyptian interests to prevail over Jordan's. Egypt abused its command of the Eastern Front, which included the Jordanian–Israeli border, by issuing commands which were intended to benefit the war in Egypt rather than the war in Jordan. The stream of misinformation and misdirection coming from Cairo proved catastrophic for Jordan. On the morning of the first day of war Jordan's carefully planned strategy was replaced by one which bore no reality to the requirements on the ground. Jordan acted on the basis of help which did not come, of troop movements which did not take place and air cover which was non-existent. Under these circumstances it is hardly surprising that within three days Israel had overrun the West Bank.

The events described in this text highlight a central paradox about Jordan's role in the 1967 war. The Hashemite regime had always declared that it was committed to Arabism but its moderate attitude towards Israel resulted in this commitment being constantly questioned by the more radical Arab nations and the PLO. In the 1967 war Jordan demonstrated its willingness to throw all its resources into the general Arab effort. In the name of Arab unity King Hussein agreed to place his army under the leadership of Egyptian commanders and accepted their directions despite the grave misgivings of his officers. In this way Jordan offered the ultimate sacrifice. However, the nation which gave the most, lost the most, and the only compensation its rulers received was Arab recognition of the depth and sincerity of Jordan's commitment to Arab unity and the Palestine cause.

Appendix: Timetable for the movement of Iraqi forces to Jordan

Date	Destination			
	Al-Ramadi	Al-Muhammadiya	H3	Jordan
4.6.67	27 infantry brigade 6 armoured brigade	1 infantry brigade	8 mechanized brigade	
5.6.67	6 armoured brigade	27 infantry brigade	1 infantry brigade	8 mechanized brigade
6.6.67		6 armoured brigade	27 infantry brigade	1 infantry brigade 8 mechanized brigade
7.6.67			6 armoured brigade	27 infantry brigade 1 infantry brigade 8 mechanized brigade
9.6.67				6 armoured brigade 27 infantry brigade 1 infantry brigade 8 mechanized brigade

Distances		
	Jalula'a to Al-Ramadi	320 km
	Al-Ramadi to Al-Muhammadiya	160 km
	Al-Muhammadiya to H3	60 km
	H3 to Jordan border	330 km
	Jordan border to Jordan valley	430 km

Biographical notes

WASFI TAL

Born in 1921, the eldest son of the famous poet Mustafa Wahbi Tal. He won a scholarship to the American University of Beirut where he read Chemistry and Physics. After graduation in 1941 he worked as a teacher, but was jailed the following year because his father's nationalist views were in opposition to those of the government.

At university Tal had been influenced by the Arab Nationalist Movement which sought to promote Arab unity and opposed Jewish migration into Palestine. In accordance with its strictures in 1942 Tal tried to join the Arab Legion, but his application was turned down by Glubb because he was a university graduate. Instead Tal joined the British Army in Palestine and served as a Lieutenant and then Captain until 1945.

For the next two years Tal worked for the Arab Bureau in London as a spokesman for Arab views on Palestine. After the UN decision to partition Palestine he resigned and joined the voluntary Salvation Army for Palestine as a Staff Officer. At the end of the 1948 war this army was absorbed by Syria and Tal was appointed a colonel. When the Syrian army entered negotiations with Israel Tal opposed this. He was arrested and later deported to Jordan where he worked as a civil servant. In 1955 Tal was appointed Director General of the Department of Press and Publications under the six-day cabinet of his friend, Hazza' Al-Majali. In Majali's next cabinet of 1959 Tal became President of the National Directorate of Information (which later became the Ministry of Information) and Director General of Radio Jordan.

In 1962, after a period as Ambassador to Iraq, at the age of 41, Tal formed his first cabinet. In 1970 he was held responsible for the Jordanian Government's confrontation with the PLO in September of that year. He was assassinated the following year by the Palestinian guerrilla organization, Black September, while attending the Arab League Council of Defence as Jordan's Minister of Defence.

Persons interviewed

ZAID RIFAI

Eldest son of Samir Rifai who was Prime Minister of Jordan several times. After graduating from Harvard, Zaid Rifai entered the Jordanian diplomatic service until his appointment as a senior aide to King Hussein in the Royal Hashemite Diwan. He was appointed Secretary General of the Diwan and eventually became Chief of the Diwan.

On 26 May 1973 he was appointed Prime Minister of Jordan and between then and 13 July 1976 he formed three cabinets. He is credited with playing a major part in the economic boom which was nicknamed 'the Rifai boom'. He resigned from the premiership in 1973 and served as a member of the House of Notables (the Senate). On 4 April 1985 he was once again appointed Prime Minister.

BAHJAT AL-TALHOUNI

Served as Chief of the Royal Hashemite Diwan several times since his first appointment in 1956. He has also been one of Jordan's longest-serving Prime Ministers, forming six cabinets between 1960 and 1970. He favoured a policy of close co-operation with Nasser and after the first Arab summit of 1964 he was appointed the King's personal representative in its follow-up committees which were concerned with executing the summit decisions. In the 1970s Talhouni served as President of the House of Notables (the Senate) and headed many pan-Arab Parliamentary committees at international events and conferences.

ABDUL MUNIM RIFAI

Served in various capacities in the Royal Hashemite Diwan under King Abdullah. He was appointed Minister of State for Foreign Affairs on 7 October 1967, a position which he held until 25 April 1968. On 24 March 1969 he was appointed Prime Minister, and between 1969 and 1970 he formed two cabinets. He has also served twice as Deputy Prime Minister. Rifai was Jordan's Permanent Representative at the United Nations for many years, including the critical period after the June war. In addition he has been Jordan's Ambassador to the Arab League and to Egypt. He was a member of the House of Notables (the Senate) until his death in October 1985. He was also a renowned poet.

DR HAZEM NUSSAIBAH

Foreign Minister of Jordan four times between 1962 and 1966. His other Cabinet appointments include Minister of State for Cabinet Affairs and Minister of Reconstruction and Development. He was Minister of the Royal Court several times and served as Jordan's Permanent Representative at the United Nations for many years. He has also been Jordan's Ambassador to a number of Arab countries and to the Arab League. He is currently a member of the House of Notables.

ADNAN ABU ODEH

Began his political career as a major in the Department of General Intelligence. In 1970 he was appointed Jordan's Minister of Information and Culture. On 11 October 1972 he was appointed Secretary General of the Jordanian National Union. This was a political group launched by Wasfi Tal. It sought to replace the tribes and the army as the mainstay of the political regime by a new generation of intellectuals. On 21 August 1973 Abu Odeh was appointed Chief of the Royal Hashemite Diwan until his appointment as Minister of Information on 10 November 1973. Between that time and 1980 he has held this position many times. In 1984 he was appointed Minister of the Royal Court.

MARWAN AL-KASSEM

As well as serving as Chief of the Royal Hashemite Diwan, Marwan Al-Kassem has held other Cabinet posts. He has been Jordan's Foreign Minister several times since 1976.

ÀKEF AL-FAYEZ

Member of the Chamber of Deputies (Parliament) since 1957. He has served as a Cabinet Minister several times and has also been Deputy Prime Minister. He is currently Jordan's Speaker of the Chamber of Deputies.

AKRAM ZUAITER

Renowned Arab historian. He is the Chairman of the 'Save Jerusalem Council'. He was appointed Foreign Minister in 1966 and was Minister of the Royal Court in 1967.

ABDUL RAOUF AL-FARES

Member of the Chamber of Deputies (Parliament) for Nablus from the 1950s until his death in 1985.

MURAIWED TAL

Brother of Wasfi Tal (see above). During the 1967 war he served as First Secretary in the Royal Hashemite Diwan. He also served in the Zaid Rifai cabinet as adviser to the Prime Minister. Currently he is director general of the Co-operative Organization.

FIELD MARSHALL HABES MAJALI (RTD)

Commander-in-Chief of the Jordanian Armed Forces during the 1967 war. He is known as the 'Hero of Latrun' because of his successful defence of the strategically vital salient of Latrun in the region of Ramallah during the 1948 Arab–Israeli war. At that time he was a Lt Colonel and in command of the 4th Regiment.

Field Marshall Majali retired from active service after the 1967 war and was appointed Minister of Defence. He has served as Cabinet Minister several times. He was reinstated as Commander in Chief of the Jordanian Armed Forces in 1970, a post he held for several years.

LT GENERAL AMER KHAMMASH (RTD)

Chief of Staff of the Jordanian Armed Forces during the 1967 war. He has served as Minister of Defence and Transport in two Cabinets between 30 June 1969 and 19 April 1970. He also served for many years as Minister of the Royal Court after 1970. He is currently a Member of the Chamber of Notables (the Senate).

LT GENERAL MASHOUR HADITHA

Commander of the Eastern Front (the Jordanian forces in the East Bank) during the 1967 war. After the war he was appointed a Divisional Commander. In 1969 he was promoted to Lt General and appointed Chief of Staff of the Jordanian Armed Forces. He became known as the 'Hero of Karama' for his part in the Battle of Karama (21.3.68), when his forces beat off an Israeli attack on the town in the Jordan Valley.

MAJOR GENERAL MUHAMMAD AHMED SALIM (RTD)
Commander of the Western Front (the forces in the West Bank) during the 1967 war.

MAJOR GENERAL YUSUF KAWASH (RTD)
Served as a Staff Officer to General Abdul Munim Riad at the Advanced Post GHQ in Amman during the 1967 war. He was a member of Jordan's delegation to the unified Arab Command in Cairo between 1964 and 1967 and served as the Staff Officer in charge of operations for the Central Front (Jordan) in the UAC.

IBRAHIM AYOUB
Ex-Minister of Supplies in the Jordanian Government. He served as Jordan's Director of Military Intelligence at GHQ during the 1967 war.

MAJOR GENERAL ALI ABU NAWAR
Jordan's Chief of Staff in 1957.

BRIGADIER FAWZI EBEIDAT
Jordan's Director of Military Operations at GHQ until July 1985 when he was appointed Commander of Jordan's newly established Royal War College.

BRIGADIER SHAFIK EJAILAN
Currently Jordan's Military Attaché at the Jordanian Embassy in London. He served as a Staff Officer attached to Eastern Command during the 1967 war.

AIR FORCE BRIGADIER HUSAM ABU GHAZALEH
Currently Jordan's Deputy Commander of the Royal Jordanian Airforce.

COLONEL YUSUF AL-DALABIH
Regimental Commander of the 40th armoured brigade during the 1967 war.

Notes

1 The decision-making process in Jordan

1 H. Sharabi, *Government and Politics of the Middle East in the Twentieth Century*, Princeton, New Jersey: Van Nostrand, 1962, chapter 1.
2 M. Hudson, *Arab Politics: The Search for Legitimacy*, New Haven and London; Yale University Press, 1977, p. 19.
3 *25 Years of History, the Complete Collection of H.M. King Hussein Ben Talal's Speeches 1952–1977* vol. 2, London: Samir Mutawi and Associates Publishing, 1979, in Arabic, p. 314. Hereafter referred to as *Speeches*.
4 Hudson, *Arab Politics* 1977, p. 166.
5 Ibid., p. 167.
6 For an informative study of ruling elite theory, see R. A. Dahl, 'A Critique of the Ruling Elite Model', American Political Science Review, vol. 52, no. 2, June 1958.
7 Interviews with Bahjat Talhouni, Zaid Rifai, Abdul Munim Rifai, Dr Hazem Nussaibah and Adnan Abu Odeh.
8 Interview with A. M. Rifai.
9 Interview with H. Nussaibah.
10 Interview with King Hussein.
11 Interview with H. Nussaibah.
12 Hudson, *Arab Politics* 1977, p. 26.
13 Hussein, *My Profession as a King*, Amman: Ghaleb Toukan, 1978, in Arabic; and Hussein, *My War with Israel*, London: Peter Owen, 1969.
14 The *Daily Telegraph*, 15.7.66.
15 Interview with H. Nussaibah.
16 S.A. El-Edroos, *The Hashemite Arab Army, 1908–1979*, Amman Publishing Committee, 1980, p. 310.
17 Hussein, *My Profession* 1978, pp. 70–2.
18 Hudson, *Arab Politics* 1977, p. 25.
19 Ibid.
20 Interview with A. Abu Odeh.
21 Hussein, 1978, op. cit., p. 212.
22 Abu Odeh confirms that 'army affairs are the King's domain and his alone'. Interview with A. Abu Odeh.
23 *Speeches* 1979, p. 587.
24 Interview with A. Abu Odeh.

25 Ibid.
26 Out of a total of 154 speeches made by King Hussein between January 1962 and December 1967, 49 were concerned with foreign policy.
27 *The New York Herald Tribune* 18.11.64.
28 *Middle East Record 1967* (Jerusalem: Israel Universities Press, 1971), p. 404; also interview with King Hussein.
29 Interview with Z. Rifai. The same point was made by many other Jordanian politicians.
30 Interview with A. Abu Odeh.
31 Interview with Marwan Al-Kassem.
32 Interview with H. Nussaibah.
33 Interview with Muraiwed Tal.
34 Hussein 1978, p. 69.
35 Interview with A. Abu Odeh.
36 Interview with Z. Rifai.
37 Interview with A. M. Rifai.
38 Interview with H. Nussaibah.
39 Interview with A. Abu Odeh.
40 Interview with A. M. Rifai.
41 Ibid.
42 Interview with Z. Rifai.
43 R. H. Dekmejian, *Egypt Under Nasser*, London: University of London Press, 1972, p. 10.
44 For an interesting study of these weaknesses see J. W. Spanier, *World Politics in an Age of Revolution*, New York: Praeger, 1967, pp. 151–95.
45 Dekmejian, *Egypt* 1972, p. 13.
46 See P. J. Vatikiotis, *Politics and the Military in Jordan*, London: Frank Cass, 1967, p. 134.
47 Interview with A. Abu Odeh.
48 Interview with Lt Gen. Amer Khammash.

2 The principles and practice of Jordanian foreign policy

1 J. Morris, *The Hashemite Kings*, London: Faber and Faber, 1959, p. 214; King Hussein, *Uneasy Lies the Head: An Autobiography*, London: Heinemann, 1962, p. 81.
2 Interviews with Zaid Rifai and Dr Hazem Nussaibah.
3 Interview with Z. Rifai.
4 Interview with Adnan Abu Odeh.
5 This belief was expressed by A. Abu Odeh: 'Defence of the Arab world [is] not limited to the geographical borders, but also [includes] the adoption of more moderate Arab policies, particularly in relation to Israel.' Interview.
6 For example, this was clearly stated by the Syrian head of state, Nuridin Atasi, on 7 December 1966: 'The elimination of the Jordanian throne which is protected by US–British imperialism is the only course for progressive forces in the Jordan to liberate the two Banks of the country on both sides of the Jordan River and thus clear

the way to return to Palestine.' These inflammatory statements were followed by others pledging support for the rebellion in Jordan against 'the traitor King Hussein'. *Radio Jordan Bulletin*, 7.12.66.

7 Hussein, *Autobiography* 1962, p. 105.

8 Ibid., p. 80.

9 A. Dawisha, 'Jordan in the Middle East: The Art of Survival' in P. Seale, ed., *The Shaping of an Arab Statesman: Sharif Abdul Hamid Sharaf and the Modern Arab World*, London: Quartet, 1983, p. 65.

10 Interview with Z. Rifai.

11 Interview with H. Nussaibah.

12 *The Guardian* 31.3.64.

13 King Abdullah of Jordan, *My Memoirs Completed*, London: Longmans, 1981, p. xiii.

14 P. Mansfield, ed., *The Middle East: A Political and Economic Survey*, London: Oxford University Press, 1973, p. 391.

15 Interview with Abdul Raouf Fars.

16 Ibid.

17 However, in many quarters it is recognized that his subjection of the Palestinians was 'the product not of the ruthless mind of a military dictator, but of an agonizing process of decision-making'. P. Snow, *Hussein*, London: Barrie and Jenkins, 1972, p. 251.

18 Hussein, *Autobiography* 1962, p. 78.

19 Interview with Z. Rifai.

20 The *Guardian* 31.3.64.

21 Interview with Z. Rifai.

22 For example, 'in August 1960 the pro-Western Prime Minister Hazza Al-Majali was killed when a time bomb concealed in his desk exploded. The plot was traced to Syria and further identified with Cairo'. R. Rinehart, 'Historical Setting' in R. F. Nyorp, ed., *Jordan: A Country Study*, Washington: Foreign Area Studies, American University, 1980, p. 33.

23 Interview with A. Abu Odeh.

24 N. Aruri, *Jordan, A Study in Political Development: 1921–1965*, The Hague, Martin Nijhoff, 1972, p. 68.

25 According to Aruri, 'the Circassians, although numbering only about 12,000 in 1964–5 had a tradition of government service which dated back to the Ottomans. Between 1947 and 1965 there was at least one Circassian in 26 out of the 33 Cabinets'. In fact, the accurate figure was at least one Circassian in 27 out of 36 cabinets. *Jordanian Cabinets, 1921–1976*, Amman, Ministry of Information, in Arabic, pp. 19–62. Aruri points out that the 'Circassians constitute an important element of Jordan's upper class. They are prosperous businessmen, financiers and landlords . . . they are dependent upon the regime for the protection of their status as a minority group. In return the regime is assured of their loyalty and support during upheavals.' Aruri, *Jordan* 1972, pp. 39–40.

26 The Christian Arabs, numbering about 110,000 (about 6.5 per cent of the population), normally occupied about 15 per cent of the seats in Parliament. They were also prominent in commerce and industry, but their privileges stemmed largely from their strong links with the West; thus their allegiance to a pro-Western monarchy was

assured, although they were not as homogenous a community as the Circassians or Bedouin.

27 Central Bank of Jordan, *The Adverse Effects of Israel's Occupation of the West Bank on Jordan's Economy* 1.9.75.

28 Jordan is basically an agricultural country; about one-third of the economically active population is engaged in agriculture which, on average, contributes about one-fifth of the Gross Domestic Product. However, agriculture is a highly unstable industry in Jordan because a large proportion of total agricultural output is derived from dry farming in areas subject to frequent droughts. Because of the resulting fluctuations in agricultural production and income, primary emphasis in recent years has been given to irrigation schemes and soil and water conservation programmes.

29 Ibid., p. 18.

30 S. Green, *Taking Sides*, New York: William Morrow and Co., 1984, pp. 16–46.

31 Interview with King Hussein. The King is referring to President Eisenhower's decision to cut financial aid to Israel in 1956.

32 Ibid.

33 Interview with H. Nussaibah.

34 Ibid.

35 Interview with Z. Rifai.

36 Israel, the Arabs, the USA and the USSR all recognized that the Arabs had no chance of winning a military confrontation with Israel. Although numerically weaker, in terms of technical sophistication, skilled personnel and ability to mobilize, the Israelis had the upper hand. They were also unified while the Arabs not only had weapons which were not necessarily compatible with each other, but were also drawn from many different armies with no experience of working together in either training or active combat. King Hussein describes how in 1964 the Arabs made a comparative study of Arab/Israeli military capability and the conclusions that were drawn:
'the Unified Arab Command ... was created with the best available military capabilities in terms of people of experience to study the problem. The results were clear – clear to us because we had always lived with the problem – but were horrifying at the same time. Nothing could be done and in fact a number of us were required to build up Arab strength to a degree of parity with Israel to begin with, and if nothing happened during that period of time the Arabs could then begin to gain superiority.' Interview with King Hussein.

37 Cited in M. Brecher, *Decisions in Crisis*, London, University of California Press, 1980, p. 40.

38 Interview with King Hussein.

39 W. Tal, *Writings in Arab Affairs*, Amman: Dar al-Liwa, 1980, in Arabic, pp. 108–126 and pp. 150–5; S. Juma'a, *The Conspiracy and the Battle of Destiny* (Beirut: Dar al-Kateb al-Arabi, 1968, in Arabic, p. 145.

40 Aruri, *Jordan* 1972, p. 39.

41 D. Pevety, 'The Arab Refugee: A Changing Problem', *Foreign Affairs* vol. 41, 1963.

42 Aruri, *Jordan* 1972, p. 188.

43 Hussein, *My Profession as a King*, Amman: Ghaleb Toukan, 1978, in Arabic, pp. 208–9.
44 P. J. Vatikiotis, *Politics and the Military in Jordan*, London: Frank Cass, 1967, p. 5.
45 Ibid., p. 20.
46 S. A. El-Edroos, *The Hashemite Arab Army: 1908–1979*, Amman: Publishing Committee, 1980, p. 310.
47 It is a curious fact that all attempted coups by army officers have been plotted by urban Transjordanians.

3 Friends and enemies

1 M. I. Faddah, *The Middle East in Transition: Jordan's Foreign Policy 1948–1967*, London: Asia Publishing House, 1974, p. 73; Y. Harkabi, 'Fedayeen Action and Arab Strategy', Adelphi Papers, no. 53, December 1968, London, Institute for Strategic Studies, p. 19.
2 Nasser's speech of 2.1.62, *Al-Ahram* 3.1.62.
3 Nasser's speech of 23.12.62, *Al-Ahram* 24.12.62.
4 This was expressed by Nasser on many occasions. See his speech of 22.2.67, *Al-Ahram* 23.2.67.
5 Interview with Adnan Abu Odeh.
6 J. Badeau, Introduction to G. A. Nasser, *Philosophy of the Revolution*, Buffalo, New York: Economica Books, 1959, p. 14.
7 P. J. Vatikiotis, *Conflict in the Middle East*, London: George Allen and Unwin, 1971, pp. 19–20.
8 Nasser's speech of 22.2.64, *The Egyptian Gazette* 23.2.64.
9 A. I. Dawisha, *Egypt in the Arab World*, London: Macmillan Press, 1976, p. 141.
10 Nasser's speech of 22.2.64, *The Egyptian Gazette*, 23.2.64; *Arab Political Documents*, Beirut: American University of Beirut, 1964, p. 52.
11 Interview with King Hussein. Here the King is referring to the Syrian Ba'ath Party in the 1960s.
12 Ibid.
13 Harkabi, 'Fedayeen Action' 1968, p. 5.
14 *Arab Political Documents* 1964, p. 57.
15 Ibid.
16 Interview with King Hussein.
17 N. Safran, *Israel: The Embattled Ally*, Cambridge, Massachusetts and London: The Belknap Press of Harvard University Press, 1978, p. 385.
18 Interview with A. Abu Odeh.
19 P. J. Vatikiotis, *Conflict* 1971, p. 133.
20 Nasser's speech of 23.12.63, *Al-Ahram* 24.12.63, also cited in M. Kerr, *The Arab Cold War*, London: Oxford University Press, 1971, p. 100.
21 Interview with King Hussein.
22 Ibid.
23 Hussein, *My Profession as a King*, Amman: Ghaleb Toukan, 1978, in Arabic, p. 211.
24 Interview with A. Abu Odeh.
25 Interview with Dr Hazem Nussaibah.

26 Hussein, *My War with Israel*, London: Peter Owen, 1969, p. 14.
27 Interview with H. Nussaibah.
28 *25 Years of History, The Complete Collection of H.M. King Hussein Ben Talal's Speeches 1952–1977*, London: Samir Mutawi and Associates Publishing, 1979, in Arabic, vol. 2, p. 250, hereafter referred to as *Speeches*.
29 Ibid., p. 251.
30 *Arab Political Documents* 1964, p. 8.
31 Interview with A. Abu Odeh.
32 M. Riad, *The Struggle for Peace in the Middle East*, London: Quartet, 1981, p. 12.
33 S. Juma'a, *The Conspiracy and the Battle of Destiny*, Beirut: Dar al-Kateb al-Arabi, 1968, in Arabic, pp. 119–20.
34 W. Tal, *Writings in Arab Affairs*, Amman: Dar al-Liwa, 1980, in Arabic, p. 326.
35 Interview with Lt General Amer Khammash.
36 Hussein, *My War* 1969, p. 19.
37 *Speeches* 1979, p. 542.
38 Interview with H. Nussaibeh.
39 Interview with A. Abu Odeh.
40 *Speeches* 1979, p. 374.
41 *Al-Jihad* 22.6.65; also *Arab Political Documents* 1965, p. 242.
42 Ibid., p. 243.
43 Kerr, *Arab Cold War* 1971, p. 106.
44 *Speeches* 1979, p. 548.
45 Ibid.
46 Ibid.
47 Interview with King Hussein.
48 Ibid.
49 Interview with King Hussein in *Al-Ra'yul al-Aam* 3.2.67.
50 Interview with King Hussein.
51 Juma'a, *Conspiracy* 1968, p. 121.
52 Safran, *Israel* 1978, p. 385.
53 Harkabi, 'Fedayeen Action' 1968, contains a detailed exposition of Fatah doctrine and criticism of Arab leaders.
54 Interview with A. Abu Odeh.
55 *The New York Times* 8.12.66.
56 *The New York Times* 3.12.66; *The Guardian* 2.12.66.
57 *Arab Political Documents* 1964, pp. 382–3.
58 R. Stephens, *Nasser: A Political Biography*, London: Allen Lane, The Penguin Press, 1971, p. 451.
59 *Speeches* 1979, p. 365.
60 Ibid, p. 369.
61 For King Hussein's attitude to subversion see *Arab Political Documents* 1965, p. 358.
62 Interview with A. Abu Odeh.
63 Interview with King Hussein.
64 Interview with A. Abu Odeh.
65 *PLO Information Bulletin*, vol. 2, no. 8.
66 Harkabi, 'Fedayeen Action' 1968, p. 7.

67 *Speeches* 1979, p. 400.
68 Hussein, *My War* 1969, pp. 21–2.
69 Ibid., p. 23.
70 *Speeches* 1979, p. 510.
71 P. Mansfield, *Nasser's Egypt*, Harmondsworth: Penguin, 1969, p. 16.
72 Cited in A. Dawisha, *Egypt in the Arab World*, London: Macmillan Press, 1976, p. 47.
73 Interview with A. M. Rifai.
74 Nasser's speech of 23.7.66, *The Egyptian Gazette*, 24.7.66.

4 Samu

1 J. B. Glubb, *The Middle East Crisis*, London: Hodder and Stoughton, 1967, p. 16.
2 Interview with Adnan Abu Odeh.
3 *25 Years of History, The Complete Collection of H.M. King Hussein Ben Talal's Speeches, 1952–1977*, London: Samir Mutawi and Associates Publishing, 1979, in Arabic, p. 541, hereafter referred to as *Speeches*.
4 King Hussein's speech at the UN on 26.6.67 in *Speeches* 1979, p. 607–13.
5 Interview with Dr Hazem Nussaibah.
6 This policy had been reflected in Jordan's defence arrangements since 1954. That year Jordan joined the Arab Joint Defence Treaty. The following year Hussein did his best to bring Jordan into the Baghdad Pact; when that proved impossible he brought the country into the Arab Mutual Defence Agreement. Two years later Jordan formed an alliance with Iraq.
7 Issued in Beirut on 24.1.64 and published in *Al-Hayat* 25.1.64.
8 Interview with Lt General Amer Khammash.
9 For text see *Arab Political Documents*, Beirut: The American University of Beirut, 1964, p. 8.
10 A. Eban, *An Autobiography*, London: Weidenfeld and Nicolson, 1977, p. 312.
11 Interview with A. Abu Odeh.
12 *The Times* 24.5.66.
13 *The New York Times* 12.5.66.
14 *The Economist* 23.7.66.
15 See chapter 3.
16 Nasser's speech, *Radio Jordan Bulletin* 23.12.63.
17 Cited by M. Kerr, *The Arab Cold War* (New York: Oxford University Press, 1971), pp. 99–100.
18 Ibid., p. 100.
19 Interview with A. Khammash.
20 Interview with A. Abu Odeh.
21 Interview with A. Khammash.
22 Interview with A. Abu Odeh.
23 Interview with Major General Yusuf Kawash.
24 Interview with King Hussein.
25 For example, see S. Juma'a, *The Conspiracy and the Battle of Destiny*, Beirut: Dar al-Kateb al-Arabi, 1968, in Arabic, p. 140–2.

26 *New York Herald Tribune* 9.10.66.
27 *Palestinian Diaries*, Beirut: PLO Research Centre, 1966–7, vols. 4 and 5, in Arabic, 20.5.67.
28 Glubb, *Middle East Crisis* 1967, p. 17.
29 See chapter 6 for an account of how Russia's actions precipitated the war.
30 *The Economist* 19.6.66.
31 Hussein, *My Profession as a King*, Amman: Ghaleb Toukan, 1978, in Arabic, p. 206.
32 *The Economist* 25.2.67.
33 *The Observer* 9.12.66; Kerr, *Arab Cold War* 1971, p. 115.
34 Statement of the Syrian Foreign Minister, 13.5.67. SWB/ME/2466/A7–9. The point was also confirmed by the Syrian Foreign Minister to the American Ambassador in Damascus. *Palestinian Diaries* 1966–7, 29.5.67.
35 Hussein, *My Profession* 1978, p. 206.
36 Interview with A. Khammash.
37 W. Tal, *Writings in Arab Affairs* Amman: Dar al-Liwa, 1980, in Arabic, p. 241.
38 According to Dupuy '18 Jordanian soldiers were killed and 54 wounded'. T. Dupuy, *Elusive Victory: The Arab–Israeli Wars of 1947–74*, New York: Harper and Row, 1978, p. 227. According to Abu Nuwar, Jordanian losses were 'two officers killed and two wounded and, of other military personnel, 13 killed and 22 wounded. The inhabitants of Samu sustained five martyrs and six wounded'. M. Abu Nuwar, *For the Sake of Jerusalem*, Amman: Moral Guidance Directorate, Army GHQ, 1968, in Arabic, p. 23.
39 According to Abu Nuwar: 'the enemy sustained 50 casualties, killed and wounded'. Abu Nuwar, *Jerusalem* 1968, p. 23.
40 According to Abu Nuwar, the Israelis sustained 'the destruction of several tanks and armoured cars and two aircraft were hit'. Abu Nuwar, *Jerusalem* 1968, p. 23.
41 *The Economist* 19.11.66.
42 *The Egyptian Gazette* 23.11.66; The *Guardian* 19.11.66.
43 Interview with A. Khammash.
44 Interviews with King Hussein and A. Khammash.
45 Interview with King Hussein.
46 Interview with A. Khammash.
47 Tal, *Arab Affairs* 1980, p. 241; *The New York Times* 22.11.66.
48 Tal, *Arab Affairs* 1980, p. 327.
49 Interview with A. Abu Odeh.
50 Tal, *Arab Affairs* 1980, p. 241. The same feeling was expressed by King Hussein. Interview.
51 *Al-Manar* 22.11.66.
52 Tal, *Arab Affairs* 1980, p. 242.
53 Interview with King Hussein. The same point was made by Abu Nuwar, *Jerusalem* 1968, pp. 18–19.
54 Interviews with H. Nussaibah, A. Abu Odeh and M. A. Salim.
55 Tal, *Arab Affairs* 1980, p. 242; *Al-Manar* 22.11.66.
56 Interview with A. Khammash.
57 Ibid.
58 Interview with King Hussein.

59 Tal, *Arab Affairs* 1980, p. 327.
60 Ibid., p. 336.
61 This account is drawn from descriptions in *The Egyptian Gazette* 23 and 24.11.66; *International Documents on Palestine*, Beirut: The Institute for Palestine Studies, 1967, p. 494; H. Kosut, ed., *Israel and the Arabs: The June 1967 War*, New York: Facts on File, 1968, pp. 30–2; *The New York Times* 22.11.66; P. Snow, *Hussein: A Biography*, London: Barrie and Jenkins, 1972, p. 168.
62 P. Snow, *Hussein* 1972, p. 168.
63 This information was given to the author by a Jordanian well-informed source who prefers to remain anonymous.
64 Interview with H. Nussaibah.
65 Tal, *Arab Affairs* 1980, p. 243.
66 *The New York Times* 12.12.66.
67 The *Guardian* 10.12.66.
68 *The New York Times* 12.12.66.
69 *Middle East Record: 1967*, Jerusalem: Israel Universities Press, 1971, p. 117.
70 Ibid., *Middle East Record* 1971, p. 118.
71 Kerr, *Arab Cold War* 1971, p. 117.
72 The *Daily Telegraph* 28.12.66.
73 *Radio Jordan Bulletin* 14.11.66–5.6.67.
74 Interview with Z. Rifai.
75 A. Nutting, *Nasser*, London: Constable, 1972, p. 393.
76 *Radio Jordan Bulletin* 18–19.5.67.
77 *Speeches* 1979, p. 549.

5 The gathering crisis

1 *The Jerusalem Post* 9.4.67. The Syrians claimed that their fighters shot down five Israeli planes compared with losing four of their own, three of which a Jordanian military spokesman announced had fallen onto Jordanian territory. *Palestinian Diaries*, Beirut: PLO Research Centre, 1966–7, vols. 4 and 5, 7.4.67.
2 *Al-Dastour* 10.5.67.
3 T. Dupuy, *Elusive Victory: The Arab-Israeli Wars 1947–74*, New York: Harper and Row, 1978, p. 226.
4 Ibid.
5 Hussein, *My Profession as a King*, Amman: Ghaleb Toukan, 1978, in Arabic, p. 205.
6 *Radio Jordan Bulletin*, December 1966–May 1967; A. Nutting, *Nasser*, London: Constable, 1972, p. 392.
7 W. Tal, *Writings in Arab Affairs*, Amman: Dar al-Liwa, 1980, in Arabic, p. 336.
8 Interviews with Dr Hazem Nussaibah and Muraiwed Tal; S. Juma'a, *The Conspiracy and the Battle of Destiny*, Beirut: Dar al-Kateb al-Arabi, 1968, in Arabic, pp. 169, 195, 225.
9 Interview with Adnan Abu Odeh.
10 Tal, *Arab Affairs* 1980, p. 329.
11 Ibid., p. 325.
12 Interview with Zaid Rifai.

13 Speech of Field Marshall Abdul Hakim Amer on the 11th anniversary of the Egyptian Revolution, 23.7.63.
14 M. Howard and R. Hunter 'Israel and the Arab World: The Crisis of 1967' *Adelphi Papers* no. 41, October 1967, London: Institute of Strategic Studies, p. 50.
15 Ibid. Dupuy gives different figures. Dupuy, *Elusive Victory* 1978, p. 337.
16 Howard and Hunter also provide figures for the balance of forces between Israel and the Arabs. Howard and Hunter, 'Israel' 1967, p. 50.
17 Cited in W. Laqueur *The Road to War: 1968* London: Weidenfeld and Nicolson, 1968, p. 68; *Palestinian Diaries* 20.5.67.
18 Dupuy, *Elusive Victory* 1978, p. 231.
19 S. Green, *Taking Sides*, New York: William Morrow and Co., 1984, p. 193.
20 Ibid., p. 199.
21 Ibid., p. 200.
22 Interview with H. Nussaibah.
23 Ibid.
24 Radio broadcast from Cairo, *Radio Jordan Bulletin* 23.5.67.
25 Interview with Major General Ahmad Salim.
26 Interview with Lt General Amer Khammash.
27 Juma'a, *Conspiracy* 1968, p. 164.
28 Interview with Marwan Al-Kassem.
29 Juma'a, *Conspiracy* 1968, p. 164.
30 Interview with A. Khammash.
31 Interview with A. Abu Odeh.
32 Nasser's speech to Arab Trade Unionists on 26.5.67, *Al-Ahram* 27.5.67; also *Palestinian Diaries* 25.5.67.
33 Statement of Government policy, 6.5.67, *Radio Jordan Bulletin* 6.5.67.
34 *International Documents on Palestine*, Beirut: The Institute for Palestine Studies, 1967, p. 486.
35 *Jordanian Documents*, Amman: Ministry of Information, 1967, in Arabic, p. 10.
36 *Palestinian Diaries*, 11.5.67; H. Kosut, ed., *Israel and the Arabs: The June 1967 War*, New York: Facts on File, 1968, p. 40.
37 Mapai was the ruling party at that time.
38 A. Eban, *An Autobiography*, London: Weidenfeld and Nicolson, 1977, p. 319.
39 Laqueur, op. cit., p. 59; *International Documents on Palestine*, *Road to War* 1968, p. 7.
40 Eban, *Autobiography* 1977, p. 319.
41 M. Riad, *The Struggle for Peace in the Middle East*, London: Quartet, 1981, p. 17, *Palestinian Diaries* 14.5.67.
42 Riad, *Struggle for Peace* 1982, p. 17.
43 Howard and Hunter, 'Israel' 1967, p. 15.
44 Interview with A. Khammash.
45 Nasser's speech, 22.5.67 at UAR Advanced Airforce HQs; *Palestinian Diaries* 22.5.67; Howard and Hunter, 'Israel' 1967, p. 15.
46 A UN spokesman announced: 'According to reports received from Lt General Odd Bull, Commander of the UN Armistice Supervisory Forces in the Middle East, the Secretary General is not aware of any troop movements or concentration on any of the

armistice lines in a way that may be worrying.' *Palestinian Diaries* 17.5.67; Dupuy, *Elusive Victory* 1978, p. 227; Howard and Hunter, 'Israel' 1967, p. 16.

47 *Palestinian Diaries* 25.5.67; *The Jerusalem Post* 24.5.67.

48 *Radio Jordan Bulletin* 18–19.5.67; Nutting, *Nasser* 1972, p. 401.

49 In a statement to the Knesset. Eshkol estimated Egyptian troops in Sinai to be around 80,000 men. *Palestinian Diaries* 22.5.67; General H. Herzog in the weekly supplement of *The Jerusalem Post* cited in *Palestinian Diaries* 2.6.67.

50 *The Times* said that until 17 May all the signs indicated that the UAR's request for UNEF to withdraw was a mere bluff and that it was not likely that the UAR was seriously considering engaging Israel in war. *Palestinian Diaries* 18.5.67. *The New York Times* also reported that Western observers in Cairo were of the opinion that Cairo wished to avoid military confrontation with Israel. They believed that Cairo was hoping that a show of force would deter Israel from taking any step it might have been contemplating. *Palestinian Diaries* 18.5.67. The same point was made by *The Jerusalem Post* which noted that the size of the Egyptian troop build-up was not large enough to undertake a full-scale attack. Ibid.

51 C. Yost, 'The Arab–Israeli War: How it Began', *Foreign Affairs*, New York, vol. 46, no. 2, January 1968.

52 Hussein, *My War with Israel*, London: Peter Owen, 1969, p. 34.

53 Interview with A. Abu Odeh.

54 Ibid.

55 Nasser's speech, 22.5.67, *Al-Ahram* 23.5.67.

56 Nasser's speech, 26.5.67, *Al-Ahram* 27.5.67.

57 *Al-Ahram* 26.5.67; *Radio Jordan Bulletin* 26.5.67.

58 Ibid.

59 Tal, *Arab Affairs* 1980, p. 330.

60 The United Press International quoted political reports from London which indicated that all circumstances confirmed that the Soviet Union was determined to benefit from the Middle East crisis to the maximum in order to strengthen its position in the area, *Palestinian Diaries* 25.5.67; *The New York Times* 30.5.67.

61 *The New York Times* 29.5.67.

62 Riad, *Struggle for Peace* 1981, p. 23.

63 *Palestinian Diaries* 18.5.67.

64 Abdul Majeen Farid, *Records, Secrets and Deliberations of Hussein–Nasser Talks: 1967–1970*, *Al-Rai* 6.4.83.

65 The Egyptian Intelligence had received news that the Israeli army would concentrate five divisions on the Egyptian border, but the Egyptians were ready to face any challenge, according to the Egyptian Land Forces Commander-in-Chief, General Al-Mortagi, who said that Israel had no firm defences and that Egypt had superiority in tanks and in the air. The Egyptian missile system was safeguarding the whole area. 'All the enemy knows we know too, and we are prepared for quick and strong counter action'. *Al-Musawar* 20.4.67.

66 Juma'a, *Conspiracy* 1968, p. 171.

67 *Al-Musawar* 18.5.67.

68 Nutting, *Nasser* 1972, p. 409.

69 Nasser's speech to members of the National Assembly, 29.5.67, *Al-Ahram* 30.5.67.

70 Nutting, *Nasser* 1972, p. 407.
71 Juma'a, *Conspiracy* 1968, p. 171.
72 D. Kimche and D. Bawly, *The Sandstorm*, London: Secker and Warburg, 1968, p. 109.
73 Nutting, *Nasser* 1972, p. 409.
74 Cited in S. Juma'a, *Conspiracy* 1968, pp. 172–3; also *Palestinian Diaries* 29.5.67.
75 Nutting, *Nasser* 1972, p. 408.
76 Ibid., p. 398.
77 Interview with A. Abu Odeh.
78 Interview with A. Khammash.
79 *The New York Times* 29.5.67.
80 Interview with King Hussein.
81 Hussein, *My Profession* 1978, pp. 208–9.
82 Interview with A. Khammash.
83 Interview with King Hussein.
84 *Palestinian Diaries* 22.5.67.
85 Interview with H. Nussaibah.
86 Interview with A. Abu Odeh.
87 Ibid.
88 Eban, *Autobiography* 1977, p. 328.
89 S. Juma'a, *Conspiracy* 1968, p. 174.
90 A. Eban, *Autobiography* 1977, p. 389.
91 *Palestinian Diaries* 30.5.67.
92 *The Jerusalem Post* 21.5.67.
93 *The New York Times* 29.5.67.
94 Interview with A. Khammash.
95 Interview with Z. Rifai.
96 Hussein, 1979, p. 36.
97 Interview with King Hussein.
98 Hussein, 1979, p. 45.
99 Ibid.
100 Interview with Abu Odeh.
101 This was confirmed in interviews with army commanders, including Major General M. A. Salim, Field Marshall Habes Majali and Lt General Mashour Haditha.
102 This is the King's cousin and Commander-in-Chief of the Jordanian army. In 1967 he commanded the army's 60th armoured brigade. Hussein, *My Profession* 1978, p. 209.
103 Ibid., p. 208.
104 Interview with H. Nussaibah.
105 Interview with King Hussein.
106 Hussein, *My Profession* 1978, p. 209.
107 Ibid.
108 Interview with Z. Rifai.
109 Interview with A. Abu Odeh.
110 *Palestinian Diaries* 18.5.67.
111 Hussein, *My War* 1969, p. 36.

112 *Jordanian Documents* 1967, p. 11.
113 Interview with King Hussein.
114 *Jordanian Documents* 1967, p. 17.
115 Eban, *Autobiography* 1977, p. 184.
116 Interview with A. Khammash.
117 Juma'a, *Conspiracy* 1968, pp. 186–7.
118 *Palestinian Diaries* 15.5.67; Juma'a, *Conspiracy* 1968, p. 187.
119 Interview with King Hussein.
120 Nasser's speech, 22.5.67.
121 Interview with A. Khammash.
122 Hussein, *My Profession* 1978, p. 210.

6 On the brink of war

1 For text see *Jordanian Documents*, Amman: Ministry of Information, 1967, pp. 19–21; also *The New York Times* 31.5.67.
2 Interview with Lt Gen. Amer Khammash.
3 Interview with King Hussein.
4 Hussein, *My War with Israel*, London: Peter Owen, 1969, p. 55; H. Mustafa, *The June 1967 War: The Eastern Front*, Beirut: Al-Mu'assasa Al-Arabia Lil Dirasat Wa Al-Nashr, 1973, in Arabic, p. 13.
5 Hussein, *My War* 1969, p. 55.
6 S. Juma'a, *The Conspiracy and the Battle of Destiny*, Beirut: Dar al-Kateb al-Arabi, 1968, in Arabic, p. 172. These expressions of confidence should be seen in the light of Juma'a's recognition that America would never allow the Arabs to overrun Israel. Ibid.
7 Interview with A. Khammash.
8 Interview with King Hussein.
9 Speech at signing ceremony, *The Daily Telegraph* 31.5.67; *Jordanian Documents* 1967, pp. 23–4.
10 *The Daily Telegraph* 31.5.67.
11 *Jordanian Documents* 1967, p. 29.
12 Juma'a, *Conspiracy* 1968, p. 173.
13 U. Narkiss, *The Liberation of Jerusalem*, London: Vallentine and Mitchell, 1983, p. 81.
14 *Palestinian Diaries* 1967, Beirut, PLO Research Centre, 3.6.67.
15 Interview with King Hussein; Juma'a, *Conspiracy* 1968, p. 175.
16 Jordanian Armed Forces *GHQ Report*, hereafter referred to as *GHQ Report*; interview with A. Khammash.
17 *The Times* 5.6.67; Hussein, *My War* 1969, p. 54.
18 *GHQ Report*.
19 Y. Kawash, *The Jordanian Front: The June 1967 War*, Amman: Al-Dar, Al-Asriyah Lil Sahafa Wal Nashr, 1980, in Arabic, p. 19.
20 Ibid., p. 29.
21 Major General Muhammed Ahmed Salim points out that 'the Israelis had the strength and capability to change their tactics and this made the task of the Jordanians even more difficult'. Interview.

22 The towns of Lydda and Ramla, which military strategists agree were almost indefensible, fell in 1948. A thin strip of land near Nablus was seized by Israel after the 1949 Rhodes Armistice Agreement and the premature withdrawal of Iraqi troops from the area.
23 This stretched from Irbed in the north to Aqaba in the south.
24 Interview with Brigadier Fawzi Ebeidat.
25 According to Brigadier Ebeidat the Jordanian army had never possessed more than one-third of the force needed for either of these defence requirements.
26 *GHQ Plans*, Al-Hussein Operation. Military Instruction no. 1/65, 4.9.65.
27 King Hussein points out that 'all we had in Jordan was a plan of defence. An offensive action was out of the question, particularly with the limited forces available at that time. Hussein, *My War* 1969, p. 56.
28 Interview with A. Khammash.
29 W. Tal, *Writings in Arab Affairs*, Amman: Dar Al-Liwa, 1980, in Arabic, p. 332.
30 Odd Bull, *War and Peace in the Middle East*, London: Leo Cooper, 1973, p. 63 and Appendix 2, Mount Scopus Agreement, p. 196.
31 Ibid., p. 66; R. and W. Churchill, *The Six Day War*, London: William Heinemann, 1967, p. 124.
32 General Odd Bull observed that 'its military significance is obvious. Whoever controls Mount Scopus controls the road northwards to Ramallah and Nablus and eastwards towards Jericho and Amman. If Israel managed to get control of Mount Scopus it would mean that Jerusalem was more or less encircled'. Odd Bull, *War and Peace* 1973, p. 63.
33 Narkiss, *Liberation* 1983, p. 23.
34 Y. Kawash confirms that all the army's situation assignments anticipated that an Israeli column would seek to push through Jenin to Qabatiya down to the Damia Bridge and from there block the Jerusalem–Jericho road. Interview.
35 *GHQ Plans* 4.9.65.
36 Interview with M. A. Salim.
37 Interview with F. Ebeidat.
38 Interviews with King Hussein and A. Khammash.
39 Ibid.
40 GHQ Operations Directive no. 6.
41 Hussein, *My War* 1969, p. 57.
42 Interviews with A. Khammash and Y. Kawash.
43 Interviews with King Hussein and A. Khammash.
44 Hussein, *My War* 1969, p. 58.
45 Ibid., p. 59.
46 *GHQ Plans*, Military Instruction no. 1/67, 23.5.67.
47 Hussein, *My War* 1969, p. 57; interviews with A. Khammash and Y. Kawash.
48 Interview with Y. Kawash.
49 The Jerusalem Corridor is the narrow western path which connects Jerusalem with Tel Aviv.
50 See Appendice 1 for the proposed deployment of the Iraqi forces.
51 Interview with A. Khammash.

7 The war

1 S. Juma'a's speech to Parliament on 5.7.67 in *Jordanian Documents*, Amman: Ministry of Information, 1967, p. 119 and interviews with Zaid Rifai and Lt General Amer Khammash.
2 S. Juma'a, *The Conspiracy and the Battle of Destiny*, Beirut: Dar al-Kateb al-Arabi, 1968, in Arabic, p. 176; Hussein, *My War with Israel*, London: Peter Owen, 1969, p. 55.
3 Interview with Lt General Amer Khammash.
4 Ibid.; Hussein, *My War* 1969, p. 55; Juma'a, *Conspiracy* 1968, p. 176. Observers argue that it should have been obvious that Israel would open hostilities in this way. Mustafa writes that 'anyone who correctly assessed the air power situation must have necessarily concluded that the enemy would first attack the Egyptian air force and air fields with a view to destroying them and to securing air supremacy.' H. Mustafa, *The June 1967 War: The Eastern Front*, Beirut: Al-Mu'assasa Al-Arabia Lil Dirasat Wa Al-Nashr, 1973, in Arabic, p. 13. The Jordanians had always been aware of this possibility. Major General Y. Kawash comments that in the spring of 1966 at a meeting held at the office of Brigadier Atef Majali in the UAC GHQs in Cairo 'we discussed the possibility of an air strike against the Egyptian air force to start with, followed by the bulk of Israel's land forces being directed to put Egypt quickly out of action'. Interview.
5 According to General Fawzi the signals corporal in charge of the Air Defence Signals station directly connected to Ajloun through a transmitting reception station had changed the reception frequency. M. Fawzi, *The Three Year War – 1967–1970: General Fawzi's Diary*, Beirut: Dar Al-Wahda, 1983, pp. 131–3.
6 According to the Churchills the turnaround time of the Israeli planes was 7½ minutes. R. and W. Churchill, *The Six Day War*, London: William Heinemann, 1967, pp. 82–7. For a detailed description of Israel's air attack see ibid., pp. 78–94.
7 Nasser's confidante, the journalist Haykal, later wrote: 'the air disaster was the first blow . . . and we were unable to protect ourselves against it . . . The rest collapsed as an inevitable result of a blow to the nerve centre guiding the battle. After that, all the power in our hands was a heap of destroyed or waste iron that could not be controlled.' *Al-Ahram* 10.11.67.
8 In his report on the war General Riad wrote:
'The surprise suffered by the air force of the UAR resulted in the air superiority of the enemy in general from the first few hours of the battle. This resulted in the Syrian air force suffering major losses which virtually excluded them from the battlefield. Consequently the battle on the Jordanian front was fought without provision for air cover or assistance . . . The enemy could destroy our forces from the air and then proceed with land forces without trouble.'
General Abdul Munim Riad, *GHQ Reports*, *Objective Discussion of Operations on the Jordanian Front*.
9 *GHQ Reports*, *Operations on the Jordanian Front*, hereafter referred to as *Operations on the Jordanian Front*; Hussein, *My War* 1969, pp. 60–1; Y. Kawash, *The Jordanian Front: The June 1967 War*, Amman; Al-Dar Al-Asriyah Lil Sahafa Wal Nashr, 1980, in Arabic, pp. 38–9.

10 Hussein, *My War* 1969, p. 66; Juma'a, *Conspiracy* 1968, p. 198; *Jordanian Documents* 1967, pp. 91–2.
11 Hussein, *My War* 1969, p. 66.
12 Ibid., p. 71.
13 W. Tal, *Writings in Arab Affairs*, Amman: Dar Al-Liwa, 1980, in Arabic, p. 331.
14 This is apparent from the instruction sent by Lt General Khammash on the morning of the war. He stated that fighting units should not start operations until 11.00 p.m. that night. *GHQ Cables*: cable sent by A. Khammash to Western Front GHQs on the morning of 5.6.67. In fact, the Jordanians were ordered by Cairo to start operations later that morning.
15 W. Tal, *Arab Affairs* 1980, p. 332.
16 Ibid., pp. 331–2.
17 Ibid., p. 338.
18 Operation Directive no. 7.
19 W. Tal, *Arab Affairs* 1980, p. 331.
20 *Operations on the Jordanian Front*. King Hussein's account of the joint Arab air raids is in Hussein, *My War* 1969, p. 65.
21 Hussein, *My War* 1969, p. 63.
22 Ibid.
23 The runways at Amman and Mafraq were bombed to such an extent that they were unusable. The Israelis used time bombs that kept exploding after the attacking planes had departed. Consequently the runways were impossible to repair immediately.
24 Hussein, *My War* 1969, p. 69 gives a description of this attack.
25 Mustafa, *June 1967 War* 1973, p. 76; M. Riad, *The Struggle for Peace in the Middle East* London: Quartet, 1981, p. 26; Hussein, *My War* 1969, p. 80; R. and W. Churchill, *The Six Day War* 1967, p. 93; T. Dupuy, *Elusive Victory: The Arab–Israeli Wars 1947–74*, New York: Harper and Row, 1978, pp. 246–7.
26 Mustafa, *June 1967 War* 1973, p. 25; Kawash, *Jordanian Front* 1980, p. 72; Interview with King Hussein.
27 Kawash, *Jordanian Front* 1980, p. 39; *Operations on the Jordanian Front*.
28 U. Narkiss, *The Liberation of Jerusalem*, London: Vallentine Mitchell, 1983, pp. 204–5; Kawash, *Jordanian Front* 1980, p. 72; S. El-Edroos, *The Hashemite Arab Army: 1908–1979*, Amman: Publishing Committee, 1980, p. 396; Hussein, *My War* 1969, p. 58.
29 The principal source used for this section are *GHQ Reports*, *Operations on the Jordanian Front*. Other sources are El-Edroos, *Hashemite Arab Army* 1980, pp. 372–90; T. Dupuy, *Elusive Victory* 1978, pp. 293–315; U. Narkiss, *Liberation* 1983, pp. 103–267; R. and W. Churchill, *Six Day War* 1967, pp. 123–47; *Middle East Record* vol. 3, 1967, Jerusalem: Israel Universities Press, 1971, pp. 223–7 and interviews with Jordanian military commanders.
30 Interview with A. Khammash.
31 Interviews with A. Khammash, Y. Kawash and Brigadier Fawzi Ebeidat.
32 Interview with F. Ebeidat.
33 Narkiss, *Liberation* 1983, p. 45.
34 Dupuy, *Elusive Victory* 1978, p. 287.

35 Ibid.
36 The Israelis had long-standing plans for its capture. Narkiss, *Liberation* 1983, p. 50.
37 This section is based on interviews with front-line commanders and other military personnel involved in the war, as well as El-Edroos, *Hashemite Arab Army* 1980, pp. 372–90.
38 Two of Central Command's brigades in the north had been transferred to Northern Command.
39 Narkiss, *Liberation* 1983, p. 111.
40 Interview with F. Ebeidat.
41 Kawash, *Jordanian Front* 1980, p. 45.
42 *Operations on the Jordanian Front*; Dupuy, *Elusive Victory*, 1978, p. 293; interview with M. A. Salim.
43 Dupuy, *Elusive Victory* 1978, p. 295.
44 Narkiss, *Liberation* 1983, p. 107.
45 Ibid., p. 108.
46 Ibid., p. 107.
47 Ibid., p. 108.
48 Ibid., p. 112; Kawash, *Jordanian Front* 1980, p. 50.
49 *Middle East Record* 1971, p. 224; R. and W. Churchill, *Six Day War* 1967, p. 134.
50 General Dayan commented that the battle for Ammunition Hill was the toughest in the war against the Jordanians. 'More than half of the troops and the majority of the officers who fought at Ammunition Hill and the Police School were wounded.' M. Dayan, *The Story of My Life*, New York: William Morrow, 1976, pp. 295–6. In the battle for the Police School alone the Israelis counted 106 dead Jordanian soldiers. R. and W. Churchill, *Six Day War* 1967, p. 135.
51 Operations on the Jordanian Front.
52 Ibid.
53 Dupuy, *Elusive Victory* 1978, p. 305.
54 El-Edroos, *Hashemite Arab Army* 1980, p. 381.
55 Ibid.
56 *Operations on the Jordanian Front.*
57 Ibid.; Hussein, *My War* 1969, p. 78.
58 According to El-Edroos, the IAF 'unleashed a storm of bombs, rockets and cannon-fire on the defenceless and helpless Jordanian tanks deployed within the narrow confines of the Dotan Valley'. El-Edroos, *Hashemite Arab Army* 1980, p. 386.
59 Hussein, *My War* 1969, pp. 80–1.
60 Interview with H. Majali.
61 This is the conversation which was intercepted by Israel and of which an edited version was broadcast to the world.
62 Hussein, *My War* 1969, p. 81; *Jordanian Documents* 1967, p. 51.
63 Hussein, *My War* 1969, p. 88; *Jordanian Documents* 1967, pp. 52–3.
64 *Operations on the Jordanian Front.*
65 Jordanian Documents op. cit. p. 54.
66 *Operations on the Jordanian Front.*
67 Interview with A. Khammash.
68 See Hussein, *My War* 1969, p. 105; *Objective Discussion of Operations.*

8 The war in perspective

1 This was the view of King Hussein, H. Majali, M. A. Salim, Dr Hazem Nussaibah, M. Haditha, Y. Kawash and A. Khammash; also W. Tal, *Writings in Arab Affairs*, Amman: Dar al-Liwa, 1980, in Arabic, p. 335.
2 Hussein, *My War with Israel*, London: Peter Owen, 1969, p. 110.
3 Interview with Y. Kawash.
4 Interviews with M. Haditha and M. A. Salim.
5 Y. Kawash, *The Jordanian Front: The June 1967 War*, Amman: Al-Dar Al-Asriyah Lil Sahafa Wal Nashr, 1980, in Arabic, pp. 68–9.
6 Interview with A. Khammash.
7 Ibid.
8 Kawash, *Jordanian Front* 1980, p. 30; H. Mustafa, *The June 1967 War: The Eastern Front*, Beirut: Al-Mu'assasa Al-Arabia Lil Dirasat Wal Nashr, 1973, in Arabic, p. 75. The slow arrival of the Iraqis was also an important factor. King Hussein commented: 'had the Iraqis arrived sooner our position would have improved . . . but the vanguard elements of an Iraqi Division started to cross the Jordanian border on the night of 4 June'. Hussein, *My War* 1969, p. 57.
9 Interview with King Hussein.
10 Interview with Y. Kawash.
11 Interview with M. Haditha.
12 Interview with H. Majali.
13 Interview with M. A. Salim.
14 Interview with H. Majali.
15 Ibid.
16 Ibid.
17 Interview with H. Nussaibah.
18 Interview with H. Majali; Tal, *Arab Affairs* 1980, p. 338.
19 Interview with M. Haditha.
20 Hussein, *My War* 1969, p. 107.
21 Interview with K. Kawash.
22 Interview with A. Khammash.
23 Interview with M. A. Salim.
24 Hussein, *My War* 1969, pp. 65–6.
25 Mustafa, *June 1967 War* 1973, p. 43.
26 Interview with H. Majali.
27 Interview with M. A. Salim.
28 Tal, *Arab Affairs* 1980, p. 334.
29 Ibid., p. 331; S. Juma'a, *The Conspiracy and the Battle of Destiny*, Beirut: Dar al-Kateb al-Arabi, 1968, in Arabic, pp. 192–3; Hussein, *My War* 1969, p. 65; interviews with M. Haditha, M. A. Salim and Y. Kawash.
30 Mustafa, *June 1967 War* 1973, p. 14.
31 H. Majali is critical of General Riad for agreeing to wait for the Syrians. He argues that on observing their delaying tactics he should have ordered the strike to go ahead without them since the Jordanians were losing precious time. Interview.
32 *Operations on the Jordanian Front*.

33 *GHQ Reports, Jordanian Documents* 1967, pp. 114–5.
34 Juma'a, *Conspiracy* 1968, p. 198.
35 Hussein, *My War* 1969, p. 84.
36 Ibid.
37 Tal, *Arab Affairs* 1980, p. 332; interviews with M. A. Salim and H. Majali.
38 Interview with H. Majali.
39 General Abdul Munim Riad, *GHQ Reports*, *Objective Discussion of Operations on the Jordanian Front*.
40 Mustafa, *June 1967 War* 1973, pp. 127–8.
41 Ibid., p. 89.
42 Tubas is 20 km from Jenin, 15 km from Nablus and 15 km from the crossroad south of the armistice line opposite Bissan. According to M. A. Salim it would take tanks about an hour to cross these distances. Interview.
43 Mustafa, *June 1967 War* 1973, p. 90.
44 Interview with F. Ebeidat.
45 Mustafa, *June 1967 War* 1973, p. 115.
46 Interview with Brigadier Shafik Ejailan.
47 Interview with King Hussein.
48 Interview with H. Majali.
49 Ibid.
50 Interviews with H. Majali, M. Haditha and F. Ebeidat.
51 Interviews with A. Khammash and S. Ejailan.
52 Interview with King Hussein.
53 Interview with S. Ejailan.
54 *GHQ Cables* 6.6.67.
55 Interviews with H. Majali and M. Haditha.
56 Interview with M. Haditha.
57 Ibid.
58 Ibid.
59 Ibid.
60 Interviews with H. Majali and M. Haditha.
61 Interview with Y. Kawash.
62 Kawash, *Jordanian Front* 1980, pp. 82–3.
63 *Operations on the Jordanian Front*.
64 Interview with M. A. Salim.
65 S. El-Edroos, *The Hashemite Arab Army: 1908–1979*, Amman: Publishing Committee, 1980, p. 433.
66 Interviews with H. Nussaibah and Abdul Munim Rifai.
67 M. Riad, *The Struggle for Peace in the Middle East*, London: Quartet, 1981, p. 96.
68 Interview with H. Nussaibah.
69 Hussein, *My War* 1969, p. 96.
70 Interviews with A. Khammash, Y. Kawash and M. A. Salim; *Objective Discussion of Operations*.
71 Interview with King Hussein.
72 Interview with A. Khammash.
73 *Objective Discussion of Operations*.

74 Hussein, *My War* 1969, pp. 56–7.
75 Interview with Y. Kawash.
76 Hussein, *My War* 1969, p. 81.
77 Mustafa, *June 1967 War* 1973, p. 23.
78 Interview with Muraiwed Tal; also Tal, *Arab Affairs* 1980, p. 337.
79 Interviews with King Hussein and A. Khammash.
80 Tal, *Arab Affairs* 1980, p. 337.
81 Ibid.; Hussein, *My War* 1969, p. 127.
82 Hussein, *My War* 1969, p. 59.
83 Interview with A. Khammash.
84 This information was provided by a source who prefers to remain anonymous.

9 The aftermath

1 This discussion is based on the following army records: Army *General Headquarter's Post-War Reports File*, hereafter referred to as *GHQ Reports*; Army *General Headquarter's Cables File*, hereafter referred to as *GHQ Cables*; Army *General Headquarter's Operations Directives File*, hereafter referred to as *Operations Directives*; Army *General Headquarters Defence Plans: 1965–1967* hereafter referred to as *Army Defence Plans*; *Reports by the Pakistani Military Advisory Mission*, hereafter referred to as *Advisory Mission*.
2 Interview with Dr Hazem Nussaibah.
3 Richard Cox in *The Daily Telegraph* 23.11.67, citing the Institute of Strategic Studies, gives the figure of 20 per cent. According to Jordanian army records, the figure was 80 per cent. *GHQ Reports*.
4 According to El-Edroos only three were functional. S. El-Edroos, *The Hashemite Arab Army: 1908–1979*, Amman: Publishing Committee, 1980, p. 434. From army records it appears that the Hittin brigade and six tanks of the 60th armoured brigade were still able to operate. *GHQ Reports*.
5 El-Edroos, *Hashemite Arab Army* 1980, pp. 430–2.
6 Ibid.
7 Syria and Egypt began to receive help from the Soviet Union in October 1967. Seventy per cent of Egypt's losses were made up and both countries were re-equipped with sophisticated aircraft, tanks and warning systems. Soviet advisers also flooded in to the countries.
8 *Advisory Mission*. One of its members was the current President of Pakistan, General Zia ul Haqq.
9 El-Edroos, *Hashemite Arab Army* 1980, p. 444.
10 Ibid., p. 445.
11 Central Bank of Jordan, *The Adverse Effects of Israel's Occupation of the West Bank*, September 1975.
12 *Middle East Record* vol. 3, 1968, Jerusalem: Israel Universities Press, 1971, p. 412.
13 Central Bank of Jordan 1975.
14 Ibid.
15 *Middle East Record* vol. 3, 1967, Jerusalem: Israel Universities Press, 1971, p. 412.
16 *Jordanian Documents*, Amman: Ministry of Information, 1967, in Arabic, p. 216.

17 Central Bank of Jordan 1975.
18 Official statistics of the Jordanian Ministry for the Occupied Territories, Amman; El-Edroos, *Hashemite Arab Army* 1980, p. 43; according to Juma'a, by 5.7.67, 200,000 refugees had fled to the East Bank, *Jordanian Documents* 1967, p. 125.
19 S. Juma'a, *The Conspiracy of Silence and the Battle of Destiny*, Beirut: Dar al-Kateb al-Arabi, 1968, in Arabic, p. 200.
20 El-Edroos, *Hashemite Arab Army* 1980, p. 443.
21 *Jordanian Documents* 1968, p. 48.
22 El-Edroos, *Hashemite Arab Army* 1980, pp. 446–7.
23 M. Riad, *The Struggle for Peace in the Middle East*, London: Quartet, 1981, p. 46.
24 Ibid, p. 46; See also *Jordanian Documents* 1967, p. 98.
25 Abdul Majeed Farid, *Records, Secrets and Deliberations of Hussein–Nasser Talks: 1967–1970*, *Al-Rai* 9.4.83.
26 Riad, *Struggle for Peace* 1981, pp. 46–7.
27 Ibid., p. 47.
28 H. Kosut, ed., *Israel and the Arabs: The June 1967 War*, New York: Facts on File, 1968, p. 166.
29 Interview with King Hussein.
30 Hussein, *My Profession as a King*, Amman: 1978, Ghaleb Toukan, in Arabic, pp. 221–2.
31 Interview with King Hussein; see also Riad, *Struggle for Peace* 1981, p. 48.
32 Farid, *Records* 11.4.83.
33 Ibid.
34 Interview with King Hussein; Farid, *Records* 11.4.83; Riad, *Struggle for Peace* 1981, pp. 54–5.
35 Riad, *Struggle for Peace* 1981, pp. 54–5. See also Farid, *Records* 9.4.83 and 11.4.83.
36 *The International Herald Tribune* 7.9.67.
37 Riad, *Struggle for Peace* 1981, p. 53.
38 Ibid., p. 73
39 Interview with Zaid Rifai.
40 Riad, *Struggle for Peace* 1981, p. 53.
41 Hussein, *My Profession* 1978, p. 223.
42 King Hussein's speech at the Washington National Press Club 7.11.67.
43 *Jordanian Documents* 1967, pp. 307–8.
44 R. Stephens, 'Jordan and the Powers' in P. Seale, ed., *The Shaping of an Arab Statesman*, London: Quartet, 1983, pp. 53–4.
45 Interview with Abdul Munim Rifai.
46 Riad, *Struggle for Peace* 1981, pp. 64–5.
47 Riad, *Struggle for Peace* 1981, pp. 67–8.
48 Interview with King Hussein.
49 Eban writes that he 'pointed out that there was no similar consensus concerning the future peace terms between Israel and Jordan'. A. Eban, *An Autobiography*, London: Weidenfeld and Nicolson, 1977, p. 436; also M. Dayan, *The Story of My Life*, New York: William Morrow, 1976, p. 444; Y. Rabin, *The Rabin Memoirs*, London: Weidenfeld and Nicolson, 1979, p. 105.
50 Farid, *Records* 11.4.83.

51 Rabin, *Rabin Memoirs* 1979, p. 106; also Dayan, *Story of My Life* 1976, p. 454.
52 Quoted by Riad, *Struggle for Peace* 1981, p. 64.
53 *Middle East Record*, p. 275.
54 Ibid.
55 Ibid.
56 Riad explains that the Resolution was not designed to deal with the problem of Palestine as a whole but that 'it confined itself to the consequences of the 1967 June war'. Riad, *Struggle for Peace* 1981, p. 74.

Bibliography

Primary sources

PERSONS INTERVIEWED	DATE OF INTERVIEW
H.M. King Hussein Ben Talal	25.4.84; 18.5.84
Airforce Brig. Husam Abu Ghazaleh	30.12.84
Adnan Abu Odeh	10.10.83; 15.10.83; 16.10.83; 12.2.84
Salah Abu Zeid	various occasions between 1983 and 1985
Ibrahim Ayoub	18.10.83
Colonel Yusuf Al-Dalabih	25.7.84
Brig. Fawzi Ebeidat	7.7.84; 14.9.84; 11.2.85; 4.4.85
Brig. Shafik Ejailan	7.4.85; 15.5.85
Abdul Raouf Al-Fares	8.5.84
Akef Al-Fayez	7.9.84
Lt General Mashour Haditha	11.10.83
Marwan Al-Kassem	6.3.84; 7.4.85; 20.5.85
Major General Yusuf Kawash	5.10.83
Lt General Amer Khammash	25.3.84; 4.7.84
Major General Ali Abu Nuwar	17.5.84
Ahmed Louzi	various occasions between 1983 and 1985
Field Marshall Habes Majali	14.4.84
Dr Hazem Nussaibah	2.11.83; 5.11.83; 12.11.83
Abdul Munim Rifai	10.11.83; 15.11.83; 21.4.83
Zaid Rifai	3.11.83; 12.11.83
Major General Muhammad Ahmed Salim	13.10.83; 7.9.84
Bahjat Talhouni	4.11.83; 6.11.83; 9.11.83
Muraiwed Tal	various occasions between 1983 and 1985
Akram Zueiter	27.11.83

DOCUMENTS

Arab Political Documents, 1964, Beirut: American University of Beirut.

Central Bank of Jordan, 1967, *4th Annual Report*, Amman.

1 September 1975, *The Adverse Effects of Israel's Occupation of the West Bank on Jordan's Economy*.

International Bank for Reconstruction and Development, 1957, *The Economic Development of Jordan*, Baltimore.

Jordanian Army General Headquarters Reports:
Cables File 1967
Defence Plans: 1965 and 1967
Military Instruction no. 1/65
Military Instruction 1/67
Munaqasha Mawduiyah Li Sair Al-Amaliyat Ala Al-Jabha Al-Urduniyah 1967 (Objective Discussion of Operations)
Operational Directive no. 6
Operations Directives File
Operations on the Jordanian Front File
Reports by the Pakistani Military Advisory Mission

Jordanian Documents 1967, 1968, 1969, 1970, Amman: Ministry of Information, in Arabic.

Khamsatun Wa Ishruna Aman Min Al-Tarikh Al-Majmua'a Al-Kamilah Li Khutab Jalalatu Al-Malek Al-Hussein Ben Talal: 1952–1977 (25 Years of History, The Complete Collection of H.M. King Hussein Ben Talal's Speeches 1952–1977) 1979, London: Samir Mutawi and Associates Publishing, in Arabic.

Middle East Record 1967, 1971, Jerusalem: Israel Universities Press.

Nasser, G.A., 1959, *Philosophy of the Revolution*, Buffalo, New York: Economica Books.

PLO Information Bulletins.

Proceedings of the Chamber of Deputies Amman: Ministry of Information.

Radio Jordan Bulletin.

Studies on Selected Development Programmes in Various Countries in the Middle East, 1967, paper presented to the United Nations Symposium on Industrial Development in Arab Countries held in Kuwait, 1–10 March 1966, New York: United Nations.

Al-Wazarat Al-Urduniyah, 1976, (Jordanian Cabinets, 1921–1976) Amman: Ministry of Information, in Arabic.

Al-Yaomiyat Al-Filestiniyah (Palestinian Diaries), Beirut: Maktab Al-Abhath, Munazzamat al-Tahrir, al-Filestiniyah, 1966–7, vols. 4 and 5, in Arabic.

Yearbook of Labour Statistics, 1966, International Labour Office.

NEWSPAPERS AND JOURNALS

Al-Ahram, Cairo daily.
The Daily Telegraph, London daily.
Al-Dastour, Amman daily.
The Economist, London weekly.
The Egyptian Gazette, Cairo daily.
The Guardian, London daily.
The Jerusalem Post, Jerusalem daily.
Al-Jihad, Jerusalem daily.
Al-Manar, Jerusalem daily.
Al-Musawar, Cairo weekly.
The News Chronicle.
The New York Herald Tribune, New York daily.
The New York Times, New York daily.
Al-Rai, Amman daily.

Al-Ray'ul al-Aam, Kuwait daily.
Al-Safa, Beirut daily.
The Scotsman.
The Sunday Times, London weekly.
The Sunday Telegraph, London weekly.
The Times, London daily.
Washington Post, Washington daily.

MEMOIRS AND BIOGRAPHIES

Abdul Majeed Farid, *Mahader Wa Asrar Wa Waqa'eh Muhadathat Al-Hussein Wa Abdul Nasser: 1967–1970* (Records, Secrets and Deliberations of Hussein–Nasser Talks: 1967–1970) serialized in *Al-Rai*, 1983.

Abdullah, King of Jordan, 1981, *My Memoirs Completed*, London: Longmans.

Fawzi, M., 1983, *The Three Year War – 1967–1970: General Fawzi's Diary*, Beirut: Dar Al-Wahda.

Glubb, J. B., 1983, *The Changing Scenes of Life: An Autobiography*, London: John Murray.

Hussein, H.M. King of Jordan, 1962, *Uneasy Lies the Head*, London: Heinemann.

1969, *My War with Israel*, London: Peter Owen.

1978, *Mihnati Ka Malek* (My Profession as a King), Amman: Ghaleb Toukan, in Arabic.

Jarvis, C. S., 1934, *Arab Command: The Biography of Lt. Col. F. G. Peake Pasha*, London: Hutchinson.

Rabin, Y., 1979, *The Rabin Memoirs*, London: Weidenfeld and Nicolson.

Stephens, R., 1971, *Nasser: A Political Biography*, London: Allen Lane, The Penguin Press.

SECONDARY SOURCES

Abu Jaber, K. S., 1966, *The Arab Ba'ath Socialist Party: History, Ideology and Organization*, Rochester, New York: Syracuse University Press.

Abu Nuwar, M., 1968, *Fi Sabil Al-Quds* (For the Sake of Jerusalem), Amman: Mudiriyat Al-Tawjeeh al-Ma'nawi, Al-Kiyadah Al-Ammah Lil Quwat Al-Musallaha, in Arabic.

1969, *Al-Liwa' Al-Mudarra'a Al-Arba'in* (The Fourtieth Armoured Brigade), Amman: Mudiriyat Al-Tawjeeh al-Ma'nawi, Al-Kiyadah Al-Ammah Lil Quwat Al-Musallaha, in Arabic.

Anonymous, 1958, *Hussein Ben Talal*, Amman: Department of Publications and Press, in Arabic.

Apter, D. E., 1965, *The Politics of Modernisation*, Chicago: University of Chicago Press.

Aresvik, O., 1976, *The Agricultural Development of Jordan*, New York: Praeger.

Aruri, N., 1972, *Jordan: A Study in Political Development 1921–1965*, The Hague: Martin Nijhoff.

Boulding, K. E., 1956, *The Image*, Ann Arbor, Michigan: University of Michigan Press.

Brecher, M., 1980, *Decisions in Crisis*, London: University of California Press.

Churchill, R. and W., 1967, *The Six Day War*, London: William Heinemann.

Dawisha, A. I., 1976, *Egypt in the Arab World*, London: Macmillan Press.
Dayan, M., 1976, *The Story of My Life*, New York: William Morrow.
Dekmejian, R. H., 1972, *Egypt Under Nasser*, London: University of London Press.
Dupuy, T., 1978, *Elusive Victory: The Arab–Israeli Wars of 1947–74*, New York: Harper and Row.
Eban, A., 1977, *An Autobiography*, London: Weidenfeld and Nicolson.
El-Edroos, S. A., 1980, *The Hashemite Arab Army: 1908–1979*, Amman: Publishing Committee.
Faddah, M. I., 1974, *The Middle East in Transition: Jordan's Foreign Policy 1948–1967*, London: Asia Publishing House.
Gilmour, 1980, *The Dispossessed*, London: Sidgwick and Jackson.
Glubb, J. B., 1957, *A Soldier with the Arabs*, New York: William Morrow.
1967, *The Middle East Crisis*, London: Hodder and Stoughton.
Green, S., 1984, *Taking Sides*, New York: William Morrow and Co.
Gubser, P., 1983, *Jordan, Crossroads of Middle Eastern Events*, London: Croom Helm.
Hudson, M., 1977, *Arab Politics: The Search for Legitimacy*, New Haven and London: Yale University Press.
Juma'a, S., 1968, *Al-Mu'amarah Wa Ma'rakatul Masir* (The Conspiracy and the Battle of Destiny), Beirut: Dar al-Kateb al-Arabi, in Arabic.
Kawash, Y., 1980, *Al-Jabha Al-Urduniyah – Harb Husairan 1967* (The Jordanian Front – The June 1967 War), Amman: Al-Asriyah Press, in Arabic.
Kerr, M., 1971, *The Arab Cold War*, London: Oxford University Press.
Kimche, D. and Bawly, D., 1968, *The Sandstorm*, London: Secker and Warburg.
Kosut, H., ed., 1968, *Israel and the Arabs: The June 1967 War*, New York: Facts on File.
Laqueur, W., 1968, *The Road to War: 1967*, London: Weidenfeld and Nicolson.
Lall, A., 1970, *The UN and the Middle East Crisis*, New York and London: Columbia University Press.
Madi, M. and Musa, S., 1960, *Tarikh al-Urdun Fil Karn al-Ishreen* (History of Jordan in the 20th Century), Amman: M. Madi and S. Musa, in Arabic.
Mansfield, P., 1969, *Nasser's Egypt*, Harmondsworth: Penguin.
Mansfield, P., ed., 1973, *The Middle East: A Political and Economic Survey*, London: Oxford University Press.
Mazur, P., 1979, *Economic Growth and Development in Jordan*, Boulder: Westview Press.
Morris, J., 1959, *The Hashemite Kings*, London: Faber and Faber.
Mustafa, H., 1973, *Harb Huzairan 1967 – Al-Jabha Al-Sharkiyah* (The June 1967 War – The Eastern Front), Beirut: Al-Mu'assasa Al-Arabia Lil Dirasat Wa Al-Nashr, in Arabic.
Narkiss, U., 1983, *The Liberation of Jerusalem*, London: Vallentine Mitchell.
Nutting, A., 1972, *Nasser*, London: Constable.
Nyorp, R. F., ed., 1980, *Jordan: A Country Study*, Washington: Foreign Area Studies, The American University.
Odd Bull, 1973, *War and Peace in the Middle East*, London: Leo Cooper.
Patai, R., 1958, *The Kingdom of Jordan*, Princeton: Princeton University Press.
Peake, F. G., 1958, *History and Tribes of Jordan*, Florida: Coral Gables.
Peretz, D., 1963, *The Middle East Today*, New York: Holt, Rinehart & Winston.
Riad, M., 1981, *The Struggle for Peace in the Middle East*, London: Quartet.

Sayigh, Y. A., 1972, *The Economies of the Arab World*, London: Croom Helm.

Safran, N., 1978, *Israel: The Embattled Ally*, Cambridge, Massachusetts and London: The Belknap Press of Harvard University Press.

Seale, P., ed., 1983, *The Shaping of an Arab Statesman: Sharif Abdul Hamid Sharaf and the Modern Arab World*, London: Quartet.

Sharabi, H., 1962, *Government and Politics of the Middle East in the Twentieth Century*, Princeton, New Jersey: Van Nostrand.

Shwadran, B., 1959, *Jordan: A State of Tension*, New York: Council for Middle Eastern Affairs Press.

Snow, P., 1972, *Hussein: A Biography*, London: Barrie and Jenkins.

Spanier, J., 1967, *World Politics in an Age of Revolution*, New York: Praeger.

Tal, W., 1980, *Kitabat Fi Al-Qadaya Al-Arabia* (Writings in Arab Affairs), Amman: Dar al-Liwa, in Arabic.

Vatikiotis, P. J., 1967, *Politics and the Military in Jordan*, London: Frank Cass and Co.

1971, *Conflict in the Middle East*, London: George Allen and Unwin.

1972, *Politics of the Fertile Crescent*, New York: American Elsevier Publishing Co. Ltd.

ARTICLES

Boulding, K., 'National Images and International Systems', *The Journal of Conflict Resolution* vol. III, no. 2, June 1959.

Dahl, R. A., 'A Critique of the Ruling Elite Model', *American Political Science Review* vol. 52, no. 2, June 1958.

Dawisha, A., 'Intervention in the Yemen', *The Middle East Journal* vol. 29, no. 1, winter 1975.

Harkabi, Y., 'Fedayeen Action & Arab Strategy', *Adelphi Papers* no. 53, December 1968, London: Institute for Strategic Studies.

Howard, M. and Hunter, R., 'Israel and the Arab World: The Crisis of 1967', *Adelphi Papers* no. 41, October 1967, London: Institute of Strategic Studies.

Pevety, D., 'The Arab Refugee: A Changing Problem', *Foreign Affairs* vol. 41, 1963.

St John Philby, H., 'Trans-Jordan', *Journal of the Royal Central Asian Society*, vol. XI, June 1924.

Yost, C., 'The Arab–Israeli War: How it Began', *Foreign Affairs* vol. 46, no. 2, January 1968, New York: Council on Foreign Relations.

Index

Note. Names beginning with 'al-' or 'el-' are indexed under the next part of the name.

Index

Index